Oil & Gas in Africa

A Legal and Commercial Analysis of the Upstream Industry

Consulting Editors **Marc Hammerson** and **John C LaMaster**

Consulting editors
Marc Hammerson
John C LaMaster

Managing director
Sian O'Neill

Editorial services director
Carolyn Boyle

Production manager
Neal Honney

Group publishing director
Tony Harriss

Oil and Gas in Africa: A Legal and Commercial Analysis of the Upstream Industry
is published by
Globe Law and Business
Globe Business Publishing Ltd
New Hibernia House
Winchester Walk
London SE1 9AG
United Kingdom
Tel +44 20 7234 0606
Fax +44 20 7234 0808
www.GlobeLawandBusiness.com

Print and bound by CPI Antony Rowe

Oil and Gas in Africa: A Legal and Commercial Analysis of the Upstream Industry
ISBN 9781909416680

Table of contents

Preface

General James L Jones (USMC, ret)

The world energy market is in the midst of an historic transformation that is poised to have profound economic and geopolitical effects. The emergence of transformative technologies has allowed new sources of oil and gas to come to the market, particularly in the United States, where oil production has increased by 80% since 2008. America's surprising upsurge in energy production will change global energy patterns, with important implications for key regions of the world.

Much of the West's attention has focused on how America's energy abundance can be used to alleviate geopolitical tensions and energy disputes elsewhere in the world. Others still wonder whether the Middle East's growing reliance on China and India for oil exports will change the historic 'security for energy' alliance that has linked Washington and the Persian Gulf since the end of World War II. In the northern hemisphere, meanwhile, Mexico's historic energy reforms have attracted significant attention among international investors.

The familiar pattern of political turmoil and unrest in the Middle East, and recent sanctions against certain state-owned Russian producers, have perhaps overshadowed Africa's growing role in the energy markets. Africa's substantial reserves of oil and gas hold the potential to help fulfill what I believe is Africa's enormous promise as the continent of the future.

The projections for Africa's future energy impact are impressive. The continent currently accounts for 10% of worldwide production and holds 7.7% of the world's proven reserves. BP's most recent *Energy Outlook* predicts that African oil production will grow by 47% by 2035. Africa is, however, poised to be more than just a major supplier of oil in the decades to come. It is expected to undergo significant population growth in the coming decades. The UN predicts that by the end of the century, nearly 40% of all humans and half of all children will be Africans. As Africa experiences ongoing population growth, continued urbanisation and rapid economic expansion, it will also experience the fastest growth in energy demand of any region in the world.

Yet these optimistic forecasts for African oil and gas development are not pre-ordained. Numerous hurdles stand between Africa's oil and gas resources and a future in which they serve as a platform for the continent's continued economic growth and development. In particular, significant security, regulatory, political and geopolitical challenges will confront international investors seeking to harness Africa's energy potential – as well as governments hoping to translate these resources into national economic prosperity.

Successfully navigating these challenges will require companies to plan carefully, maintain a healthy appetite for risk and retain expert counsel capable of navigating the political, legal and regulatory challenges that are sure to arise throughout the course of any investment. To cope with these same challenges, regional governments must develop political systems built on the rule of law and the consent of the governed. Marc Hammerson and John LaMaster's edited volume *Oil & Gas in Africa: A Legal and Commercial Analysis of the Upstream Industry* provides expert insights on both the opportunities and challenges inherent in investing in oil and gas in Africa. It provides particular insights to companies seeking to navigate the various security, regulatory, legal, governance and environmental challenges to operating in Africa's oil and gas industry.

Both traditional and emerging security threats will challenge oil and gas investors in Africa during the coming years. We have seen dramatic attempts to attack oil and gas infrastructure in Africa, most notably the Al-Amenas attack in Algeria in 2013, which resulted in 38 civilian deaths. That attack, which occurred on the heels of France's military intervention in Mali to fight the spread of terrorism, revealed the depth of the jihadist challenge facing north and sub-Saharan Africa.

The collapse of former Libyan strongman Muammar al-Qaddafi's regime, while successful in liberating the Libyan people from a ruthless tyrant, unleashed a flow of militants and weapons throughout north Africa. Much attention focused in 2014 on the emergence of the self-styled 'Islamic State' in Iraq and Syria, but its emergence should not overshadow the dangerous rise of extremism in Africa as well. The turmoil has deeply impacted upon the consistency of hydrocarbons production in Libya, which holds Africa's largest proven reserves and is an important supplier of energy to Europe. The alarming rise of Boko Haram in Nigeria has also shaken investor confidence in that country's bright future. Indeed, Libya, Algeria, Nigeria and other African energy producers are likely to become even more important suppliers of energy to Europe as it seeks to diversify its sources of supply.

Closely linked to the terrorist challenge is the security threat posed by smugglers and other common criminals on the continent. Oil theft in Nigeria not only undermines the economy and national security of the country, but also encourages corruption and impedes good governance. Some estimates show that smuggled oil may cost the Nigerian economy – now estimated as Africa's largest – up to $8 billion per year and 100,000 barrels of oil per quarter. This kind of theft is damaging to governments and investors alike and also feeds drug trafficking and piracy throughout the region.

Cybersecurity is another challenge that oil and gas companies investing in Africa should be prepared to confront. Until now, the most high-profile cyber-attacks on energy have taken place in the Gulf. Sooner or later, however, African critical infrastructure will become the source of disruptive cyber-espionage or potentially even a cyber-attack from an unfriendly government. It is critical for African countries that are rapidly adopting new technologies also to stay at the forefront of network security and human capital development in information technology.

Lagging health care infrastructure in many parts of Africa poses yet another security concern for the people of the continent as well as foreign investors. The outbreak of Ebola in west Africa has highlighted the strides in health care that still must be made in many parts of the continent, while also showing the notable progress made in countries such as Nigeria. Regardless of the progress made, the tragic outbreak of the disease has negatively impacted upon perceptions of Africa around the world and has harmed businesses even beyond west Africa.

Regulatory and political risk may be of even greater concern to investors seeking to develop Africa's oil and gas resources. Corruption remains a significant concern for major western investors in Africa's oil and gas industry, both as a source of possible legal problems with home governments and as a source of waste and inefficiency with their investments in a country.

Corruption undermines the widely shared goal of advancing good governance and political reform, which is imperative for governments that seek to survive demands for scrutiny and accountability in the digital age. Sub-Saharan Africa is the fastest growing mobile communications market in the world, and an ever-more connected citizenry is demanding greater transparency and accountability from its political leaders. These citizens will demand good governance not only from local governments but also from companies doing business in Africa. Particularly in the energy industry, where foreign investors come under close scrutiny, companies should take extra care to serve as good corporate citizens whose operations benefit the local population as a whole and respect the local environment.

The United States and its democratic allies would do well to remain closely engaged in supporting Africa through trade, investment and a commitment to undertaking political reform. This is true, even as rising energy production in the United States reduces American oil imports from countries like Nigeria. After all, the United States' growing bounty of energy will not shield American consumers from the effects of turbulence and rising demand in global oil markets or free the country from its historic responsibilities abroad. On the contrary, the United States' own unique experience in energy should serve as an opportunity to strengthen diplomatic and commercial ties with countries in Africa seeking reliable energy partners and expertise.

In my own extensive travels through Africa, I hear often from political and business leaders that they crave American and European investment and trade linkages but have to settle for non-Western partners due to the absence of alternatives. Thanks to the strong backing of its export bank and the strategic approach of its leadership, China has proven to be a formidable competitor for investment and markets in Africa and has displaced the United States as the region's largest trade partner. This has certainly had benefits for Africa's economies, but it also has its share of drawbacks.

It is my strong belief that in the 21st century, the United States and its democratic allies must think more strategically about how we can exert influence around the world, leveraging all tools of our national power – including the private sector. Just as our own governments in the West urge African countries to continue political reform, our own systems should not lose sight of the reforms our own governments and corporations must make to remain competitive in the fierce domain of our globalised world.

President Obama's historic US-Africa Leaders Summit in the summer of 2014 was an important, if belated, recognition by the United States that its political leaders need to invest significant time and capital in the increasingly fierce competition for business and trade markets in the fast-growing economies of Africa. America's failure to do so will not only undermine our own interests but also ultimately undermine the interests of African countries who benefit from the effects of competition.

I am ultimately optimistic about the future of Africa and believe it holds great potential for foreign investors in a variety of sectors, including oil and gas. Manuals such as *Oil & Gas in Africa* will be an invaluable tool to guide foreign investors through the challenges and help them succeed in a complex but ultimately promising market.

General James L. Jones (USMC, ret.)

President and Founder, Jones Group International
Former National Security Advisor to the President of the United States
Former Supreme Allied Commander Europe and Combatant Commander, USEUCOM
32nd Commandant of the U.S. Marine Corps

Introduction

Larry Bottomley
Alex Green
Chariot Oil and Gas Limited

---

1. Introduction

What does it really mean to talk of 'oil and gas in Africa'? No geologist, geophysicist or engineer would ever think of the African continent as a homogenous area for the exploration and development of oil and gas reserves. From the geoscientist's perspective, while the underlying science remains constant, Africa is a continent with many hydrocarbon basins, each with its own unique sub-surface characteristics. The same range of diversity occurs in the legal and commercial aspects of the business perspective. By one count (the number of fiscal regimes covered in Wood Mackenzie's African upstream database), there are over 30 different African countries with oil and gas legislation, many of which have several different sub-sets of fiscal terms that may be applicable. As a result, the industry professional working in Africa will likely be faced with what may, at first, seem to be a huge variety of legal systems with which to get to grips. Although such professionals may find themselves working with exploration and production licences governed by diverse production sharing contracts or royalty and tax based systems, the same fundamental concepts apply, as with geoscience. Once these 'constants' are understood, it may be seen that variation comes in the form of changes driven by such factors as geography, water depth, the maturity of the licence area, host government ownership rights and whether the play type tends towards being oil or gas prone or even unconventional – as this book ably shows in several of its chapters.

2. Challenges and opportunities

The oil and gas industry across Africa covers the entire range of project size and maturity. This book does not attempt to discuss these by reference to individual projects or countries. Instead, it selects key commercial and economic issues and analyses these on a pan-continental basis. An important starting point involves reviewing the production sharing contract, which is now the host government instrument of choice in Africa. Chapter X [Atkins] provides examples of how funding, carry and cost recovery obligations operate in key jurisdictions. It also deals with quasi-financial obligations imposed on contractors, such as government back-in rights and work commitments. Understanding these underlying petroleum rights is key to any investment decision. This is the case whether a company is bidding in licensing rounds or acquiring a developed asset. Similar issues indirectly apply to banks and other financial institutions providing debt or equity funding. Both mergers and acquisitions (M&A) and financing are discussed in the context of

African oil and gas in the chapters on M&A by Donovan and on financing of oil and gas operations by Johnston respectively.

Investment decisions are also undertaken in the context of a country's legal, political and legislative frameworks. Each of these subjects is covered in this book.

From a legal perspective, an investor is concerned to understand how contracts (including the production sharing contract or other host government instrument) will be enforced by an arbitrator or a court. This question is particularly relevant where actions against a host government must be initiated before domestic courts. In such cases, there is the risk that a host government may assert improper influence over such proceedings (a risk that is, of course, not unique to Africa).

Expropriation has always been a concern in jurisdictions with unstable political regimes. As well as the question of enforcing petroleum rights against a host government, investors also want to know what rights a government may have to acquire an interest later in a successful oil and gas project. In some circumstances, such as back-in rights or national oil company participation, this is pre-defined, either through negotiation or legislation. Other cases may involve the host government expropriating property and will be open to legal challenge (with all the uncertainty and cost that accompanies such disputes). The chapter on dispute resolution by Beeley and on state participation/local participation by LaMaster/Moran analyse disputes and government participation in an African petroleum context.

Politically, investors are also concerned about on-the-ground security threats. These range from petty theft and vandalism to organised and politically-motivated terrorist activity. Security and community relations have long been key ingredients of successful African onshore petroleum development. More recently, in certain locations offshore from the coast of Africa, piracy has developed into a major concern. Corruption and bribery, which are prevalent in various degrees throughout the continent, may be connected with these criminal activities. These types of problem faced by oil and gas companies doing business in Africa are discussed in the chapter on security by LaMaster and on anti-corruption initiatives by Soliman *et al.*

Decommissioning and local content requirements are not unique to Africa. The former will grow increasingly important as the continent's industry matures and governments and stakeholders begin to calculate the expense and difficulty of removing infrastructure standing in deep water. Local content, on the other hand, is a topical and pressing issue. Its successful implementation is vital to the development of any nascent petroleum industry and the wider economy. Given the scale of social and economic issues in Africa, getting the balance of competing interests right on this point (without jeopardising the cost or success of projects) is an issue that will determine the future success of the continent's petroleum developments.

3. Nascent regimes

Many African countries have had an active petroleum sector for decades, with a fully developed framework of contracts and taxation legislation designed to govern the respective rights of the oil company and the state. Given the recent exploration push into frontier and under-explored areas by the industry, however, there are also countries which have found themselves with a need to either develop new or expand existing frameworks. Such nascent countries may allow a little more flexibility in negotiating terms, although this is far from always being the case and should never be taken for granted. One should also bear in mind that, if precedents have not been set by the activities of previous companies, then one may find oneself being a legislative test case. A clear, balanced contract and a sound understanding of the relevant hydrocarbon may help see off problems further down the road – particularly in an industry that has such lengthy timescales and diverse phases of activity. There is, after all, a lot that can change in the time it takes from being granted an exploration licence to the abandonment of production wells.

4. Conclusion

Finally, in the months between our having been invited to write this introduction and actually putting pen to paper, it seems that the oil and gas industry is entering into what looks to be the beginning of, if not a new business cycle, then at least a period of turbulence. The price of Brent crude has dropped by nearly 50%, reaching its lowest level since 2010. Many analysts and commentators have begun to predict a restructuring of the sector, driven both by a changing supply/demand dynamic and actions taken by many of the majors and larger independents in seeking to rebalance their portfolios with asset sales. Service providers too are apparently feeling the wind of change, with several seismic survey companies putting out profit warnings and rig companies dropping their day rates. Closer to home, the Scottish referendum on independence has come and gone, leaving behind it a vast amount of now redundant analysis on the potential consequences to the UK's oil and gas legislation should the vote have been won by the nationalists. What though, has this to do with a book titled Oil and Gas in Africa? The answer, at least in our opinion, is that while changes in the macro-economic environment may result in the start of a new cycle for the industry, the requirement for best practice remains unchanged: whether it be the negotiation of balanced, robust contracts or the successful execution of well-planned projects that will outlive such cycles, possibly by decades. Whether that business is in Africa or beyond, this book is an asset that should provide valuable assistance to achieving those aims.

Upstream agreements in Africa

Kevin Atkins
Chadbourne & Parke LLP

1. Introduction

A key feature of African oil and gas interests is the nature of rights awarded by host governments and the structure of entitlements to petroleum production. Oil and gas regimes in the majority of western Europe and the United States differ significantly from those that are prevalent in Africa. At the heart of this distinction is an investor's entitlement to production and when and where title to oil and gas vests with the investor. In the United Kingdom, for example, once oil and gas is produced at the wellhead, it is automatically owned (by operation of law) by the investors who funded the drilling operations, pursuant to a licence awarded by the UK government. In certain US states (eg, Texas and New Mexico), ownership goes one step further: title to oil and gas *in situ* vests with the landowner, such that oil and gas is owned even when it is sub-surface and sits within geological strata. By contrast, this private ownership concept is not adopted in most African jurisdictions, and investors typically take a share of either the production or the proceeds of sales, in accordance with a formula laid down in contractual arrangements with the host government.

These different systems are principally known as the 'concessionary system', which vests title to all oil and gas with the investor, and the 'production sharing system' which vests title to all oil and gas with the host government and grants investors a predetermined contractual entitlement to a proportion of the production or the proceeds of sales. While there are other forms of oil and gas licensing system in use around the world (the other common form being service contracts), the two most common systems are the concessionary form and the production sharing form; and the latter system is far more prevalent in emerging markets and very common across Africa.

This chapter looks at upstream agreements in a number of African countries (most notably the model form arrangements in Angola, Equatorial Guinea, Ghana, Liberia, Madagascar, Morocco, Namibia, Nigeria, South Africa and Uganda) and briefly addresses some of the trends that are occurring in oil and gas title documentation across Africa.

In addition, this chapter looks at some of the other forms of contractual arrangement that are prevalent in the African upstream sector, including Joint Bidding Agreements (JBAs) and Joint Operating Agreements (JOAs). While each of these documents will vary from transaction to transaction and may have its own jurisdictional precedents or prescribed model form, the differences between JBAs and JOAs adopted in Africa and elsewhere around the world are not as fundamental as those between the concessionary form and the production sharing form of licensing arrangement, and are, typically, not structural in nature but, rather, transaction-specific.

Production sharing arrangements are known by various names in different countries (such as production sharing contracts, production sharing agreements and petroleum agreements) but, for ease of reference, are referred to throughout this chapter as 'production sharing agreements' (PSAs).

2. Production sharing agreements

The concept of PSAs was created in Indonesia in the 1960s. The first PSA was entered into in 1966 between Pertamina, the Indonesian state-owned energy company, and an American oil and gas company. PSAs are popular with host governments, as ownership of the oil produced remains with the host government, which contracts with investors to explore for and develop oil and gas resources. This is a common feature of all PSAs, regardless of the host government awarding the rights.

Host governments, through their national oil companies (NOCs), will acquire a share of an oil and gas project along with investors. Their interests are, however, based on different terms. Investors operate the asset at their sole risk, bearing all the costs and expenses involved in drilling operations. Host governments and nominated local partners typically will not bear any risk at all at this stage. Each group will receive different proportions of the production once oil is produced. Investors are entitled to recover the costs and expenses incurred out of the first tranche of production. In the event that no oil is found, the risk rests solely with the investor, whose costs and expenses become irrecoverable sunk costs.

Of the countries examined for the purposes of this chapter, the majority (Angola, Equatorial Guinea, Ghana, Liberia, Madagascar, Nigeria and Uganda) typically adopt PSA structures. A minority (including Morocco, Namibia and South Africa) use the concessionary model that is customary in western Europe. Under the latter, host government benefits are derived from royalties and taxes rather than ownership of production. As a general rule, therefore, most African countries (except for those in southern Africa) tend to adopt the PSA model.

2.1 Joint and several liability

It should be noted at the outset that the liabilities of investors under a PSA are typically joint and several. Thus, where a number of different investors co-operate with one another to form a joint venture (JV) which successfully bids for and is awarded an oil and gas asset – and despite each investor expressly holding a divisible share in the JV (as laid down in the JOA) – each investor will be liable for their own obligations and those of every other investor. This means that, despite the proportionate share of obligations and liabilities for which investors have agreed to be responsible between themselves, the host government may pursue any and all of them for any breach of the PSA – even if the investor(s) being pursued were not responsible for the breach in question. This is not, however, an uncommon provision; it is certainly not unique to African PSAs and is in fact also a feature of the concession model in the United Kingdom.

2.2 Ownership of production

As noted at 1 above, oil produced under a PSA belongs to the host government. Investors are entitled to a share of oil produced only if there is a commercial discovery that results in production. Investors therefore take an economic interest in production by way of a contractual right and do not have an ownership interest in production once it is taken out of the ground. The entitlement to a share in production created by such a right can be satisfied either

- in kind (by way of a delivery of a proportionate share of barrels of oil), or
- in cash (by way of a payment of a proportionate share of the proceeds of sale of each barrel of oil produced).

This contractual right is like any other and can be breached, leaving investors with nothing but a claim for a breach of contract. An investor may be particularly reliant on contractual rights where the host government or the nominated local partner takes the lead in marketing and selling production and is therefore responsible for both handling production and the resulting revenue streams from sales. This is the case in some African jurisdictions, where local participation is taking on increasing importance in upstream projects.

This is a fundamental concept that distinguishes oil and gas projects in Africa from those elsewhere around the world. It is a key consideration when entering into an oil and gas investment in Africa, as equity backers and debt lenders alike need to be comfortable with the rights that the investor has to production before making any decision to invest in the project.

Investors often act as *de facto* or technical operators of oil and gas projects across Africa (such that they act for and on behalf of the JV and typically market and sell their own production and the production of local partners). As resource nationalism and local content requirements escalate, however, host governments (through their NOCs) may take more of an active role in this process and may take over control of the marketing and sales process. This exposes international investors to the risk of breaches of contract and failure to remit contractual entitlements to production, although any such action by a host government that was unprompted (eg, by a prior breach by the oil and gas investor) would likely be seen as an extremely nationalistic and hostile act to the international oil and gas community.

2.3 Funding and carry obligations

The costs of exploration for oil and developing discoveries under PSAs are typically borne by investors only and it is not uncommon for the scope clause of PSAs to refer expressly to the risks being accepted by investors. For example, clause 2.3 of the Ghanaian 2002 model form PSA provides that:

in the event that no Commercial Discovery is made in the Contract Area, or that Gross Production received from the Contract Area is insufficient fully to reimburse Contractor in accordance with the terms of this Agreement, then Contractor shall bear its own loss; GNPC and the State shall have no obligations whatsoever to Contractor in respect of such loss.

Further, clause 2.5 of the Liberian model form PSA provides that:

the Contractor shall bear alone the financial risk associated with the performance of the Petroleum Operations.

The period during which investors are considered solely liable for costs and project risks can vary; it may be during the exploration phase only, or during exploration and development, all the way up to production of first oil. A common feature of PSAs is that the capital intensive period of the project is borne by the investor, with the host government taking no financial risks and being 'carried' during this phase.

For example, under clause 2.4 of the Ghanaian model form the carry obligation applies as follows:

With respect to all Exploration and Development Operations GNPC's Initial Interest shall be a Carried Interest. With respect to all Production Operations GNPC's interest shall be a paid interest.

With regard to the meaning of 'development operations', the interpretation clause in that model form provides:

'Development Operations' means the preparation of a Development Plan, the building and installation of facilities for Production, and includes drilling of Development Wells, construction and installation of equipment, pipelines, facilities, plants and systems, in and outside the Contract Area, which are required for achieving Production, treatment, transport, storage and lifting of Petroleum, and preliminary Production and testing activities carried out prior to the Date of Commencement of Commercial Production, and includes all related planning and administrative work, and may also include the construction and installation of secondary and tertiary recovery systems.

This provision, therefore, specifically provides for a carry obligation which covers all costs and expenses right up to the moment that production commences, with the NOC (in the example above, Ghana National Petroleum Company) thereafter paying for costs incurred once production has commenced. Production costs will be much less capital intensive than those incurred during the exploration and development phases and will principally relate only to day-to-day operational costs, as capital expenditures required for infrastructure and equipment will already have been paid for as part of the development operations).

By contrast, under clause 10 of the 2008 model form Angolan PSA, costs are borne as follows:

The costs and expenditures incurred in the Petroleum Operations, as well as any losses and risks derived therefrom, shall be borne by the Contractor Group and Sonangol shall not be responsible to bear or repay any of the aforesaid costs and expenditures.

The interpretation clause in that model form provides:

'Petroleum Operations' means the activities of Exploration, Appraisal, Development and Production which constitutes the object of the Agreement.

This means that even during the production phase in Angola, the host government is carried and does not bear any financial risk.

2.4 Local partners

Host governments will typically invest in oil and gas projects through their NOCs. Local partners will normally form part of the contractor group that is awarded an oil and gas asset and will be party to the PSA. As noted above, however, they typically do not bear the costs of operations and are usually carried throughout some or all of the pre-production phase. Depending on the circumstances, host governments may also require further local participation in oil and gas JVs and nominate other local vehicles to participate in the project.

As part of any JV operation, international investors should conduct financial and legal due diligence on the partners to the project (whether those partners are other international investors or local participants). Among other things about which investors should be concerned are the financial capabilities of each project partner to fund its commitments as and when they arise (whether from day one or upon the expiry of any applicable carry period). Furthermore, given the scope of US and English laws relating to corruption and money laundering (where parties 'associated' with another party can be liable for the actions of that party), investors should, as a matter of course, conduct integrity due diligence on each project partner with which they are unfamiliar, in order to ensure that they are comfortable with the source of funds available to and the corporate governance policies of such partner and each of such partner's related parties. For example, if there is a concern as to the sanctity of the oil and gas project award process, international investors can be held liable and investigated for corruption breaches if US or English laws apply, which could lead to extremely heavy fines and sanctions.

2.5 Back-in rights

In addition to the carried interests which they hold, it is not uncommon for host governments also to be able to back-in to an oil and gas asset and acquire an additional share in the project. The extent of such back-in right will usually be prescribed by law (ie, the maximum host government take will be capped by law), but the exercise of any back-in right will inevitably impact upon deal economics as each investor's share of production will be proportionality reduced. Under clause 2.5 of the Ghanaian model form of PSA, the back-in right is laid down as follows:

> *GNPC shall have the option in respect of each Development and Production Area to contribute a proportionate share not exceeding [ ]% of all Development and Production Costs in respect of such Development and Production Area, (or make arrangements satisfactory to Contractor to that effect) thereby acquiring an Additional Interest of up to [ ]% in Petroleum Operations in such Development and Production Area. GNPC shall notify Contractor of its option within ninety (90) days of the Date of Commercial Discovery.*

Clause 2.10 of that form provides:

> *Contractor's participating Interest in all Petroleum Operations and in all rights under this Agreement shall be ninety per cent (90%), reduced proportionately at any given time any in any given part of the Contract Area by the participating Interest of GNPC pursuant to Article 2.5.*

Back-in rights are negotiated rigorously, as they cut to the heart of the JV economics and directly affect the proportionate take to which each commercial party is entitled. Typically, as is the case with the Ghanaian model form provision, back-in rights are exercisable within a certain timeframe, commencing on the date of first production, and are conditional on the payment of some proportion of past costs of which the host government did not pay its share. In the event of a carry arrangement lasting until production, this means that the host government can pay zero costs for its share of the project and also increase its share in the project as and when production is achieved.

As can be seen from the example Ghanaian clause given above, the back-in right typically arises only in relation to a specified Development and Production Area and not in relation to the entire licence area. Thus, despite the carry obligation in clause 2.5 ceasing to apply to 'Production Operations', the exercise of a back-in right in Ghana does not mean that the host government will thereafter fund its share of any future exploration costs (if any) elsewhere in the licence area, but will only in fact fund its enlarged share of future production costs (which, as noted above, will be substantially less than exploration and development costs) in the 'Development and Production Area' that has been identified.

Back-in rights are not exclusive to PSAs, but exist also under concession regimes. South Africa, for example, implements a back-in right for up to 10% upon production.

2.6 Cost recovery

Given that ownership of production belongs to the host government and that costs prior to production are borne by the investors, with the host government and local partner being carried, investors will need a mechanism to recover their own past costs and the past costs that they have paid for and on behalf of the host government under the carry obligation. Production is, therefore, split and allocated for different purposes and will typically be allocated in the following order – firstly, to settle any taxes arising from such production, secondly, to recover a proportion of past costs, and thirdly, to be shared between the host government and the investors.

For example, the Equatorial Guinean model form PSA provides as follows:

The Contractor shall pay Royalties to the State from the first day of Production based on the daily Total Disposable Production from a Development and Production Area. (Clause 7.1.1)

After deducting Royalties, the Contractor shall be entitled to up to [ ]% of the Total Disposable Production remaining in any Calendar Year for recovery of its Petroleum Operations Costs (Cost Recovery Oil). (Clause 7.2.1)

The quantity of Total Disposable Production remaining every Year after the deduction of Royalties and Cost Recovery Oil will hereafter be referred to as Net Crude Oil, which will be shared between the State and the Contractor in the following proportions [ ]. (Clause 7.3)

The costs incurred will often amount to multi-million US dollar sums; consequently, the first months of production will not generate enough oil to extinguish fully and amortise those past costs incurred. They will, instead, be recovered over time, as and when more production is generated. Some of the key questions to ask, therefore, when investing in an African oil and gas project are as follows.

- What amounts are required to be deducted prior to recovery of project costs?

- What is the acceptable cap for each cost recovery period (ie, how much of each month's production can be applied to recover past costs)?
- What is the proportionate share of profit oil that an investor will take after deducting costs?
- Are there any types of cost that are not entitled to be recovered?
- How frequently and by whom are cost recovery statements examined?

Royalty rates will commonly be laid down by applicable local law, whereas recovery caps and profit sharing will be open to negotiation as part of any oil and gas project bidding process and will be one of the fundamental criteria used by the host government to determine which JV should be awarded a particular project. Notwithstanding the foregoing, it should be noted that some countries specifically prescribe cost recovery caps in their model form documentation – examples are Madagascar and Liberia, which have a 60% and 70% cap respectively. Marginal or frontier fields (where oil recoverability may be riskier and exploration more costly) may require higher cost recovery caps.

The extent to which costs are permitted to be recovered also provides fertile ground for discussion as this inevitably directly impacts upon each party's deal economics. Cost recoverability is usually dealt with in the accounting procedures annexed to the PSA. The following types of cost are normally not recoverable:

- bonuses paid during the life of the project (such as signing bonuses or discovery bonuses);
- sanctions and fines imposed on investors under applicable laws; and
- budget over-expenditures that have not been approved by the host government.

Certain countries may also include other amounts which are deducted prior to costs being recovered. For example, some countries provide for an additional host government entitlement to production where a certain rate of return is received by the investors on their investment in the project. Typically, shares in production are taken in cash and not in barrels of oil, such that production is assigned a value pursuant to a formulation laid down in the PSA although, as discussed at 2.9 below, valuation mechanisms can be heavily negotiated.

2.7 Booking reserves

Cost recovery also directly affects reserves statements, as booking reserves under PSAs is not as simplistic as under concession regimes, and increases in oil prices will inevitably impact upon:

- when the costs incurred by investors can be recovered from the proceeds of sales of production;
- when a project becomes cash positive; and
- how much profit oil is shared on a sliding scale basis.

Booking reserves under PSAs can also sometimes be advantageous, however – for example, decreases in oil prices may not correspondingly decrease reserves, which would obviously be the case under a concession regime, as recovery of costs will take more barrels to achieve.

2.8 Profit sharing

After costs are deducted, the balance of production in any period is considered profit oil and is shared between the host government and the investors, pursuant to a predetermined formula laid down in the PSA. There are two main methodologies for sharing profits:

- a straight line basis (which, for example, is adopted in the Liberian and Equatorial Guinean model forms), and
- a rate of return basis (or R-factor), which takes into account the expenses and revenues of the project (which is adopted in the Angolan model form).

On a straight line basis, the sharing of profit oil is based on a table of escalating production figures whereby, as and when certain production thresholds are achieved and an increased volume of profit oil is generated, the sharing ratios change and the host government's share increases with no decreases (ie, the host government's share only ever escalates over time). On an R-factor basis, however, profit sharing is calculated on the basis of a formula whereby project revenues are divided by project expenses or some other rate of return on the investor's investment is calculated.

From an investor's perspective, R-factor calculations are likely to be preferable, as they value the actual cost of the investment and adjust sharing ratios depending on costs and liabilities incurred, as opposed to a straight line escalating profit share for the host government over time. For example, in the event of a slowdown in production (eg, a blockage) that requires operational expenditure and remedial works:

- on a straight line basis, the host government's profit share would still escalate as barrel thresholds are reached, while
- on an R-factor basis, profit sharing may even adjust in favour of the investor as a result of any additional expenditures incurred to relieve the project of the slowdown in production.

2.9 Minimum work commitments and relinquishment

As is consistent across the oil and gas industry, any award of drilling rights and title to oil and gas projects (whether by way of a concession arrangement in the United Kingdom or a PSA in Africa) will necessarily include a minimum work commitment to be performed during the exploration phase of the project. In similar fashion to oil and gas projects elsewhere in the world, host governments across Africa want to ensure that an agreed minimum level of work is performed in the licence area during the first phase of the project.

As with the levels of cost recovery and profit sharing, the scale of minimum work commitments that investors are prepared to pursue will be an important factor that host governments take into consideration when determining to whom licence areas should be awarded. Typically, these will involve acquiring 2D and/or 3D seismic imaging data over certain areas and drilling at least one exploration well (although these commitments will be increased where the exploration phase of the project is extended, and for each extension it is not uncommon for another exploration well to be drilled).

Minimum work commitments are also customarily given a cash equivalent value, which sum is then secured by way of credit support (whether by way of a corporate guarantee from the investor's parent company or a drawable performance bond or letter of credit). In the event of a failure to perform the required minimum work commitments or the encountering of technical difficulties which suspend exploratory drilling prior to incurring the cash equivalent value of the well commitment, the host government will be entitled to draw down the balance of the funds under the credit support instrument.

In the event that no discoveries are made, the JV may decide to abandon the project and elect not to continue into the development and production phase. Where a discovery is made which the investor would like to pursue, however, the investor will be required to relinquish a certain proportion of the initial licence area which it does not intend to appraise or develop. Again, the proportion to be relinquished is open to negotiation, and is considered by the host government when determining to whom to award licence areas, but is generally for no less than 50% of the initial licence area, the idea being that investors should focus on the prospective areas they have identified and relinquish under-explored areas back to the host government so that they can be awarded to other investors in subsequent award processes.

Absent express relinquishment obligations, licence areas will remain in the hands of investors and can become fallow if they remain under-explored. Host governments obviously want to avoid this, as they will typically be unable to award those areas to new investors. One way of avoiding this outcome is by implementing marginal field programmes and awarding those original investors royalties over any subsequent production that new investors, to whom such marginal acreage might be awarded, may generate.

2.10 Management committee

Unlike concession structures, under a PSA the host government is directly involved in operational matters and carries voting rights in a management committee established under the PSA. The management committee comprises an equal number of representatives of the investor and the host government. Decisions therefore cannot be taken without the vote of at least one representative of the host government (although host government representatives will usually vote as a unified block) and, in most cases, unanimity may be required.

The management committee will be responsible for approving all work programmes and budgets and expenditures. Fertile ground for negotiation during the course of the award of a PSA is, however, the scope that investors have to conduct day-to-day operations without prior host government approval, especially where investors are carrying the costs of the host government and incurring all of the project risks.

When coupled with the JOA structure discussed at 6 below, it can be seen that there is a effectively a dual committee process, as follows:

- one committee, appointed under the JOA, solely comprising representatives of the JV partners; and
- the second (management) committee, appointed under the PSA, comprising, in equal numbers, representatives of the JV and the host government.

In practice, this means that JVs agree what work programmes and budgets they wish to pursue under the JOA and then discuss these matters with the management committee under the PSA. Minority JV investors should be aware that they may not necessarily get a seat on both the JOA committee and the PSA management committee, though to the extent that the management committee agrees any changes to work programmes and budgets, those changes would then in practice be agreed at the JOA committee level under the JOA terms and conditions.

2.11 Valuation of production

Production will be valued for the purposes of recovering costs and profit sharing, pursuant to specific valuation mechanics. While calculating the value of oil produced may sound simple, in practice this clause in the PSA is vigorously negotiated, as the value ascribed to production underwrites the economics of the entire project and investors want to have control over the marketing and sale of their production in order to ensure that they get the best price possible (although, in certain countries, the host government takes control for marketing and sales).

The general principle in most model forms is that production is valued on the basis of an arm's length transaction with a third party (normally on a free-on-board basis, using the Incoterms applicable to international sales practices, and excluding non-cash purchases and swaps), which is the concept adopted in Equatorial Guinea, Ghana and Liberia. Where a sufficient proportion of volumes in a particular month are not sold to third parties on such basis, however, some countries, such as Equatorial Guinea and Uganda, refer to benchmark industry reference standards (such as Brent crude or American Petroleum Institute figures) of an equivalent grade and quality.

This can frequently lead to disputes, however, as determinations of equivalency and available sales markets against which comparisons can be made can be ambiguous and open to interpretation and, as noted above, volatile oil prices can lead to faster recovery of costs and therefore a greater share of profits by investors. Disputes relating to valuation mechanics are frequently referred to expert determination.

2.12 Title to equipment

It is customary in PSAs for title to equipment that is acquired by investors for operations to vest with the host government. Any rig or drilling equipment that is acquired by the investor will therefore belong to the host government upon expiry of the project and the investor will no longer be able to use the asset acquired unless it leases the same from the host government.

For example, clause 19.2 of the Ugandan model form PSA provides that equipment belongs to the host government once the acquisition costs of such equipment have been recovered:

All equipment and other assets, whether fixed or movable, acquired and owned by Licensee for use in the Petroleum Operations hereunder shall become the property of the Government upon the earlier of that date upon which: (i) such equipment and assets have been fully depreciated for Income Tax purposes, or the costs thereof have been fully recovered; or (ii) this Agreement is terminated.

Clause 32 of the Angolan model form also provides as follows, to the effect that equipment belongs to the host government immediately:

Physical assets purchased by Contractor Group for the implementation of the Work Plan and Budgets become the property of Sonangol when purchased in Angola or, if purchased abroad, when landed in Angola.

Despite ownership vesting with the host government, during the life of an oil and gas project, it will be an obligation of the investor (not the host government) to ensure that the equipment is in good condition and working order and, in the event of a breakdown of any such equipment, the investor will be responsible for ensuring that new replacement equipment can be accessed and utilised. In addition to equipment and assets used for joint operations, it is not uncommon for all technical information and know-how developed through the project also to belong exclusively to the host government and to be distributed to new prospective investors in future award rounds.

In the light of these provisions, a practice has developed for affiliates of investors to acquire equipment and assets and to lease the same to JV parties for the purposes of the oil and gas project although, as noted at 6 below, contract awards and tendering processes under JOAs will affect the terms and conditions on which affiliates can transact with one another.

2.13 Domestic supply

PSAs also frequently impose domestic supply obligations on investors. Under the model form PSA applicable in Madagascar, each overseas investor active in the oil and gas sector bears a proportionate share of the domestic supply obligation relative to the aggregate production of all other overseas investors active in the oil and gas sector in Madagascar, subject to a monthly cap on required volumes of no more than 10% more than the volumes required in the previous month. A similar construct is adopted in the Ghanaian model form, albeit without the cap on 10% month-on-month increases, while the Liberian model form arrangement mandates up to a predetermined amount each month and not a proportionate share across the industry.

Each project is, however, confidential and production figures from project to project are unlikely to be publicly available, which means that calculations of proportionate shares will need to be performed by the host government (being the only consistent party to each project) and are unlikely to be independently verifiable prior to payment. While both the Ghanaian and Malagasy model forms require domestic supplies to be at the same price at which production is valued pursuant to the PSA, it is common for domestic supplies to be at a discount to market prices. This is another potential ground for disputes.

2.14 Bonuses

Investors will be required to pay bonuses (typically in multi-million US dollar sums) to the host government upon the occurrence of certain events under a PSA – typically:

- upon signing,
- upon achieving first production, and thereafter
- upon achieving certain production thresholds.

As with cost recovery caps and profit sharing ratios, the bonus levels being offered are another key criterion that the host government takes into consideration when determining to whom an oil and gas project should be awarded. The scale of such bonuses will obviously affect the net present value and prolong the rate of return of a project, particularly given that, as discussed at 2.6 above, these bonuses are not cost recoverable.

2.15 Governing laws and stabilisation

Whereas JOAs and JBAs are commonly governed by English or New York law, PSAs are always governed by the laws of the host country and host governments never accept any other choice of law. The only exceptions to this may be a failed state or a country seeking international recognition in which no body of domestic law currently exists.

Given the mandatory local law formulation, investors normally insist on robust stabilisation provisions and on structuring their investments to use and maximise the benefits of bilateral investment treaties (BITs), which protect investors from nationalistic actions and changes in law that adversely affect the project.

By way of examples, the following stabilisation provisions are included in the Ghanaian and Liberian model forms respectively:

> *As of the Effective Date of this Agreement and throughout its Term, the State guarantees Contractor the stability of the terms and conditions of this Agreement as well as the fiscal and contractual framework hereof specifically including those terms and conditions and that framework that are based upon or subject to the provisions of the laws and regulations of Ghana.* (Clause 26.2)
>
> *In the event of any changes in circumstances from those existing at the Effective Date, that have a significant material effect on the terms of this Contract, either NOCAL or the Contractor shall at the request of the other consult together. If it mutually established* [sic] *that such Profound Changes in Circumstances have occurred, then the Parties shall effect such changes in or clarifications to this Contract that they agree are necessary. The Parties shall meet in good faith to make the necessary revisions and adjustments to the Contract in order to maintain such expected economic benefits to each of the Parties, provided that the economic benefits to the Parties shall not be reduced as a result of exercising the terms of this article.* (Clause 36.3)

While having a stabilisation provision is better than not having one at all (particularly where a project is to be financed, as banks are unwilling to lend to a project with an underlying lack of certainty), the manner of implementation of each such provision is frequently contested, as most fiscal changes will have knock-on economic effects throughout the remainder of the document and the changes are, in any event, subject to mutual agreement.

BITs are international treaties between countries, whereby each country agrees to provide certain protections within its territory to the investors and investments of the other country. As a general rule, BITs protect foreign investors from adverse governmental conduct, such as unlawful expropriation, discriminatory treatment, and failure to provide "full protection and security" and "fair and equitable treatment" and enable investors to bring claims against host governments in international arbitration proceedings where such protections are breached. Additionally, many BITs also require host countries to treat investors and their investments no less favourably than they treat their own nationals. By way of example, Nigeria has over 20 BITs in force with (among others) the United Kingdom, Germany, France, Netherlands, Spain and Sweden.

2.16 Financing

As noted above, banks will need robust stabilisation provisions and investor protections before lending funds to a project. Financing an upstream oil and gas project in Africa will, however, require close scrutiny of the PSA in question in order to determine what consents are required for the creation of security interests and what security can be taken (eg, if revenues from production are required to be repatriated in-country and cannot be held offshore in a charged account, share pledges under local law will be required).

It is common for there to be an absolute prohibition on assignments (except to affiliates, in which case the assignor remains liable in any event), without the prior consent of the host government (which is unlikely to be qualified by reasonableness). Lenders will typically look to take security over the entire value chain and require security over the shares in the investor as well as over the PSA and the revenue stream from sales arrangements (as failure to take security over any of these elements of the project will jeopardise the ability of the lender to generate revenues upon an enforcement event or may otherwise structurally subordinate the lender). If, however, an assignment or pledge cannot be taken over the PSA, lenders will need to get comfortable with security over the shares and the revenue streams only, and with covenants and negative pledges from the investor that it will not do anything to prejudice its rights under the PSA.

2.17 Trends

The last few years have seen a rise in resource nationalism across Africa as discoveries are made and investors earn vast profits from production and corporate transactions. This has caused host governments to assert more rights and exert more control over oil and gas projects. This has led to a number of African countries, notably Angola, Ghana and Nigeria, implementing local content policies and prioritising local service providers and contractors over international competitors. In some cases, the advent of local content policies has led to corporate transactions being stalled, and sometimes even withdrawn, in the face of challenges by local players.

At the project management level however, local content affects day-to-day operational matters. Local partners and service providers are given preference in tender processes, as a minimum proportion of project contracts must be with local parties. In some countries, such as Mozambique, NOCs are also taking more control over marketing and sales of production in order to regulate the revenue stream and cash flow generated by a project.

At a project structuring level, the rise of local players participating in oil and gas projects has also led to an increase in synthetic ownership structures, as many local players may lack sufficient financial and technical resources to carry out operations and are, therefore, supported and effectively guaranteed by investors who fund the obligations of those local players (without taking a direct interest under the PSAs) and, in return, take a share of the profit oil of the local player being funded (which is effectively a type of back-to-back production sharing arrangement). This type of structure obviously comes with its own risks, as the investor funding operations does not have a vote at management committee level under the PSA, such that contractual measures have to be included in the funding arrangement in order to ensure that the local player votes as agreed between itself and the investor. Furthermore, the investor is also exposed to the risk of a breach by the local player of its profit sharing obligations (as this is merely a contractual entitlement) and the additional risk that the local player does not apply the funds paid by the investor for the required needs.

3. Other types of arrangement and other key considerations

As noted at 1 above, PSAs are not the only form of oil and gas title document in use in Africa. The concession form is adopted in certain countries (though far fewer than the countries that adopt the PSA form – see 2 above) while service contracts are awarded from time to time in others.

3.1 Concessions

Under concession arrangements, investors take all the risk and benefits of an oil and gas project and conduct operations as they see fit, albeit subject to the oversight of and regulation by the host government. Unlike with PSAs, host governments do not take an active role in operational management and decision-making procedures and are certainly not involved in the day-to-day management regime. As noted at 1 above, however, the key distinction between concessions and PSAs is that, under a concessionary regime, the investor takes the title to production and the host government's revenue stream is derived from fiscal terms (such as royalties and taxes) charged on production in the hands of the investor.

In some jurisdictions (such as South Africa), even though a concessionary system is adopted, a technical advisory committee comprising representatives of the host government and the investors is still established, although this is less of a management and decision-making body than under a PSA and mostly performs advisory functions. Given the broader control over operations in a concession structure than under a PSA, concession holders are under general obligations to keep the host government informed of all material developments (typically with a quarterly update).

3.2 Service contracts

Aside from the PSA model and the concession model, certain countries occasionally also implement service contract structures. These are similar to PSAs, in that they do not vest any title in production with the investor, but rather, as the name suggests, the investor is engaged to perform oil and gas services (similar to the obligations of investors under PSAs), in return for which the investor is paid a fee (in similar fashion to a contractual entitlement to a share of production). While historically, service contracts gave oil and gas investors no control or say over operational matters (with investors simply performing the required services laid down by the contract), over the last 5-10 years most service contract arrangements are now in fact much closer in style to PSAs.

3.3 Local law

Each PSA or concession or service contract will need to be examined in the light of the local oil and gas laws applicable to the project. Among other things, and aside from the contractual terms applying to each project, local laws may include statutory restrictions (such as back-in rights and local participation, which may be required as a matter of law). Local law may also provide for certain set criteria that oil and gas investors in the country concerned must satisfy (eg, listing on a domestic stock exchange or incorporation in a certain country). Additionally, in some African countries, PSAs are ratified by the local parliament and thereby given effect as if they are local law instruments.

Laws are, however, organic and change over time, hence the importance of robust stabilisation provisions and proper investment structuring to ensure the continued economic viability of an oil and gas project, especially, as noted above, given the rise of resource nationalism in oil and gas-rich countries across Africa and the corresponding changes this brings about to local law. For example, in 2014 alone, both Mozambique and South Africa passed new petroleum laws governing their oil and gas industries, while both Gabon and Nigeria have been debating new petroleum laws for a number of years.

4. Arrangements prior to joint bidding agreements

In addition to entering into a JBA, parties to JVs will also typically enter into a number of other ancillary agreements at the outset of JV operations.

4.1 Confidentiality agreements

Parties will customarily enter into a confidentiality agreement which governs any exchange of confidential information between the parties, and an area of mutual interest (AMI) agreement which creates an alignment between the parties over opportunities in areas of mutual interest. While a confidentiality agreement is not a principal agreement dealing with title interests, nor does it vest exploration and production rights, it is nonetheless frequently negotiated as the scope of confidentiality protections afforded are key where, as is frequently the case, certain parties to the proposed venture have more technical knowledge or sensitive and proprietary information than others.

Confidentiality agreements will also be applicable to various corporate transactions (such as acquisitions and disposals) throughout the life of an oil and gas project. As part of any disclosure process relating to such a transaction, sellers will require buyers to enter into a confidentiality agreement to ensure that documents disclosed to buyers are kept confidential. Sellers should, however, scrutinise the confidentiality provisions of their PSA to ensure that the disclosures are permitted under the terms of the PSA, as certain host governments in Africa have been known to enforce confidentiality restrictions rigorously. For example, sellers will not want to be deemed to be in breach of their PSA confidentiality obligations (eg, because the PSA permits disclosures to asset buyers but not share buyers) and buyers will want to avoid any potential implication that they have procured breaches by sellers (thereby laying themselves open to potential claims for tortious interference). It is, therefore, customary for confidentiality agreements to include a warranty from the seller that the disclosure of information is permitted and that all consents and approvals that may be required to permit such disclosure have in fact been obtained and are in force.

4.2 AMI agreements

An AMI agreement signifies broad alignment between different companies and a desire to work together in the event that certain areas become available for development. Such agreements can vary from loose statements of principle to rights of first refusal or exclusivity when acreage comes up for licensing. They can be structured either as an upfront right of first offer before a company takes any steps towards a new oil and gas opportunity, or as a matching right whereby a company offers a share of newly acquired oil and gas opportunities to its AMI partners. There may be several AMI agreements between different parties, relating to different and/or overlapping areas (which may not be identical to the area for which rights are being offered) and containing a variety of terms. Checking which AMI agreements relate to the bid area, and negotiating between the parties to those agreements to create the appropriate bidding group while preserving the rights under each AMI agreement, can prove challenging.

4.3 Funding agreements

As noted above, local content and local participation plays a key role in upstream JVs in a number of African jurisdictions. It is therefore common for separate funding arrangements to be agreed between the JV parties whereby the nominated local partner in the JV is carried and funded for a certain period of time (ie, the local partner does not pay its share of JV costs, which are in fact paid by the other JV parties). This form of funding arrangement is typically agreed in advance of the bidding process in the form of a separate funding agreement.

The term of such a funding arrangement will vary from transaction to transaction, and is a matter for commercial negotiation between the JV parties. Local partners are typically funded through the exploration and development phases of operations and the associated high capital costs up to production (when ongoing costs are significantly cheaper and mostly operational only). These costs are recoverable by the funding parties as and when production is obtained, but unless and until production occurs, the costs are borne by the paying JV partners, who bear in its entirety the risk of any failure to produce.

One important consideration to bear in mind as part of any funding arrangement is the risk of corruption. JV parties should conduct a full integrity due diligence process on any entity that is nominated as a local partner, in order to ensure that there are no allegations of corruption or nepotism that could tarnish the joint venture and give rise to proceedings under the US Foreign Corrupt Practices Act 1977 or the UK Bribery Act 2010.

5. Joint bidding agreements

A JBA is entered into where a consortium of bidders intends to apply to a regulatory body for the issue of rights to explore for and extract petroleum and aims to share risks, liabilities and financial commitments between bidders and to establish the rights, decision-making mechanics and operational objectives of the bidding group.

Applications for the grant of rights to explore for and extract petroleum take place in a number of different ways around the world, although most African jurisdictions are now frequently awarding drilling rights by offering acreage onshore and offshore to companies in regular licensing rounds (for example, both Angola and Liberia held licensing rounds during 2014). Where two or more companies join together to seek the award of such rights, it is common for them to enter into a JBA to govern their relationship during the application period and the sharing of costs.

In grouping together bidders, different strengths and areas of expertise are commonly sought in order to create a successful bidding team, with technical and financial capabilities commonly being key requirements mandated by the local law applicable in the host country. Obviously not all participants will have all of the characteristics in equal measure, and understanding what each player brings to the team is essential for developing the JBA.

The JBA itself is a precursor to a JOA and shares many of the same features. While JBAs are focused on bidding processes and how to agree proposals to be submitted to host governments, they also typically set out the basic terms of any subsequent JOA that would be entered into upon a successful award following the bid. Indeed, pending finalisation of a JOA, operations may proceed on the basis of the JBA, with costs and liabilities shared in accordance with the basic JBA terms.

The JBA's primary function is to set out the terms on which the parties will make their bid for the oil and gas rights. It will need to delineate the area and type of rights being applied for and the timetable and actions required to prepare and submit the bid (and deal with competing proposals for the bid put forward by each JV party). A JBA will usually also prohibit the parties from making any application for petroleum rights within the specified acreage separately from the group, and may contain warranties as to non-conflict with existing AMIs and other relationships.

Once the preferred bid proposal is voted through by the JV parties, most JBAs will provide for a period during which any party that does not wish to proceed with such a proposal can withdraw from the JV. That party's interest will either be absorbed by the remaining parties or some of them (typically in proportion to the existing interests of the non-withdrawing parties), or a new party acceptable to the co-venturers will need to be found. To enable a new party to join the group, the JBA will have to deal with:

- the approval of the new party by the existing parties (which will usually require unanimity);
- the financial terms on which the new party joins, including whether it is responsible for a share of past costs of the group; and
- the mechanism by which the new party will accede to the JBA.

The withdrawing party will generally be required not to make a competing bid for the same acreage on its own or with another group, and to treat the terms of the application as confidential.

As discussed previously, the JBA should provide details sufficient to enable it to be used to operate the development in the early stages while a fully-formed JOA is being negotiated. JBAs commonly deal with:

- the decision-making procedures of the bidding group and situations where the required votes cannot be reached;
- the appointment of an operator and establishment of an operating committee to decide operational matters;
- thresholds for approvals for expenditure;
- the consequences of a failure by a party to pay (typically, the ejection of such party from the group);
- transfer rights and withdrawal/relinquishment;
- *force majeure* events; and
- the treatment of data derived from joint operations.

While the terms of JOAs are discussed at 6 below, the level of detail required in the JBA for each of these terms should be driven by how fast the development will proceed and an informed view of how quickly a JOA can be agreed.

6. Joint operating agreements

The day-to-day management and operation of an oil field is reflected in the JOA, which lasts for the duration of an upstream oil and gas project and is referred to regularly for guidance on voting procedures and tender processes for contract awards and the adoption of annual work programmes and budgets.

The JOA is one half of a pair of documents (the other being the PSA) from which a company's oil and gas rights in Africa are derived. As noted above, where more than one company is granted upstream rights over the same area, the grant will impose joint and several liability on the parties, often referring to them as a single entity (the 'contractor'). The key principle of any JOA is, therefore, to separate that joint liability into several percentage interest shares in the JV. Such separation operates between the JV participants only and not against the grantor of the oil and gas rights (ie, the host government), which remains free to pursue claims against any and all of the JV partners and will most commonly take action against those members of the group that it considers to have the deepest pockets.

While oil and gas title documents differ significantly around the world (with PSAs very common in Africa but not in western Europe and the United States), this is not the case with JOAs. Many of the JOAs in force across Africa today are based on forms adopted in western Europe and the United States (such as the model form maintained by the Association of International Petroleum Negotiators (the 'AIPN')). Some countries have, in particular licensing rounds, published a preferred model form JOA that they would like investors to adopt (which Mozambique did for the 2006 licensing round). Those forms have not, however, deviated substantially from the international model form discussed below and are normally based on it.

6.1 Operatorship and operating committees

A JOA creates a contractual, unincorporated JV. One party is appointed under the JOA as 'operator', with the role of carrying out joint operations, representing the JV to the government and third parties and managing the internal affairs of the group, including meetings and accounting. The operator performs these roles on a no win/no loss basis, taking no additional risk and obtaining no additional reward for performing the role (over and above its separate percentage interest share in the JV). The JOA will set the standard to which the operator should perform. The more recent trend has been for JOAs to define this standard by reference to "good and prudent petroleum industry practices and field conservation principles".[1] This arguably imposes a higher standard than was previously the case, as the previous standard having been that of a "reasonable and prudent operator".[2] Replacing the term 'reasonable' with 'good' gives operators less flexibility and is more burdensome.

Because the operator is meant to function on a not-for-profit basis, however, the JOA will provide that the operator is only liable in excess of its percentage interest share when guilty of gross negligence or wilful misconduct. The term 'gross negligence or wilful misconduct' is carefully negotiated and defined in the JOA; it usually includes intentional or reckless acts or acts of wanton indifference to harmful consequences that the operator knew or should have known about. JOAs typically provide, however, only for specific operator liability over and above its percentage interest share where senior supervisory management at a certain level has behaved with gross negligence or wilful misconduct. The level at which such liability is triggered is, commonly, rigorously negotiated. The AIPN model form JOA includes a proviso, which operates even in the event of gross negligence or wilful misconduct, excluding the operator from any liability for consequential or environmental loss (this was also included in the Mozambican model form JOA adopted for the 2006 licensing round). Notwithstanding the Deepwater Horizon accident in 2010 at the Macondo wellsite, the most recent model form JOA published by the AIPN has not deviated from this limitation of liability concept, the rationale being that any such deviation would deter oil and gas companies from taking on the role of operator and disrupt the future development of oil and gas resources.

1 Clause 4.2(B) of the AIPN model form JOA from 2012.
2 This formulation was previously widely adopted across a number of upstream operating documents and was more common in JVs featuring US companies, as the US formulation tended to refer to 'reasonable' as opposed to 'good'.

The JOA also creates an operating committee, comprising representatives from all JV participants, which is responsible for delineating which matters that have been delegated to the operator must be considered by the operating committee. The operating committee is essentially the brain of the JV.

Voting in the committee will be on the basis of the separate percentage interest held by each party. Accordingly, establishing the aggregate percentage interest required to agree a proposal (the 'passmark') will be hotly negotiated in the group. Passmarks may differ according to the separate phases of operations reached, and key decisions such as relinquishment of the asset, dismissal of the operator or surrender of parts of the acreage may require higher passmarks or even unanimity. JOAs vary significantly in the complexity of their voting arrangements, particularly with regard to techniques for avoiding a deadlock; for example, the passmark may be lowered if a proposal is repeatedly brought back to a committee. It is not, however, uncommon to find three different passmarks for different types of operations:

- a basic passmark for routine operational matters;
- a higher passmark, or even unanimity, for certain specific matters that are considered to be critical by the participants (ie, those activities that a party does not want to be compelled to perform, such as relinquishment); and
- a lower passmark for operations that are necessary to ensure that the PSA is not revoked and that stipulated minimum work obligations are in fact performed.

The other way in which an operator can be supervised is through the control of expenditure, which is achieved in a number of different ways. An annual work programme and budget will customarily be agreed (although in some cases they can be agreed on a multi-year basis). In addition, the operating committee will reserve the right to approve expenditure within the budget of more than a specified figure or type. This concept of authorisations for expenditure enables non-operators to review and control the operator's discretion, even if the expenditure were included within an approved budget. Of course, the authorisation for expenditure procedure is potentially open to abuse, with non-operators being able to block plans that are otherwise within the overall agreed programme and budget. Setting out the types and levels of expenditure for which authorisation for expenditure is required, and the circumstances in which an objection is deemed genuine, can provide fertile ground for negotiation. By way of example, the Mozambican model form required authorisations for expenditure for amounts in excess of $1 million during the exploration phase and $3 million during the development or production phase.

In addition to controls on expenditure, the operator is usually required to observe set procedures with regard to contracting for certain types of work, including a competitive tendering process for contract awards in excess of a certain amount. Under the Mozambican model form, tendering was required for contract awards exceeding $500,000 during the exploration phase, $1 million during the development phase and $750,000 during the production phase. Requirements for local content, minimum environmental and health and safety standards and other matters may lead to an approved list of contractors. While the operator will want to maximise its ability to operate the field, other parties (including the host government) will want to ensure that they are protected not only against bad operations but also poor operations. In practice, dissatisfaction with the performance of contractors can be a source of tension between operators and non-operators.

Access to information and a right to audit accounting information are crucial to enabling non-operators to monitor the conduct of operations. The accounting procedure normally forms a significant part of the JOA and establishes the nature and categorisation of expenditures that are chargeable to the joint account and recoverable as cost oil under the PSA. Given the level of detail involved in this section of the JOA and the input provided by the accounting teams of each JV party, drafting the accounting procedure can take a significant amount of time. Critical areas include the scope of general and administrative costs (including overheads born by the operator and potentially by its parent company), the extent to which information should be provided to non-operators and the frequency and terms on which the accounting records may be audited.

6.2 Sole risk and non-consent

Over the life of an upstream oil and gas project, the interests and commercial sensitivities of JV parties vary sufficiently that JOAs normally reserve the right for parties:

- not to participate in joint activities where they did not vote in the affirmative in the relevant operating committee meeting or where they did affirmatively vote but changed their mind within a certain number of days of the vote ('non-consent'); or
- to undertake activities without the participation of all the joint venture parties ('sole risk').

Whereas parties might have been willing to do everything together at first, their understanding of the field, its risks and costs and their own position (economically and commercially) may have changed over time. Parties with smaller interests may not wish to fund larger commitments than they expected and larger parties may wish to press ahead with more costly or risky developments even though they do not achieve the passmark for joint action.

Non-consent is usually not permitted for mandatory obligations under the PSA and may be limited to other specific types of project. Certain JOAs require that if a party elects non-consent, the consenting participants may convene another operating committee meeting, following which they can have a second opportunity to elect non-consent. If, at a later date a non-consenting party wishes to rejoin that part of the project (which would in the meantime have been conducted on a sole risk basis – see below), it will normally have to buy its way back in by picking up its share of the cost, commonly together with some sort of time-based additional charge.

Sole risk clauses are also frequently limited to certain types of project (such as further exploration or appraisal operations or deepening or side-tracking existing well holes – as was the case with the Mozambican model form), and it is rare for JOAs to enable any type of operation to be conducted on a sole risk basis. It is, however, possible under some JOAs for those operations that are part of an approved work programme and budget, and for which an authorisation for expenditure was required but not obtained, to be conducted on a sole risk basis. This can obviously cut across approved operating committee work programmes and budgets and force parties to proceed on a sole risk basis where an authorisation for expenditure for such an operation is not approved. The operator will usually operate the sole risk project, particularly if joint property is used, and there will be provisions to ensure that joint operations take priority, so that a sole risk project cannot adversely affect a joint operation. As with non-consent, there will be additional costs for rejoining a particular sole risk project at a later time, commonly based on a multiple of the original cost incurred by the participating sole risk parties (which can be up to 10 times the original cost of the expenditure and, in the case of the Mozambican model form, seven times the original cost).

6.3 Withdrawal and default

There are normally three ways in which a party can leave a JOA:

- transferring its interest;
- withdrawing from the JV; or
- where that party is in default of its obligations, compulsorily forfeiting its interest.

Forfeiture is the ultimate price paid for failure to contribute to a percentage interest share of the cost of the JV (which now typically includes any failure to indemnify, in addition to the more common failure to fund costs). The consequences of default usually escalate over time, beginning with the party losing all rights under the JOA for a period of time after the default has occurred. For so long as the default continues, a party in default will not receive information, be entitled to attend and vote at JOA meetings or take its share of petroleum. If the default continues for a further specified period (which can be as little as 30 days after the date of the default notice, as was the case under the Mozambican model form), the defaulting party may be obliged to forfeit its interest under the JOA and transfer that interest to its co-venturers.

If one party is in default, the other parties to the JOA will be required to pay the sums in default, each in the proportion that its percentage interest bears to the total of the non-defaulting parties' percentage interests. Any failure to pay these additional sums is treated as a default in and of itself. Upon a defaulting party forfeiting its rights, the non-defaulting co-venturers will have the right to acquire the defaulting party's interest in the proportion that their percentage interests bear to the total percentage interests of those parties exercising their right to acquire. In circumstances where other parties do not wish to take up the defaulting party's interest, the JV normally dissolves and the asset interest is relinquished.

A party may also decide, even without defaulting on its obligations, that it wishes to withdraw from the JV and the PSA. In these circumstances, the other parties will be entitled to take up the departing party's interests in proportion to their percentage interests, as in the case of default. Participants are, however, typically restricted from withdrawing from the JV before mandatory obligations under the PSA have been fulfilled.

6.4 Transfers

All JOAs require that the continuing parties consent to the identity of the proposed purchaser of an interest. Consent is frequently qualified by an obligation on the other parties to be reasonable, or by a more detailed statement saying that consent may only be refused on grounds of the financial and technical capability of the proposed transferee. It is worth noting that this provision requires the consent of each other co-venturer (ie, the passmark is irrelevant for this purpose), and will generally require suitable information on the proposed transferee to be provided in order to enable the co-venturers to make a determination as to the technical and financial capabilities of the new joiner. Parties are also normally permitted to assign rights under the JOA as security for financing.

Some JOAs will, however, limit the minimum percentage interest that a party may own and, therefore, restrict the part of a percentage interest that may be transferred, such that neither the transferor nor the transferee may hold less than the minimum percentage interest following the transfer (this is commonly 5% or sometimes, as in the case of the Mozambican model form, 10%), which obviously also limits the total number of JV parties.

Additionally, transfers to affiliates are usually permitted without consent being required, provided that the transferor remains secondarily liable for the performance of obligations under the JOA. There is usually a supplementary provision requiring reassignment to the original party if the affiliate ceases to be part of the same group as the original party.

6.5 Pre-emption

Many JOAs provide co-venturers with the right to pre-empt the sale of an interest in the venture to a third party. While on the one hand, parties need their oil and gas rights to be tradeable assets, selling out of the venture runs the risk of breaking up the original cohesiveness of the group. Although highly contentious, pre-emption rights can actually be seen as a compromise: they allow a party to sell its interest while still preserving the culture of the JV by preventing an unacceptable third party from joining the group. In practice, pre-emption rights can inhibit the marketability of oil and gas assets, because potential purchasers will be put off by the prospect of having their deal swiped from them after months of hard and costly work. Historically, pre-emption rights in most JOAs only applied to sales at the asset level (ie, transfers of participating interests by JV parties) and this was certainly the case under the Mozambican model form. In recent years, however, the oil and gas industry has also tended to apply pre-emption rights to share sales and indirect transfers (ie, transfers at the corporate level of shares in the JOA parties) and it is now relatively rare to encounter a JOA entered into in the last five years or more that does not contain a right of pre-emption on both asset and share transfers. In the case of a package sale of several assets (as identified below), however, there can be difficulties in applying the provision at shareholder level.

Pre-emption clauses in JOAs vary significantly in their complexity and distinctions can be made between clauses that provide only for rights of first refusal or first offer and those that provide true rights of pre-emption (although some JOAs can contain both). A right of first offer will usually allow co-venturers a period of time in which to consider whether and when to make an offer for the interest being sold. The selling party may, of course, decide not to accept such an offer, believing that it may obtain a better price from a third party. Rights of first refusal, however, often go on to state that no sale may be made to a third party for less than the highest offer made by a co-venturer, and also typically impose deadlines within which transfers to third parties must be made.

If rights of first refusal are a relatively soft protection, a fully termed pre-emption clause is much more aggressive and gives co-venturers the right to acquire the interest on the same terms as have been negotiated and agreed with a third party. Even if no co-venturer exercises its rights to pre-empt, the waiting period can provide a significant disincentive to a potential purchaser, as completion cannot occur until such time has elapsed or the co-venturers waive their entitlement. Some pre-emption clauses require the final agreed terms and conditions, together with all supporting information, to be provided to the co-venturers, whereas others are unclear as to whether a reasonably detailed term sheet or a fully-termed agreement needs to be in place before the offer is circulated to co-venturers, who may seek to exploit any ambiguity in the pre-emption process in order to delay sale transactions and give themselves more time to consider whether or not to exercise rights of pre-emption.

Where the offer is made in cash, matching its terms is not difficult; it is not, however, uncommon to see purchasers structure their deal so as to create an unmatchable offer by including other assets in the price. The object of structuring transactions in this way is to defeat pre-emption rights by arguing that no co-venturer can pre-empt the offer because it cannot provide the same consideration (eg, the co-venturer cannot possibly own the same participating interest in an oil field that the purchaser is prepared to asset swap as consideration for the sale). Many JOAs, however (including the Mozambican model form from 2006), now provide that a cash equivalent value must be stated by the seller or can be determined (by an expert or ultimately by the courts) if the offer includes non-cash assets, in order to enable co-venturers to pre-empt validly.

Further difficulties arise where a co-venturer is selling several assets covered by more than one JOA, some of which contain pre-emption rights and some of which do not. In these circumstances, it has been argued that the package deal is unmatchable, although this argument is threatened if the sale and purchase agreement negotiated with the third party allocates separate values to each asset (which is sometimes required for tax purposes). In the context of a package deal, certain JOAs provide that a right of pre-emption will only apply if the asset to which the right relates is in excess of a set percentage of the aggregate value of the package.

The existence of rights of pre-emption over some but not all of the assets in a package may also act as a disincentive to purchasers, as they may want an all-or-nothing deal whereby they can walk away from a potential purchase if a key asset in the package is pre-empted. For this reason, purchasers may try to game asset valuations in a package deal and ascribe valuations to certain assets that either vitiate any rights of pre-emption, or allocate a prohibitively high value to those assets in order to block co-venturers from exercising their rights of pre-emption.

7. Conclusion

The legal structure of oil and gas projects in Africa differs substantially from the legal structure of oil and gas projects that exists in western Europe and the United States. Accordingly, investors and lenders alike should ensure that they fully understand the risks and rewards present in each jurisdiction in which they elect to invest, and take sufficient contractual precautions (such as robust stabilisation provisions and BIT protections). While there are a number of issues identified in this chapter, the most important differences between the production sharing system and the concessionary system are the treatment of ownership rights, local participation, profit sharing mechanics and cost recovery formulations. These features introduce an additional level of risk to oil and gas projects that are not otherwise present in the US and western European markets, and need to be thoroughly examined and factored into deal economics before any investment is made in the upstream sector in Africa.

From the perspective of host governments, the greater degree of influence and control that local players have under the production sharing system means that oil and gas projects in Africa will continue to be governed by this system instead of the concessionary system.

As noted previously, a key trend across Africa during the last few years has been the required scope and extent of local participation in upstream projects, with a number of countries having already implemented (and more countries in the process of passing legislation to implement) local content policies that prioritise local service providers and contractors. The extent to which such local participation is required is likely to rise in the near to medium term as resource nationalism takes more of a foothold across Africa, and with host governments responding to the windfall profits that oil and gas companies have been making across the continent in the last few years, following major discoveries on both the east and west coasts, at a time of (then) rising oil prices.

The drop in the oil price towards the end of 2014 may start to deter investors from investing in exploration projects and participating in licensing rounds, particularly as falling oil prices mean that technologically difficult projects (such as deep water pre-salt exploration) are closer to their break-even point as they are significantly more costly than most other projects. This may, in turn, cause host governments to postpone upcoming licensing rounds or, where oil revenue is critical to the local economy, to take measures to relieve some of the burden of local participation in order to incentivise investor participation. As ever, the fine balance between the political necessities of host governments and economic reality and commodity market prices will play a big part in the oil and gas sector during 2015 and 2016.

Local content in the African oil and gas industry

Caroline-Lucy Moran
Akin Gump Strauss Hauer & Feld LLP

1. Introduction

An international oil company (IOC) operating today will be familiar with local content policies, which have long been a feature of the global oil and gas industry. Yet, while local content initiatives have been implemented for over 40 years, it is only relatively recently that there have been holistic studies on their impact, in terms of their economic costs and benefits, and lessons for industry participants.[1]

A focus on local content in the African oil and gas industry is particularly informative to this wider discussion at a time when IOC interest across Africa is intensifying and yet developmental challenges remain significant. While Africa may be considered to be 'reaping the benefits of better macro-economic management and deepening integration into the world economy', it faces considerable and entrenched issues, such as poverty and widespread unemployment.[2] Industry's contribution to economic growth overall remains limited and there exists a disconnect between such growth and both employment and social development.[3]

Local content policies in the broadest sense are those government-imposed initiatives that seek to facilitate the oil and gas industry generating broader benefits for the domestic economy. State or locally owned equity participation in oil and gas assets may be considered to be one aspect of such interventionist policies.

As more commonly used in relation to oil and gas, the term 'local content' refers to the wider 'value added' that is sought to be created across sectors by the inputs, outputs and infrastructure requirements of the industry. It is the oil and gas industry's backward links' to the domestic economy, such as through employment, training, goods and services, that are most commonly regulated with a view to boosting growth. While local content policies often seek to realise immediate benefits for the domestic economy, a primary goal is the long-term transfer of specialist skills and knowledge to the local workforce.

This chapter will address the theoretical and historic background to local content

1 See, for example, Silvana Tondo, Michael Warner, Osmel E Manzano & Yahya Anouti, *Local Content Policies in the Oil and Gas Sector*, (2013), Washington DC: World Bank), available at http://www-wds.worldbank.org/external/default/WDSContentServer/WDSP/IB/2013/07/12/000445729_20130712141852/Rendered/PDF/789940REVISED000Box377371B00PUBLIC0.pdf.

2 *2014 Mutual Review of Development Effectiveness in Africa: Promise and Performance*, jointly prepared by the United Nations Economic Commission for Africa (ECA) and the Organisation for Economic Co-operation and Development (OECD).

3 *Economic Report on Africa 2014: Dynamic Industrial Policy in Africa: Innovative Institutions, Effective Processes and Flexible Mechanisms*, jointly prepared by the United Nations Economic Commission for Africa (ECA) and the African Union (AU).

policies and the various means by which they are implemented, taking examples from across the African oil and gas industry. This chapter will also consider the challenges posed by local content for both host governments and IOCs.

2. Local content: theory and historical background

Central to the economics of local content policies is the concept of sector links as key for economic growth. By this model, put forward by Hirschman during the 1950s,[4] industrial sectors are highly interactive. A given industry will have an impact on other domestic industries through a series of connections, including backward links, such as the demand for products and services (ie, the outputs of other industries) and forward links (ie, the output of that industry being supplied forward to other industries). Local content policies in the oil and gas industry primarily seek to regulate backward links and connected employment links, by stipulating that IOCs must source certain goods, services and employees based in the host state.

Recent studies applying global data have stressed that, while the forward links created by the oil and gas industry (eg, downstream sectors) are significantly greater than those created by other industries, in most countries few other industries create fewer backward links.[5] Without, and perhaps despite, regulation, the oil and gas industry generates limited cross-sector demand for input goods and services and wider employment. This is seen across the globe, in both developed and developing countries, for reasons which will be discussed later in this chapter. From a government standpoint, the economics seem to support the need to implement local content policies in the oil and gas industry in order to address this shortfall and maximise the potential for wider domestic growth.

Local content policies are also intrinsically linked to political as well as economic goals. From an ideological perspective, local content policies have been significantly influenced by the principle of state sovereignty over national resources, enshrined by the UN General Assembly's resolution of 1962. This stated that a nation's permanent sovereignty over its natural wealth and resources must be exercised not only in the interests of national development but also "the well-being of the people of the State concerned."[6]

It is clear that for a regime seeking to remain loyal to the principle of state sovereignty, the policies of its extractive industries must be premised not only on economic enrichment but also with a view to providing wider societal benefits for domestic citizens. In the oil and gas industry, local content policies are used by governments to encapsulate this rhetoric, by purporting to tackle at once both economic and developmental concerns.

In addition to these theoretical and ideological aspects, the widespread implementation of local content policies in the oil and gas industry also stems from the arguable historic success of the implementation of such policies in, for example, the United Kingdom and Norway.

---

4 Albert O Hirschman, *The Strategy of Economic Development* (1958, Oxford University Press).
5 Tondo *et al*, *op cit* (note 1 above), pp 5 & 167-169.
6 UN General Assembly resolution 1803 (XVII) of December 14 1962, *Permanent sovereignty over natural resources*, available at www.ohchr.org/EN/ProfessionalInterest/Pages/NaturalResources.aspx.

It was the United Kingdom that first implemented local content initiatives in the North Sea in the 1970s, in the context of wider interventionist government policies of the time. The government's Office Supplies Office (OSO), formed in 1973, led the policy drive to generate the supply chain and employment opportunities needed to extract oil domestically, and arguably succeeded in raising UK industrial participation in North Sea expenditure to approximately 70%. The OSO sought, for example, to ensure that United Kingdom-based suppliers could compete with foreign firms, to encourage the establishment of new UK suppliers and, later on, to support domestic research and development in the oil and gas industry.

In particular, the OSO introduced the Full and Fair Opportunity policy (FFO) to enable UK firms to compete for business. The FFO was advanced by several means. The then Department of Energy agreed a non-statutory memorandum of understanding and code of practice with the United Kingdom Offshore Operators Association, which set out the terms of tender documents and allowed OSO input in the tender process. The OSO was allowed, for example, to suggest additional UK bidders or make bidders provide UK content estimates.[7] Local content was also advanced by contractual means: an 'FFO clause' was included in the terms of all licence applications from the 1976/77 to 1984/85 North Sea licensing rounds. The FFO thus represented the first local content policy, "providing both the right and the mechanisms for [the OSO] to intercede in [IOC] procurement decisions".[8]

3. Local content in Africa

The United Kingdom case demonstrates the use of softer mechanisms – which were not legislated – to encourage local content in the oil and gas industry. The FFO maintained, to some extent, a free market and allowed participant IOCs to enjoy a greater level of flexibility in adopting local content. Today, there are a number of so-called 'channels' of local content policy implementation, which vary considerably across the oil and gas industry and particularly across African states. These channels, as recently identified by the World Bank, include:[9]

- legislation (primary and secondary);
- contractual provisions in petroleum agreements; and
- policy guidelines and codes of practice.

In any jurisdiction, one or several such implementation channels may be used, which methods will be highly context-specific and depend on a number of factors. In particular, the maturity of the host oil and gas industry and the relative attractiveness of the jurisdiction as a place of IOC investment may impact upon government policy. The government's wider political goals will also come significantly into play.

---

7 NJ Smith, 'Industrial Policy: Lessons from the North Sea, *Civitas Review*, Volume 10, Issue 2 (December 2013) at p 5.

8 *Ibid*, at p 6.

9 Tondo *et al*, *op cit* (note 1 above), p 37.

3.1 Legislation

Host state legislation, which is binding on all IOC participants, is the most rigid means of enshrining local content requirements in the oil and gas industry. This may be introduced by the government by way of primary legislation (ie, acts, statutes) or secondary legislation (eg, decrees, regulations, rules, orders).

In Africa, this channel of policy implementation is arguably best exemplified by the local content regimes of Nigeria and Angola, as detailed below. In the wider African context, it is important to note that these countries support the most developed oil and gas industries on the continent. Together, Nigeria and Angola accounted for 75% of sub-Saharan Africa's oil production in 2013.[10] Nigeria is the largest oil producer in Africa at the time of writing[11] and highly dependent on oil and gas exports, revenue from which represents over 90% of total export revenue.[12] Similarly, oil has been the lifeblood of the Angolan economy since its independence from Portugal in 1975, and remains so today. In 2009, the oil sector constituted over 44% of Angola's gross domestic product, over 95% of the value of exports, and around 65% of government revenues.[13]

Local content is also historically well-established in both Nigeria and Angola. The need to enhance local content in the Nigerian industry has been expressed in the country's parliament since 1959 and was advanced significantly by its wider 'indigenisation policy' of the early 1970s.[14] In Angola, local content was first enshrined in policy in the late 1970s. Most notably, neither Nigeria nor Angola struggles to attract significant IOC investment. Major and well-established IOC players in both countries include ExxonMobil, Chevron, Total, and Eni, with Shell also prominent in Nigeria and BP in Angola. There has also been significant prospective interest in both countries. The most recent Nigerian marginal fields bid round was announced in December 2013 to great industry anticipation, but has, at the time of writing, been suspended. Similarly, in recent years Angola's pre-salt discoveries have attracted significant IOC interest and it is anticipated that there will be a number of auctions of such prospects in the coming years.

With clear historical imperatives and having long secured IOC interest, it is unsurprising that the Nigerian and Angolan governments have chosen to enshrine local content policy in stringent legislation. The use of legislation as the implementation channel is not, however, reserved for well-established oil and gas regimes. Recent analysis of global data indicates that, on a country-by-country basis, it is particularly:

> *new producers, with less developed economies and/or large resource bases, [that] tend to adopt more assertive policies by imposing measures that limit investors' choices with*

---

10 Jesse Salah Ovadia 'Local content and natural resource governance: The cases of Angola and Nigeria', *The Extractive Industries and Society*, Volume 1, Issue 2 (November 2014), pp 137-146.

11 OPEC Annual Statistics Bulletin 2014, available at www.opec.org/opec_web/static_files_project/media/downloads/publications/ASB2014.pdf, p 29.

12 US Energy Administration, Nigeria online briefing (December 31 2013), available at www.eia.gov/countries/analysisbriefs/Nigeria/nigeria.pdf.

13 Tondo *et al*, *op cit* (note 1 above), p 14.

14 Uchenna Jerome Orji, 'Towards sustainable local content development in the Nigerian oil and gas industry: an appraisal of the legal framework and challenges – Part 1', (2014) *International Energy Law Review*, Volume 1, pp 30-42.

respect to employment, purchasing strategies, localization, and the transfer of knowledge.[15]

Ghana provides an example of this, as will be discussed in further detail below. Alternatively, a host government may seek a moderate approach to local content in the interests of flexibility and in order to attract IOCs, as will be shown, for example, in the case of Mozambique.

(a) *Nigeria*

The Nigerian Oil and Gas Industry Content Development Act 2010 (NCDA) is a stand-alone piece of legislation dealing specifically with local content. It defines 'Nigerian Content' as the "quantum of composite value added to or created in the Nigerian economy by a systematic development of capacity and capabilities through the deliberate utilization of Nigerian human and material resources and services in the Nigerian petroleum industry".[16] The NCDA is wide-reaching, setting out both overriding principles and quantitative requirements that are binding on all IOCs. Local content compliance is monitored by the Nigerian Content Development and Monitoring Board (NCDMB).

The NCDA enshrines the general principle that first consideration must be given to Nigerian goods and services as inputs for the oil and gas industry. In addition, the detailed Schedule to the NCDA stipulates specific mandatory quantum levels of Nigerian Content across a wide range of goods and services. For example, 85% of length of 2D seismic data and 100% of spend on 2D seismic data processing services must constitute Nigerian Content.[17] There is a catch-all that where a description of goods or services is not specified in the NCDA, the NCDMB has the mandate to set the minimum Nigerian Content level for that item, pending the inclusion of the minimum content level for those goods or services by an amendment to the NCDA.[18] The NCDA ensures that IOCs cannot avoid local content requirements simply because local equity participation is involved. For example, the NCDA requires that an IOC operating through Nigerian subsidiaries must demonstrate that a minimum of 50% of the equipment used in the execution of work is owned by the Nigerian subsidiaries themselves.[19]

Pursuant to the NCDA, Nigerians must also be given priority with respect to employment and training opportunities.[20] For example, all operators in the Nigerian oil and gas industry must employ only Nigerians in junior and intermediate employment roles,[21] and may retain a maximum of only five per cent of expatriates in management positions, which positions are also subject to approval of the NCDMB (as defined below).[22] IOCs are required to make expenditure, to the satisfaction of the NCDMB, for the promotion of education, training and research

---

15 Tondo *et al*, *op cit* (note 1 above), p xiii.
16 NCDA, section 106.
17 *Ibid*, section 11 and Schedule.
18 *Ibid*, section 12.
19 *Ibid*, section 41(2).
20 *Ibid*, section 10.
21 *Ibid*, section 35.
22 *Ibid*, sections 32 and 33.

and development. It has been commented that because the NCDA does not set out minimum monetary requirements in this regard, there is the risk that IOC expenditure may be minimal, although it seems likely that the Nigerian government will introduce specific legislation to address this shortcoming.[23]

In terms of initial requirements on IOCs, prior to commencing operations, the NCDA requires, for example, that all operators in the oil and gas industry must, before "bidding for any license, permit or interest and before carrying out any project in the Nigerian oil and gas industry... submit a Nigerian Content Plan to the [NCDMB] demonstrating compliance with the Nigerian content requirements".[24] It is only after the NCDMB is satisfied with such a plan, and subject to any public review, that an IOC will be issued a certificate of authorisation that it may proceed with the business in question. The NCDA also established the Nigerian Content Development Fund for the purpose of funding the implementation of Nigerian local content in the oil and gas industry. By law, 1% of the contract value of every contract awarded to any operator or other entity involved in the upstream sector is deducted at source and paid into the fund, which is managed by NCDMB.[25]

The local content policy of Nigeria is onerous for IOCs and may become increasingly so if the all-encompassing Petroleum Industry Bill (PIB) is enacted in the near future.

(b) *Angola*

Angola uses secondary legislation as the main channel for local content policy. While local content principles are enshrined in the Petroleum Activities Law 2004, more prescriptive requirements are detailed in a series of official government decrees. In line with local content policies across the continent, the Angolan regime seeks to regulate the oil and gas industry through two major policy objectives: the 'Angolisation' of the workforce, including in employment and training, and the domestic sourcing of goods and services.[26]

Angola also uses contractual provisions in its model form production sharing contract as a supporting device for the purposes of requiring local content compliance by IOCs. This is discussed at 3.2(a) below.

There have been local content initiatives in Angola's oil and gas industry in relation to employment since the early 1980s. For example, an official decree was issued in 1982 with the objective "to endow the People's Republic of Angola with national personnel able to assure the functioning of the economic key sectors".[27] More recently, the law was revised to accommodate advances in technological and human elements since the 1982 decree.

Decree-Law 17/09 deals specifically with rules and procedures to be observed by IOCs in the recruitment, integration, training and development of workers from the oil sector. It requires that all IOCs operating in the Angolan oil sector, whether

---

23 Uchenna Jerome Orj, *op cit* (note 14 above), at p 12.
24 NCDA, section 7.
25 *Ibid*, section 104.
26 Tondo *et al*, *op cit* (note 1 above), p 39.
27 Republic of Angola, Council of Ministers (1982), cited by Tondo *et al*, *op cit* (note 1 above), p 26.

directly or indirectly through an Angolan subsidiary, must populate their workforces in all categories and functions with Angolan citizens. Only if "there are not, demonstrably, in the domestic labor market", Angolan citizens with sufficient qualifications and experience may IOCs seek prior authorisation from the Ministry of Petroleum to hire foreign workers.[28]

There are ongoing requirements regarding training and development. For example, every IOC must prepare an 'annual program contract', subject to ministerial approval, detailing plans for the integration of Angolans into the workforce and specific training programs for Angolan personnel.[29] IOCs also have ongoing reporting obligations in this regard, to submit to the Ministry of Petroleum, in the first quarter of each year, a detailed report on the implementation of human resource development during the previous year.[30]

Operators, on behalf of each participant IOC, are also required to make annual monetary contributions to a centralised training and development fund, in accordance with criteria set out in Decree-Law 17/09.[31] While the employment regime does not otherwise enshrine quantitative targets for the Angolisation of the workforce, it sets out stringent monetary penalties on IOCs, linked to these contributions, if they do not comply with the regulations. For example, an IOC not complying with the requirement to obtain ministerial approval for the hiring of a foreign employee will be penalised by a fine of an amount in local currency equivalent to 25% of the annual contribution for training.[32]

Separate secondary legislation deals with local content requirements with regard to the procurement of goods and services, most recently Decree-Law 127/03. Under this decree, all procurement expenditure relating to activities that do not entail high capital value or specialist know-how are reserved for Angolan goods and services alone.[33] This includes, for example, the provision of transport of products from terminals to supply points.[34] Specified goods or services requiring a higher level of know-how are open to competition under a 'semi-competitive' regime, by which foreign suppliers and service providers must form joint ventures with Angolan companies prior to any procurement bid.[35] Oil and gas activities falling within this category include, for example, the purchase and/or processing of geographical data and the operation and maintenance of production installations. Remaining goods and services, typically those requiring highly specialist technologies or know-how, fall under a 'competitive regime' and may be put to international competitive tender. The Angolan NOC, Sonangol, and selected Angolan private companies have a right of first refusal to be engaged, provided that their bid is not more than 10% higher than those of other companies.

---

28 Angolan Ministry of the Interior, Decree-Law 17/09, article 4.
29 *Ibid*, articles 6 & 7.
30 *Ibid*, article 9.
31 *Ibid*, articles 12 & 13.
32 *Ibid*, article 16.
33 *Ibid*, article 2.
34 *Ibid*.
35 *Ibid*, articles 2 & 6.

(c) Ghana

By contrast with Nigeria and Angola, Ghana is in the early stages of oil and gas industry development following the first discoveries on a commercial scale in 2007. Ghana's local content policy is primarily enshrined through legislation, under the Petroleum (Local Content and Local Participation) Regulations 2013. These regulations, both in structure and content, derive significantly from the Nigerian model. The Ghanaian regulations similarly employ a Local Content Committee, established by the Petroleum Commission Act 2011 (Act 821), to oversee the application of local content rules.

The primary purpose of the Ghanaian regulations accords with those across the African continent, being to "promote the maximisation of value-addition and job creation through the use of local expertise, goods and services, businesses and financing in the petroleum industry value chain and their retention in the country".[36] Mirroring the Nigerian model, the regulations enshrine the general principle that Ghanaian companies have preference in any bidding process for the acquisition of goods and services,[37] while setting out onerous quantified minimum local content requirements per activity, as detailed in the First Schedule to the regulations.[38]

With regard to employment, it is a mandatory requirement that only Ghanaians shall be employed in junior and mid-tier roles in the oil and gas industry. Notably, the Ghanaian regulations go further than the Nigerian model by enshrining quantified local content requirements for employment criteria, as well as for goods and services. It stipulates the following targets to be obtained by certain deadlines by reference to the date of effectiveness of an IOC's petroleum agreement:[39]

Recruitment and training	Start	5 years	10 years
(a) Management staff	30%	50%- 60%	70% – 80%
(b) Technical core staff	20%	50%- 60%	70% -80%
(c) Other staff	80%	90%	100%

The Ghanaian approach certainly aligns with the notion that new producers are, perhaps surprisingly, more assertive in their approach to local content. Notably, the juxtaposition of such stringent implementation channels with an early-stage industry will likely heighten the challenges faced by government and IOCs, particularly regarding capacity, as will be discussed later in this chapter.

36 Ghanaian Petroleum (Local Content and Local Participation) Regulations 2013, regulation 1.
37 *Ibid*, regulation 11.
38 *Ibid*, regulation 10 & First Schedule.
39 *Ibid.*

(d) *Mozambique*

For the purposes of an analysis of local content, Mozambique may also be viewed as hosting a relatively early-stage oil and gas industry, for, "'though oil and gas exploration in Mozambique dates back to as early as 1904, it has been the 2012 offshore discoveries of Eni, Anadarko and their partners that has transformed Mozambique into a major new gas province with realistic ambitions at become [*sic*] a key player in the LNG market".[40] In Mozambique, local content requirements are dealt with by recent primary and secondary legislation, in particular the Petroleum Law 2014 and its associated Decree 24/2004 on Petroleum Operations Regulations.

By contrast with the local content policies discussed previously, Mozambique remains, for the moment, relatively flexible in its approach to local content, to the benefit of IOCs. The Petroleum Law 2014 requires that IOCs "must ensure the employment and the technical-professional training of Mozambican nationals, as well as their participation in the management and in the petroleum operations [*sic*]".[41] At present, this principle remains vague as there is, as yet, no underlying legislation codifying the means of its implementation, whether by way of a specific quota or otherwise. Notably, however, it is clear that more detailed provisions will follow. The Petroleum Law 2014 provides that the government shall create mechanisms and outline the conditions for national entrepreneurship in oil and gas enterprises.

The Petroleum Law 2014 and associated regulations emphasise that the procurement of goods and services in the oil and gas industry shall be carried out on an internationally competitive basis. An IOC operator must "give preferential treatment to the purchase of local goods and services when such goods and services are internationally comparable in terms of quality, availability, and quantity required and are offered at prices inclusive of taxes not higher than ten percent of the available imported goods".[42] The regulations do find a role for an overseeing body, the National Petroleum Institute, in procurement decisions: if it determines that procurement bidding procedures have not been duly complied with, it may "request the Operator to reconsider its decision".

There are also more specific, albeit at present potentially ambiguous, requirements with regard to goods and services. The Petroleum Law 2014 requires that, where their value exceeds a particular amount, they must be procured through a public tender.[43] The threshold for such requirement is unclear, and is to be determined by subsequent regulations. The law also requires that all foreign entities that provide services to petroleum operations must "associate to [*sic*] single or collective Mozambican entities". This appears to broaden the scope of the Petroleum Law to apply it beyond IOCs to services companies and construction contractors, which is potentially an onerous requirement on wider industry participants.[44] It is

---

40 Rod Chooramun 'In with the New and Out with the Old: Mozambique's New Petroleum Law, published online by Andrew Kurth LLP in *Notes From The Field – An English Law Perspective On The Oil & Gas Market*', available at www.andrewskurth.com/media/pressroom/1708_14394_AK_Notes_Mozambique_Sep2014.pdf.

41 Mozambique Petroleum Law, 21/2014, article 12.

42 Mozambique Ministry of Mineral Resources, Petroleum Operations Regulations, Decree 24/2004, article 38.

43 Mozambique Petroleum Law, 21/2014, article 41.

unclear how this principle will be implemented in forthcoming regulations and it may be that foreign entities caught by its scope may be able to incorporate Mozambican companies with the sole purpose of satisfying this legislative requirement.[45]

Taken as a whole, the recently introduced Mozambican legislation conveys a moderate approach to local content. While this must be viewed as the opening pitch by the government, with subsequent regulations to follow, it is an astute approach by a government that is no doubt aware of continent-wide competition for IOC investment. By preserving the role of market forces and a certain level of flexibility for industry operators, the Mozambique government has introduced a regime that, at least for now, stands out as a potentially workable policy from an IOC perspective.

3.2 Contractual provisions

An IOC will, at the time of investment, enter into or become bound by a petroleum agreement with the government, eg, a concession, risk service agreement or, most commonly in Africa, production sharing agreement (PSC), each of which may be referred to as a petroleum agreement. In most cases, the host government stipulates a model form of petroleum agreement to be entered into between the government or its national oil company (NOC)) and the IOC that is first granted title to oil and gas interests. The petroleum agreement is then commonly assigned to any IOCs acquiring participating interests under such title. Frequently, and particularly in the case of mature petroleum industries, such as Nigeria and Angola, the petroleum agreement is 'non-negotiable'; whether this principle is honoured, however, will depend in each case on the bargaining power of the government (or NOC) and IOC, respectively. Where the host state's oil and gas industry is in the nascent phase, such as in certain east African jurisdictions, an investing IOC may have significant scope to negotiate and tailor the terms of the petroleum agreement to its own benefit, which will in turn likely shape the evolution of the model form.

Local content policy is frequently prescribed in the terms of such model petroleum agreements, which have "traditionally been the dominant vehicle" for this purpose.[46] If primary or secondary legislation sets out local content requirements, these may be simply reiterated in the contractual provisions of petroleum agreements. Where this is the case, the IOC may take on certain specific obligations over and above the relevant legislation. In any case, it is noteworthy that, in addition to its legal obligations, the IOC will also, under the petroleum agreement, have contractual obligations to the government or its NOC.

(a) Angola

Angola is an example of an oil and gas regime which uses the PSC as a supporting channel for the implementation of well-established legislation regarding local

---

44 Clifford Chance LLP online briefing note, New Petroleum Law: *The Future of Oil & Gas in Mozambique* (October 2014), available at www.cliffordchance.com/briefings/2014/10/new_petroleum_lawthefutureofoilgasi.html.

45 Chooramun, *op cit* (note 40 above).

46 Tondo *et al*, *op cit* (note 1 above), p 40.

content. The provisions included are relatively brief. For example, a recent PSC based on the model form entered into between Sonangol and BP (among others) in relation to the 2011 pre-salt licensing round sets out concise provisions for local content in employment and training, as follows:[47]

Article 36

[Recruitment, integration and training of Angolan personnel]

1. *Contractor Group shall comply with Decree-Law No 17/09, of 26 June 2009, and ancillary regulations, as well as applicable legislation regarding the recruitment, integration and training of Angolan personnel.*
2. *In planned, systematic and various ways and in accordance with the provisions of this Article, Contractor Group shall train all its Angolan personnel directly or indirectly involved in the Petroleum Operations for the purpose of improving their knowledge and professional qualification in order that the Angolan personnel gradually reach the level of knowledge and professional qualification held by the Contractor Group's foreign workers ...*
3. *Any of the entities comprising Contactor Group that is subject to said Decree-Law No 17/09, of 26 June 2009 must deliver to Sonangol, physical and digital copy of the Program Contracts and respective revisions signed with the Ministry of Petroleum under the referred Decree-Law and its regulations, as well as the Human Resources Development Programs and all documentation and correspondence with such Ministry and third parties on the scope of said contracts and plans.*
4. *Contractor Group agrees to require in its contracts with subcontractors who work for Contractor Group for a period of more than one (1) Year and which are subject to Angolan personnel recruitment, integration and training obligations in accordance with the Law, compliance with such obligations. Contractor Group further agrees to monitor compliance with the aforementioned obligations.*
5. *Contractor Group, through the Operator shall accept, in a job assignment regime to train Sonangol technical personnel in the execution of the Petroleum Operations. Costs incurred by Contractor Group for acceptance for the job assignment and training programs for Sonangol personnel shall be considered, as applicable, Exploration, Development, Production and Administration and Services Expenditures for [the] purposes of Article 11.1.*

Notably, article 36(4) of the PSC concerned goes further than the Angolan legislative requirements previously described, in that the contractor group agrees to bind its subcontractors with regard to local content and to monitor their compliance. This is a mechanism widely used in PSCs to provide for the application of local content obligations to wider industry participants. Article 36(5) refers to the fact that amounts expended pursuant to PSCs in the fulfillment of local content criteria are ultimately cost recoverable by IOC participants.

47 Production Sharing Contract between Sociedade Nacional de Combustíveis de Angola – Empresa Pública (Sonangol EP), CIE Angola Block 20 Ltd, Sonangol Pesquisa e Procucao SA, BP Exploration Angola (Kwanza Bengula) Limited, China Sonangol International Holding Limited in the area of Block 20/11, as publicly disclosed to the U.S Securities and Exchange Commission, available at www.sec.gov/Archives/edgar/data/1471261/000104746912001183/a2207234zex-10_20.htm.

(b) *Kenya*

The Kenyan local content regime is, at present, relatively light-touch. Brief requirements set out in the Petroleum (Exploration and Production) Act[48] are further developed in the Kenyan model PSC by way of the following provisions:[49]

13. LOCAL EMPLOYMENT AND TRAINING

(1) The contractor, its contractors and sub-contractors shall, where possible, employ Kenya citizens in the petroleum operations, and until expiry or termination of this contract, shall train those citizens. The training programme shall be established in consultation with the Minister.

(2) In addition to the obligation under sub-clause 13(1) and commencing on the effective date, the contractor shall for the purposes of section 11 of the Act contribute or hold to the order of the Ministry a minimum of [•] thousand US dollars per year for the Ministry training fund established under section 11(1) of the Act. The contractor's obligation hereunder shall be increased to a minimum of [•] thousand US dollars per year commencing with the adoption of the first development plan under sub-clause 20 (3).

The requirement to contribute to a centralised government training and development fund is common to many African local content regimes, as previously exemplified by Nigerian and Angolan legislation (see 3.1(a) and (b) above). In Kenya, the amount of IOC contribution to this fund is a negotiable aspect of the PSC.

(c) *Tanzania*

The Petroleum Agreement may in some cases be a stand-alone, or otherwise primary, channel for the implementation of local content policies. This is seen, for example, in Tanzania, where the model PSA 2013 (the TPSA) and its predecessor have stipulated local content policy. Without an established legislative framework for such a policy, the provisions of the TPSA are more extensive than those found in the Angolan model. In particular, the TPSA has been used to define as well as implement local content. For example, for the purpose of obligations dealing with the sourcing of goods and services, the TPSA adopts specific definitions as follows:[50]

'Tanzanian goods' means goods manufactured, obtained or produced in the United Republic of Tanzania;

'Tanzania Services' means services provided by Tanzanians or Tanzanian companies; and

'Tanzanian Materials' means materials obtained, produced or manufactured in the United Republic of Tanzania.

There is a contrast here between the approach to goods and materials, which must merely be produced in Tanzania (by any party, whether Tanzanian or otherwise) and services, which must be provided by Tanzanians or Tanzanian companies, being defined as those entities incorporated in Tanzania and with shares being at least 51% owned by Tanzanian nationals.[51]

---

48 Petroleum (Exploration and Production) Act (Chapter 308), section 11.
49 Republic of Kenya Model Production Sharing Contract, article 13.
50 Tanzania Model Production Sharing Agreement 2013, article 20(p)(i).
51 *Ibid*, article 20(p)(ii).

In cases of ambiguity or contradiction in contractual requirements, the stand-alone contractual channel is not the most holistic or watertight means of local content policy implementation, because the interpretation of provisions is more challenging without a framework context. In such cases, IOC participants must test and negotiate any such shortcomings.

With regard to goods and services, the TPSA seeks to preserve a competitive environment. For example, the TPSA emphasises that contractors must use Tanzanian service companies and contractors only "where services of certified standards are available from such contractors at competitive prices and on competitive terms", thereby retaining the governance of market principles. This is in common with certain elements of the Mozambican and Angolan approaches.[52] The TPSA also sets out the following procedure for the tendering of goods and services, which exemplifies a common approach to procurement:[53]

Article 20

...

(l) All tenders are to be advertised, evaluated and awarded in the United Republic of Tanzania. Contractor shall apply to TPDC for prior approval where the circumstances warrant that any part of the tender process be conducted outside of [the] United Republic of Tanzania.

(m) [The Contractor shall] give preference to Tanzania companies and [sic] by ensuring access to all tender invitations and by including high weighting on local value added in the tender evaluation criteria.

(n) In order to give effect to this Article, the Contractor shall collaborate with TPDC and or any public authority responsible for local content promotion or other public body to identify a list of Tanzanian services and goods suppliers and contractors

The NOC, Tanzania Petroleum Development Corporation ('TPDC'), has a role in approving and assisting the tender process and, more generally, is obliged to monitor compliance with the TPSA on behalf of the Ministry of Energy and Minerals. Again, this is a familiar approach under model PSCs. It is, however, an approach that creates the potential for legal interpretative challenges for while the NOC is not an IOC, it is nonetheless a contractor under a PSC and, unless specified otherwise, is bound by all obligations that similarly apply to IOC participants. It is a quirk of practice that the NOC often has dual, and contradictory, roles as contractor and enforcer under a PSC, in particular in relation to local content.

The local content provisions relating to employment in the TPSA are wide-reaching but not unusual in the light of previously described legislation elsewhere in Africa. They include provisions requiring contractors to ensure that unskilled manpower roles are reserved for Tanzanian nationals only, and to impart to Tanzanian employees technology and business expertise involved in all petroleum operations activities.[54] Such obligations are not quantified, save that the contractor is obliged, on an annual basis, to expend a minimum of approximately $500,000 on

52 *Ibid*, article 20(d).
53 *Ibid*, article 20.
54 *Ibid*, article 20.

matters such as in-country training, higher education or specialist skills workshops for Tanzanian personnel, or the purchase for the government and TPDC of items such as professional publications, technical software and similar.[55]

3.3 Policy guidelines and codes of practice

While discussion thus far has focused on formal legal channels for the implementation of local content policies, IOCs must also consider the potential application of government policy guidelines and codes of practice. Most commonly, these policies give context to existing laws and regulations or imply the introduction of new local content requirements, as shown by the following examples.

(a) Tanzania

In addition to the TPSA, Tanzania introduced a draft Local Content Policy in 2014 which is "intended to provide guiding principles for the participation and transformation of Tanzanians in the development of the oil and gas industry."[56] It does not set out rules or operative terms for local content, but may set the tone for more prescriptive local content regulations in coming years. In the meantime, it appears that the TPSA will remain the key source of local content requirements.

(b) Kenya

As previously discussed, Kenyan local content requirements for the oil and gas industry are primarily set out in the model PSC and are brief by comparison with other African examples. In 2014, however, the government issued a draft National Energy Policy which identifies "inadequate manpower, technical capacity and local content in gas exploration and production activities" as key challenges for the upstream oil and gas sector.[57] The policy sets out a framework plan for the development and implementation of a local content policy in the next fifteen years, including, for example, as yet unspecified revisions to the current model PSC.[58]

(c) Namibia

Namibia has an existing legal framework for local content requirements in the oil and gas industry. This is implemented by dual channels, pursuant to the Petroleum (Exploration and Production) Act 1991 and a model petroleum agreement. An increasing amount of attention is, however, being paid by the industry to the potential application of the New Equitable Economic Empowerment Framework (NEEEF), which was adopted in 2011 but has not yet been made the subject of legislation. The stated objective of the NEEEF is to "encourage the private business sector to become more equitable and to make a greater contribution towards national economic empowerment and transformation".[59] It has a potentially wide-

---

55 *Ibid*, article 21.
56 Local Content Policy of Tanzania for Oil and Gas Industry 2014, Draft One, p 12.
57 Republic of Kenya Ministry of Energy and Petroleum, Draft National Energy Policy (February 24 2014), section 2.2.2.
58 *Ibid*, section 2.2.3.
59 NEEEF, p 6.

reaching cross-sector scope, by virtue of five 'empowerment pillars': ownership, management control, employment, equity and community investment.[60]

The scope and application of the NEEEF as it relates to the oil and gas industry remains unclear. On the one hand, it is expressed to be based on "voluntary business practice" and yet, on the other, it states that "companies that fail to comply with NEEEF targets ... will not be eligible to tender for Government ... contracts or ... other licenses and may therefore find themselves in a disadvantageous and uncompetitive position".[61] Given such ambiguity, and without a clear indication of the application of the NEEEF to the oil and gas industry, IOCs looking to invest in Namibia face regulatory uncertainty, which must be accommodated in any cost-benefit analysis taking into account the local content regime.

4. Local content – challenges for host governments and IOCs

Despite established implementation channels within the legal framework, African governments and IOCs alike may face a range of challenges in relation to local content polices which interact with the wider constraints of the oil and gas industry and the developmental and political aspects specific to each African jurisdiction.

4.1 Nature of the industry

Most fundamentally, and impacting upon both host governments and IOCs, is that the very nature of the oil and gas industry may be seen inherently to undermine the application of local content. That is:

> *the use of specialized inputs and the technological complexity of the petroleum sector often limit the possibility of developing backward and forward links into the local economy.*[62]

A key rationale for local content policies is the limited backward links arising from the oil and gas industry, yet this itself prevails as an inhibitor to their effectiveness, certainly in the short term.

For the IOC, the challenge of sourcing the requisite specialised inputs in line with local content requirements is exacerbated by ambitious yet unrealistic government-imposed expectations or targets. There are also potential business inefficiencies and additional costs that may arise from meeting local content requirements. Depending on how regulations are structured, local content may impose limits on the introduction, growth and development of new enterprises by IOCs.[63] Recent studies suggest that almost a quarter of industry participants have experienced local content requirements delaying, postponing or cancelling oil and gas projects.[64] This challenge may be alleviated to some extent by an IOC having in place a clear, long-term view and well-defined strategic plan with regard to local content. Given that local content

---

60 *Ibid*, p 7.
61 *Ibid*, p 21.
62 Tondo *et al*, *op cit* (note 1 above), p xiii.
63 IPICA report, *Local content strategy: A guidance document for the oil and gas industry* (2013).
64 PricewaterhouseCoopers (PWC), *On the brink of a boom: Africa oil and gas review* (July 2014), available at http://download.pwc.com/ie/pubs/2014-pwc-africa-oil-and-gas-review-25-07-2014.pdf, p 29.

is a worldwide oil and gas industry phenomenon, there remain limited, if any, conceptual challenges to local content requirements. Many IOCs, however, could benefit from a more clear-cut internal approach to the integration of local content into their business.

Host governments, meanwhile, face the considerable challenge of formulating local content policies that will have a tangible economic impact in light of both the specialist input requirements of the oil and gas industry and also the capacity constraints of the domestic sector. This challenge is particularly marked for early-stage African oil and gas industries, particularly where wider developmental challenges are significant.

In Angola, as discussed, the local content requirement is 100% in relation to goods and services that do not entail high technological complexity and specialist skills, while otherwise setting out a two-tiered competitive regime. This approach recognises the limits of local capacity and seeks to maximise 'backward links' to less specialist domestic sectors. By requiring that more specialised goods and services must be provided through a local-IOC joint venture, Angolan policy aims to nurture the transfer of knowledge and technology from experienced IOC operators. The success of this policy will, however, depend heavily on the active participation of suitable Angolan companies, which may be significantly undermined by issues such as 'fronting', as discussed at 4.3 below.

4.2 Formulation and implementation of policy

A challenge for host governments is balancing the juxtaposing and often contradictory economic, developmental and political goals of local content policies. As one recent analysis emphasises, "local content policy design is not solely or principally guided by considerations of economic efficiency and the need to address market failures. On the contrary, it would seem that political imperatives are key drivers, and economic efficiency is often an afterthought."[65]

It is crucial that local content is a part of wider economic and social reform. In particular, while legislative channels may enshrine principles and targets to increase local involvement, the success of these mechanisms requires broader progress, through investment in education and infrastructure, in order to create the specialised inputs required by the oil and gas industry. There is the risk that such developmental goals may be manipulated for purposes of short-term political ends, in which circumstances local content policies cannot be truly transformative for a host state's economy or its people.

While addressing domestic needs, the host government must also, in the formulation of policy, balance stringent local content requirements with flexibility, in order that IOCs may operate effectively. The use of caveats and wide government discretion in this regard is common. For example, the NCDA provides that if there is inadequate capacity to meet any of the quantum targets for Nigerian content in goods and services, the government may authorise the continued import of the relevant items. Although, under the terms of the NCDA, this exception technically

65 Tondo *et al*, *op cit* (note 1 above), p xiii.

expired in 2013, in practice it appears likely that it will continue to prevail, given the ongoing absence of sufficient local capacity to service many IOC operations.[66] Similarly, in Angola, if there are not available, "demonstrably, in the national labor market", suitably qualified Angolan citizens, an IOC may seek prior authorisation from the Ministry of Petroleum to hire foreign workers.

While this flexibility is important in the interests of attracting and retaining IOC investment, and maximising efficiency, local content policies will be significantly undermined if the host government or NOC facilitates a culture of such caveats being exercised as common practice. From an IOC perspective, if it is looking to secure ministerial or NOC authorisation for a deviation from prescribed requirements, it will need to be clear what formalities and evidence are required in this regard.

In formulating local content requirements, host governments should seek to foresee, and avoid, interpretative issues. It has been discussed that definitions of, for example, 'local content' and what constitutes 'national' companies and citizens will be particularly scrutinised and any ambiguity or contradiction may lead to confusion as to what is required. This is, of course, equally problematic for an IOC, which will require input by local legal counsel in each case, in order to understand thoroughly the interpretation and practical application of requirements, particularly in light of informal procedural steps or common practice employed in relation to local content.

Local content policies may also be problematic for host governments to implement and enforce. Primarily, they may be costly and, given that local content costs are commonly recoverable under a PSC, host governments "should be mindful of introducing measures for which the cost of compliance exceeds the social benefit."[67]

The institutional structure in place is also important. In Nigeria and Ghana, specifically formed government bodies act as overseers, particularly in relation to ongoing planning and monitoring requirements and the implementation of quantitative requirements for employment and procurement. While this centralisation of local content functions may increase efficiency, the administrative burden on the host government likely remains significant, given the interpretative and monitoring challenges of the complex local content criteria in force in both of those countries.

In Angola, both the Ministry of Petroleum and the NOC, Sonangol, have local content functions. The Ministry of Petroleum is involved in the implementation and monitoring of local content, while Sonangol negotiates the local content provisions of the PSC and is in charge of procurement. Such institutional overlap, and potential duplication of functions, may create inefficiencies and associated costs for the host government and also additional costs and procedural hurdles for IOCs. There may also be potential conflicts of interest for a NOC acting in both a commercial and local content-enforcing capacity, as discussed elsewhere in this book.

---

66 Uchenna Jerome Orji, *op cit* (note 14 above), p 9.
67 Tondo *et al*, *op cit* (note 1 above), p 141.

4.3 Corruption and 'fronting'

An equally significant challenge, and one which both exacerbates and is exacerbated by the previous discussed limitations regarding domestic capacity, is the issue of 'fronting': that is, the potential manipulation of those privileges afforded to domestic companies and individuals under local content regulation.

In Nigeria, for example, a Nigerian company purporting to act as a local service provider may in fact outsource the execution of a contract, and take a share of the contract sum without performing the contract or developing the required skills or experience to do so.[68] The government has been said to:

> *usually award strategic oil and gas contracts to indigenous firms seemingly on the basis of political patronage with regards to competency ... [which] practice has been responsible for pervasive corruption in the industry as well as the non-competitiveness of most oil-service firms in Nigeria.*[69]

Recent commentary has stressed that, in Angola too, local content policies have, as well as stimulating economic growth "also become important mechanisms for unequal growth and new forms of elite accumulation."[70] Fronting in the context of local content is problematic for host governments, in that it significantly undermines the goals of local content policies.

Concerns about corruption in general remain a key issue for IOCs, with industry commentators identifying it as the second greatest constraint to developing an African oil and gas business.[71] It is clear that host governments must prioritise efforts to maintain a transparent, efficient and enforceable regulatory regime in order to remove 'fronting' and associated corruption as systemic issues. There are several means of risk mitigation employed by IOCs in the legal context in relation to corruption, as discussed elsewhere in this book.

4.4 Regulatory uncertainty

Often perceived as equal to corruption risk for IOCs in today's oil and gas industry is the risk associated with regulatory uncertainty, which has been identified by industry commentators as the greatest constraint to IOC development, above all other factors.[72] While regulatory uncertainly may be seen as prevalent across the African oil and gas industry, it is particularly notable in the case of local content policies, which appear to be currently in flux on a continent-wide basis. As previously discussed, new legal frameworks have recently been introduced in Ghana (2013), Mozambique (2014) and Tanzania (2013 and 2014), and significant legislation and policies impacting upon local content policy remain pending with an uncertain timeframe for implementation, such as in the cases of Nigeria's PIB and Namibia's NEEEF.

---

68 Uchenna Jerome Orji, *op cit* (note 14 above), pp 2 and 12.

69 *Ibid.*

70 Jesse Salah Ovadia, 'The dual nature of local content in Angola's oil and gas industry: development vs elite accumulation', *Journal of Contemporary African Studies*, Volume 30, Issue 3 (2012), pp 395-417.

71 PWC, *op cit* (note 64 above), p 7.

72 *Ibid.*

5. Conclusion

This chapter has examined the characteristics of the legislative and contractual channels through which local content policy is implemented in the African oil and gas industry. It has been seen that stringent local content requirements that are already well-rooted in developed oil and gas economies such as Nigeria and Angola are now becoming increasingly prevalent, and legally enshrined, in emerging oil and gas states such as Tanzania and Namibia.

Inevitably, the highly specialist and technologically complex nature of the oil and gas industry poses hurdles for the fulfillment of local content objectives, and domestic capacity may struggle to innovate sufficiently to meet IOC demand. There are challenges both for host governments and IOCs in relation to the formulation and implementation of local content policies, while IOCs also face both a fronting risk in relation to local procurement and widespread regulatory uncertainty.

A key priority for an African host government must be to identify the best means of tailoring local content requirements to the unique economic and developmental circumstances of its nation. While it may be beneficial to draw upon continent-wide local content experience when formulating local content policy, too often there appears to be an adoption by African governments of a 'mirror image' policy, simply on the basis that it is applied elsewhere on the continent. Instead, it must be recognised that the success of local content policies "largely depends on their interaction and coherence with broader economic development policies and related implementation tools".[73] To this end, host governments must acknowledge that one size does not fit all.

73 Tondo *et al*, *op cit* (note 1 above), p 121.

Africa: comparative economic and financial analysis

Christopher R K Moore
Moyes & Co

1. Introduction

This chapter reviews similarities, differences and trends in upstream fiscal terms and their economic impact in Africa. It is intended to be a guide to what to expect, and what to look for, when evaluating a new upstream opportunity or the acquisition of an existing project.

At the outset, it should be pointed out that readers turning to this chapter in the expectation of finding a league table of economic metrics (such as government take and net present value per barrel, by jurisdiction) will be disappointed. Although such comparisons are occasionally useful, for example when comparing similar fields in similar geographical and geological settings, they are not very useful in the broader context of a continent-wide discussion. It is nevertheless worth noting in more detail the shortcomings of broader comparisons based on economic metrics.

Firstly, many African countries employ fiscal systems under which the terms applicable to each contract are negotiated, and which terms have indeed formed the basis for determining the winner in competitive bidding situations. It is therefore possible to have neighbouring contemporary contracts within a country or even a basin with different fiscal terms.

Secondly, fiscal terms evolve over time. It may be useful to review the most recent terms when assessing new exploration or development opportunities. Much commercial activity in the upstream sector involves merger and acquisition (M&A) activity, however. This may involve legacy assets with substantially different fiscal terms when compared to more recent contracts. Some areas of offshore west Africa are asset-producing locations in which the original contracts may be fifty years old. While Algeria's terms under Law 05-07 of 2005 consist of a royalty/tax regime with a progressive additional profits tax, most of the country's oil production arises under production sharing contracts (PSCs) executed under the older Law 86-14 regime of 1986, and this is likely to be the case for the foreseeable future.

Thirdly, there is an extremely wide range of economic performance for different oil and gas fields. This is partly a result of subsurface differences, including resource size and well production rate. More importantly, it is because of the very wide range of costs incurred, particularly, for example, when comparing onshore fields with those offshore in a variety of water depths, up to 3,000 metres in west Africa. There are two principal alternatives for comparing fiscal terms, both involving economic analysis and the derivation of metrics concerning government take and contractor economics. The first method makes the comparison using one or more identical generic or prototype fields, regardless of the characteristics of fields found in that jurisdiction. The second method is to make the comparisons using only field models typical of the jurisdiction being analysed. It should be apparent that both methods have some deficiencies. While the first method provides a 'pure' comparison, it may be of only academic interest if, for example, one jurisdiction has only onshore fields whereas the other jurisdiction is predominantly offshore. It may be argued that, in terms of value to the contractor, the second method is more useful. Under that method, however, the comparison is not only of the fiscal system and government take, but also the economics of the project before the application of fiscal terms (sometimes called the 'natural' economics).

For these reasons, this chapter does not include the results of detailed economic analysis. Instead, it focuses on qualitative differences, and on five important areas of interest – progressivity, stabilisation, state participation, assignment and natural gas terms.

2. Fiscal regimes

It is assumed that the reader has some knowledge of fiscal systems applicable to upstream oil and gas activities. There are various conventions for categorising fiscal systems, some including 'hybrids' as a category, recognising that many systems borrow from different 'pure' forms. The approach used in this chapter is based on the mechanism(s) for obtaining resource rent from those engaged in the exploitation of oil and natural gas.

Taxation is an important source of state revenue in most countries. Industrial enterprises are usually taxed regardless of whether or not they consume the state's natural resources. The concept of 'resource rent' will therefore be used in this chapter to include all forms of revenue and profit sharing accruing to the state, except taxes that are levied on all industrial enterprises. One may distinguish between three resource rent extraction mechanisms as follows.

- Royalties, including severance, *ad valorem* and similar taxes. These are levies on the value of the production (proceeds of sales) without regard to the investments required for production or to whether the enterprise is profitable. Royalties may be a fixed or variable proportion of the sales revenue. If variable, the royalty rate may increase with increasing production volumes, or sometimes with price or even profitability. Some countries allow transport, processing and/or a proportion of field operating and development costs (those beyond the wellhead or outside the contract area) to be deducted in arriving at the value for royalty purposes.
- Taxes. Given the exclusion of 'standard' corporate taxes under this mechanism, these include, firstly, the additional amount of corporate income tax due to the difference between the standard rate levied on industrial enterprises and the special rate for petroleum production, and, secondly, special taxes assessed only on petroleum production activities, in addition to corporate income tax. In both cases, taxes are based on profits (proceeds of sales less allowable costs) rather than proceeds of sales alone.
- Disproportionate sharing of production in favour of the state or its agent

before the application of taxes, if any, on the contractor's profits. Usually simply called production sharing, the word 'disproportionate' should be emphasised. In this context, it means disproportionate to the respective shares of costs. Consider a joint venture between a national oil company (NOC) holding a 51% interest, and an international oil company (IOC) holding 49%, in which both pay their respective shares of all costs and receive their respective shares of all revenues. This allocates a larger production share to the NOC, but is not 'production sharing' in the usual industry sense, because it is not disproportionate. If the IOC pays its 49% share of costs, but receives a larger share of the production, say 60%, then that is production sharing. Such high levels of state cost-sharing are relatively uncommon. The issue of state participation is discussed as a separate topic later in this chapter.

For the illustrations that follow in figures 1-6, there are three mutually exclusive categories:

- royalty, in which there are no other levies except royalty and corporate income tax at the standard rate;
- petroleum taxes, in which there are additional taxes on profits over and above corporate income tax at the standard rate. In these cases there is usually, but not always, also a royalty; and
- production sharing contracts (PSCs), which include all situations involving disproportionate production sharing, whether or not taxes are payable by the contractor and whether or not there is a royalty.

The last two types are most common in jurisdictions where significant production and therefore a working petroleum system has been established. The first type tends to be found in countries and sometimes applied to basins with (as yet) no significant petroleum production, perhaps with a mining sector in which a royalty may typically be the only method of obtaining economic rent.

The presentation of regional trends in a concise and sensible form presents a number of problems. Should one give added weight to those systems which, firstly, result in large numbers of individual contracts or, secondly, are deemed to be the most important because they are representative of the most important producing countries? Colour-coding political maps is unsatisfactory because it gives too much weight to large countries (by geographic area) and less weight to countries that are small in area but have relatively significant petroleum industries. As a compromise, the illustrations shown in figures 1-6 below are diagrammatic, with each jurisdiction allocated a rectangle of equal area and arranged alphabetically. Figure 1 shows the 50 jurisdictions researched. Figure 2 shows the type of fiscal system applied in each jurisdiction.

Figure 1: African Jurisdictions Researched

Algeria	Angola	Benin	Botswana	Burundi	Cameroon
Central AR	Chad	Congo Republic	Congo DR	Côte d'Ivoire	Djibouti
Egypt	Equatorial Guinea	Eritrea	Ethiopia	Gabon	Gambia
Ghana	Guinea	Guinea-Bissau	GB Senegal AGC	Kenya	Liberia
Libya	Madagascar	Malawi	Mali	Mauritania	Morocco
Mozambique	Namibia	Niger	Nigeria	Nigeria/São Tomé	Rwanda
SADR	São Tomé	Senegal	Seychelles	Sierra Leone	Somalia: Puntland
Somalia: Somaliland	South Africa	Sudan	Tanzania	Togo	Tunisia
Uganda	Zambia				

Figure 2: African Fiscal Systems

Petroleum tax	PSC	PSC	Royalty and Income tax	PSC	PSC
Petroleum tax	Petroleum tax	PSC	PSC	PSC	PSC
PSC	PSC	PSC	PSC	PSC	Petroleum tax
PSC	PSC	PSC	PSC	PSC	PSC
PSC	PSC	Royalty and Income tax	PSC	PSC	Royalty and Income tax
PSC	Petroleum tax	Royalty and Income tax	PSC	PSC	PSC
PSC	PSC	PSC	Petroleum tax	Petroleum tax	PSC
PSC	Royalty and Income tax	PSC	PSC	PSC	Petroleum tax / PSC
PSC	Royalty and Income tax				

The term 'jurisdiction' requires definition. For present purposes, it includes areas which, while governed by treaty, are not sovereign states, such as the joint development zones (Guinea-Bissau/Senegal and Nigeria/Sao Tomé). It also includes jurisdictions which regulate, or purport to regulate, oil and gas activities despite lack of universal recognition of their authority (Puntland, Somaliland and Sahrawi). Jurisdictions whose laws allow for alternative fiscal systems are represented on the basis of the system recently in common use, except for Tunisia where there is a choice. It should be noted that under the categories used here, Angolan PSCs and Risk Service Contracts (RSCs) are both treated as production sharing, as the RSC includes disproportionate production sharing as well as the royalty and additional petroleum tax not levied under the PSC.

Keeping up with all the changes to fiscal terms is a challenge. In some jurisdictions, the host government instruments (HGIs), which include contracts, licences, concession documents or similar, are confidential, so that complete details may not be available in the public domain. The author accepts all responsibility for any errors or omissions in the analysis shown.

Upstream fiscal systems in Africa are dominated by those based on production sharing, in use in nearly three-quarters of the fifty jurisdictions analysed. Of the balance, slightly over half include some form of special petroleum tax or a special rate of corporate income tax, and slightly less than half derive, or would derive, economic rent for oil and gas solely from royalties and corporate income tax at the standard rate.

3. Stability

Petroleum development is a long term, relatively high risk, capital intensive enterprise, in which initial revenues, let alone repayment of the capital invested, may not occur for many years. In order to make large long term capital investments, investors (such as IOCs) require contractual assurance that the fiscal terms under which they have agreed to make these investments will survive over the term of their contract. The situation is made even more complicated by two particular problems with respect to investments in petroleum projects.

Firstly, exploration investments are made under the assumption that there is a high likelihood (more than 50%, and frequently 70%-90%) that the investment will fail and generate no future income, with no tax offset in the country of investment to mitigate the loss. To account for this, the value of success (the reward) must be large enough to justify the exposure to loss. If commercially successful, however, the risk of failure is removed and the terms under which development moves forward may appear generous to the IOC. The host government, possibly under popular pressure, may wish to 're-balance' the terms in the state's favour.

Secondly, product prices have become increasingly volatile, but with an asymmetric response. Increases in prices lead to popular demands for 'windfall' taxes, but reductions in prices meet with no sympathy (although governments will respond to systemic price falls with improved terms, these usually relate to licences without commercial success or to future exploration rather than existing contracts with discoveries).

Stability is therefore of considerable importance to IOCs, particularly in states with a volatile history with regard to the stability of treatment of foreign investments. Stability can be accomplished in one of two ways, although the two mechanisms are usually not talked about together. Firstly, one can design fiscal systems that respond, preferably symmetrically, to upward or downward movements in product prices (progressive fiscal systems). Secondly, one can introduce stabilisation mechanisms into the fiscal system (contractual stabilisation).

4. Progressivity

Terms that allow host government take (as a fraction of net profits) to increase with increasing profitability are more likely to survive unexpected changes in project profitability. Such terms include royalties, production sharing terms, taxes or special taxes whose rates increase together with increases in profitability ('R Factors' or rate of return (ROR) measures) or increases in sales price. R Factors are ratios of cumulative revenues to cumulative costs, although the details of the calculation differ between jurisdictions. Government take increases either as each threshold R Factor is crossed or as a continuous function of the R Factor. Shares based on ROR typically involve compounding the cash flows at various threshold rates. When the cumulative compounded cash flow turns positive at each threshold rate (when the project has achieved that rate of return), government take is increased.

Figure 3: Incidence of some element of fiscal progressivity

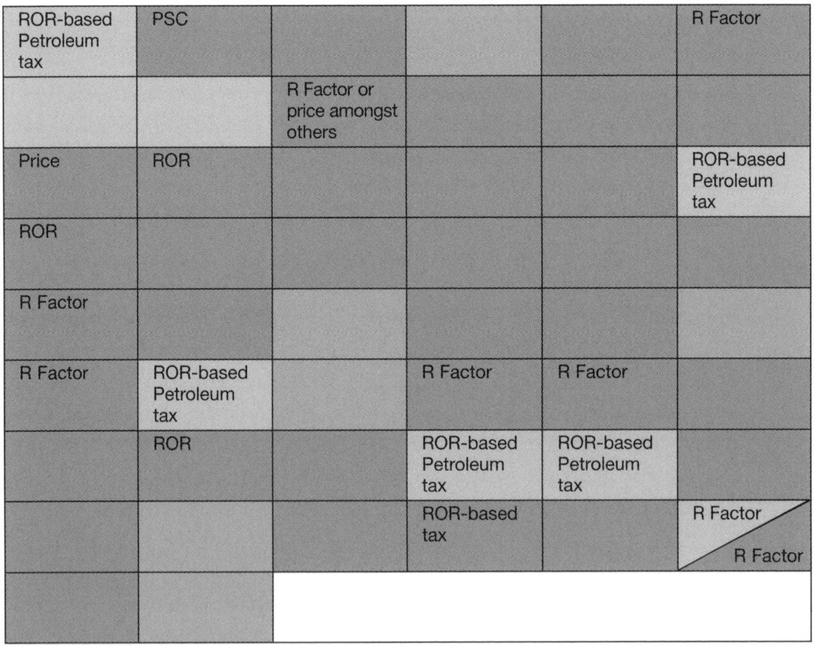

Figure 3 shows the incidence of progressive elements of fiscal terms superimposed on the same colour-coded template used in Figure 1. This is qualitative. A progressive element does not guarantee that, overall, the system is progressive with respect to price (meaning in this regard that host government take increases as a fraction of profits as oil prices increase).

It should be noted that progressive fiscal terms are rarely found in jurisdictions where royalty and income tax are the only forms of government take. Conversely, fiscal systems relying on special petroleum taxes typically contain progressive elements. Perhaps surprisingly, only about a third of systems with production sharing terms include a progressive element. This is despite the fact that methods and examples have been around for over thirty years. The result is that the majority of fiscal systems are regressive, such that government take falls as a fraction of profit as product price increases. It is therefore not surprising that price increases lead to host government discontent and host governments are tempted to introduce changes or additional terms to capture what is seen as a resulting windfall to the IOCs.

5. Contractual stabilisation

Host governments have generally been sympathetic to IOC demands for stabilisation, because the state's basic need for industry knowledge combined with large amounts of foreign direct investment in the petroleum sector was, and continues to be, paramount. Stabilisation is therefore fairly common. It is reasonable to ask why one should worry about stabilisation in the context of reviewing comparative economic terms. The answer is that any analysis of the economic performance of a project should include sensitivity to product price changes. The progressive or regressive nature of the terms is only one part of sensitivity to price. One should also consider the likelihood that the existing fiscal terms will survive a significant change in price. The extent to which there is a risk that the terms will be changed and adversely affect the IOC's interest, disrupting investment and project development, is the complement to the extent to which the existing terms are stabilised.

Systems with fixed terms provide that the fiscal system is fixed by the HGI, either with explicit rates or by reference to the terms in force at the time the instrument is enacted. Importantly, however, such terms are usually incorporated with regard to existing taxes (usually corporate income taxes) and this only stabilises the overall fiscal regime if it is accompanied by an exemption from all other taxes (including new taxes in the future). Included in this category are those contracts which are enacted as laws, giving them seniority compared to subsequent more general laws.

'Tax paid' systems are limited to PSC regimes. These taxes are part of the overall resource rent taken by disproportionate production sharing. Taxes (and sometimes royalties) are paid out of the host government share of production and the IOC is immunised from changes in rates. Again, though, this only stabilises the overall fiscal regime if it is accompanied by an exemption from all other taxes. Such tax paid systems are part of broader 'risk allocation' stabilisation mechanisms, in which there is a prescribed remedy for changes that must be absorbed by the state or its NOC, the risk having been transferred from the IOC. In Africa, no other types of risk allocation clause are known to the author.

An increasingly popular approach is to include an 'equilibrium' clause. This states that if circumstances change (usually laws and regulations, but occasionally any material change in circumstances) to the detriment of the contractor ('asymmetric' clauses) or either the contractor or the state ('symmetric' clauses), then the parties will renegotiate to restore the economic equilibrium.

Figure 4: Contract Stabilisation Types

None specified	Equilibrium	Tax paid and Equilibrium	None		Equilibrium
	Fixed	Tax paid	Tax paid and fixed	Tax paid and Equilibrium	
Tax paid, fixed and Equilibrium	None	Equilibrium	None	Equilibrium	None
Fixed and Equilibrium	Tax paid and Equilibrium	Equilibrium		Tax paid and Equilibrium	Fixed and Equilibrium
	None			Fixed	Equilibrium
Exemption from new taxes only	None	Fixed	Tax paid and Equilibrium	Fixed and Equilibrium	
Fixed	Equilibrium	Fixed	None	Fixed and Equilibrium	
Fixed and Equilibrium	Fixed	Tax paid	None	Tax paid	Tax paid
None	None				

Figure 4 shows the incidence of the various types of stabilisation mechanism on the same template. Blank squares represent where information is lacking. Where a jurisdiction deliberately chooses not to provide any form of stabilisation, this shown in a 'None' square. Care should also be exercised because, in some jurisdictions, contract provisions such as stabilisation clauses may be left in, taken out or amended, leading to differences between otherwise similar contracts. Where possible, Figure 4 shows the model form, if one is available.

6. State participation

States are actively involved in upstream petroleum activities, both in management (through the regulatory process and/or under the contractual framework of the HGI) and ownership of production (whether by taking royalties in kind or having a production entitlement under a PSC).

Many HGIs provide for an additional form of state involvement, frequently in

PSC systems and less frequently in royalty/tax systems. The state, or more usually its NOC, may become a working interest holder in the HGI. This is referred to, perhaps confusingly, as 'state participation'. When the expression 'no state participation' is used with regard to HGI terms, it is this working interest participation to which it refers. An important difference from the IOC's working interest is that the state participation is usually 'carried' through either the exploration and appraisal phase (to project sanction) or through the exploration, appraisal and development phases (to production). This means that the state rarely pays its share of the at-risk exploration costs, and sometimes does not pay its share of development costs in advance in the event of a commercial discovery.

The carried state share is a burden on the IOC and substantially affects the attractiveness of an exploration opportunity. Before considering risk aversion, an IOC must be provided with double the reward (the value of a successful outcome) to carry a 50% state participation entitlement in order for a project to meet the same economic criteria compared to one where there is no state participation. Risk aversion exacerbates the problem, as the IOC's valuation is dominated by the expected cost of failure (the cost of failure times the likelihood of failure). The reward must therefore be set at an appropriately higher level to compensate for the increased cost of failure. The required reward may be so high that it aggravates the previously stated problem where, given success, the contractor's risk is forgotten and its reward seems too high.

In the case of success, however, the IOC is indifferent to the addition of a paying partner, provided that it can pay its cash calls in a timely fashion. It is no different to having another IOC partner. The state, in the event of success, may reimburse the 'carry', or else the IOC receives the tax deduction or cost recovery for the costs it has carried on the state's behalf.

From a host country perspective, there are advantages and disadvantages to participating in a development. Much has been made of the 'information asymmetry' between the sophisticated IOC and the supposedly naïve NOC or state. Participation by the NOC on the same side of the table as the IOC reduces that imbalance. It also provides a mechanism for the knowledge transfer necessary to develop NOC competence. There are, however, disadvantages. Participation by the NOC as part of the contractor group is an inefficient way to participate in the revenue generated by the project, as its share of the project generally suffers the same resource rent extraction burdens as the other members of the contractor group. It also requires substantial investments by the state in the upstream sector, in competition with other state responsibilities and social burdens.

Nevertheless, state participation is a global phenomenon. Figure 5 shows the incidence of state participation in Africa. In many cases, the level of state participation is a negotiable or biddable element. It should be noted that state participation is not limited to production sharing regimes. Again, blanks indicate a lack of information, whereas 'None' indicates those jurisdictions with no state participation.

Two recent innovations have provided the state with opportunities to acquire additional working interests. In the first case, not only does the state have a carried interest, but it also has the option to acquire an additional interest at market value. This right is usually exercisable at the same time as the carried interest is crystallised. The second case arises through a preferential right to purchase triggered by the assignment of a working interest (jurisdictions with the circled numeral 1 in Figure 5) or even a change of control of a working interest owner (*ibid*, circled numeral 2). Further fiscal issues related to assignments are discussed in the following section.

Figure 5: State Participation

51% part carried to sanction	30% carried to sanction	15% caried through exercise	None		15% carried to sanction
20% carried	None	20% carried to production	10% carried to production	15% carried through Expl	
None	20% carried to sanction	Negotiable carried to sanction	Negotiable carried to sanction	E20% to prod + 15% buy at FMV	20% option to purchase
15% carried to production	15% carried to sanction	15% carried to sanction	17% carried to sanction	Negotiable carried to sanction	15% carried to production
50% carried to production	None	None	20% carried to production	18% carried to production	20% carried to sanction
Negotiable 10% + carried to sanction	10% carried to production	10% carried to sanction	None	None	
Biddable	Biddable carried to production	30% carried to sanction	None	None	
10%-20% carry undefined	20% carried + 30% right to purchase	8% carried to sanction	25% carried to sanction	10% to sanction + 10% to prod	50% / None
15% carried to production					

7. Assignment

Historically, the assignment of interests, particularly before production start-up, typically did not trigger any tax liabilities. Host government attitudes have, however, started to change in the light of a number of high profile sales or attempted sales of interests in significant discoveries prior to production start-up. Host government concern stems from an observation that the proceeds of such sales represent value generated by the exploitation of the state's natural resources. In the absence of any transaction tax, the investor is monetising its rights to those resources substantially ahead of the state receiving any revenues from production.

It is not clear to what extent either capital gains or income tax regulations would have to be modified to legitimise tax gains from such transactions. Tanzania's latest model contract expressly provides for capital gains tax on transfers. Other jurisdictions have adopted alternative approaches. Algeria has introduced a transfer tax of 1% of the value of the transaction for all assignments. Madagascar has introduced a modest sliding scale fee. Fees similar to bonuses are now payable in Sierra Leone.

If the state's argument for taxing such transactions is to share in accelerated resource monetisation, then it should result in just that, an acceleration rather than an increase in government take. If the state were only accelerating government take, there should be a corresponding reduction in future government take by allowing the acquisition cost as a deduction against the purchaser's tax liability. Only 8% of jurisdictions (17 out of 206), however, have depletion allowances for the treatment of expenditures such as acquisition costs[1] To the author's knowledge, none of these jurisdictions are in Africa.

8. Natural gas

Unlike crude oil and other liquid forms of hydrocarbon product, natural gas is neither fungible nor priced on a consistent global basis with differences due only to quality and transportation requirements. Natural gas pricing varies according to circumstances, from oil equivalence on a calorific value basis in selected parts of the world, to worthless or a negative value in areas with no market nor any opportunity for commercial development. In the latter areas, it is called 'stranded' gas. Many areas of the world, including Africa, once included large regions where most or all of the gas was stranded. This picture is changing with growing regional demand to use such gas, and discovered resources becoming sufficient for gas monetisation plans that require large resources, such as LNG plants. Increasingly, therefore, terms for natural gas are required where none were required before.

Associated gas does not normally require special terms because it is a by-product of a presumably commercial oil field. Non-associated natural gas may be more challenging. For non-associated gas fields, contemporary fiscal terms may be divided into two species of approach. Under the first approach, which represents about two-thirds of jurisdictions, existing terms include terms for natural gas. These may be identical to the terms for oil, but with volumes converted, usually by reference to calorific value. Alternatively, the terms may be structurally similar, but with different values for cost petroleum limits or production shares, reflecting the need for less onerous terms for what is usually a commodity with a lower value. Under the second approach, which represents about one-third of jurisdictions, the parties agree to negotiate terms for commercial development, but within a similar structure to that for liquids. In a PSC, the language may include a right to recover costs and to share profits (production). There is one exception that belongs to neither of these approaches. Angola continues to exclude from its contracts the right of the contractor to produce and sell natural gas, although the contractor is obliged to develop and deliver excess associated gas to the state.

Figure 6 shows these types of gas terms on the same template. Once again, a blank space indicates a lack of information, not a lack of terms. The initialism 'TBD' indicates 'To be determined', as opposed to 'Included', where the terms for natural gas are covered by the instrument.

---

1 Steve Parish, HIS course notes, *Fundamentals of Cash Flow Analysis*, Association of International Petroleum Negotiators Oil & Gas Asset Evaluation Workshop, Houston, September 8-9 2014.

Figure 6: Terms for Natural Gas

Included	Gas rights excluded	TBD	Included		Included
Included	TBD	TBD	TBD	Included	
Included	Included	TBD	TBD	TBD	
Included	Included			Included	Included
	TBD		Included	Included	Included
Included	Included	Included	TBD	TBD	
	TBD	Included	TBD	TBD	
Included	Included	Included	Included		
Included	Included				

It is not clear that having a fiscal system with predetermined terms for natural gas is advantageous if there is no agreement on the gas sales price. Most HGIs define the price of natural gas for fiscal purposes as the actual sales price, to be negotiated with the end user. There are several degrees of freedom in such a structure. Firstly, there is a trade-off between price and government take. The same contractor revenue can be generated with a low price and low take as with a higher price and higher take. Secondly, stranded gas monetisation plans usually involve one or more end users. The transfer price may be arbitrarily set to apportion value (before or after government take) between upstream and downstream parts of the value chain. Since, in most jurisdictions, the downstream plant will not be subject to petroleum fiscal terms, this provides another opportunity for apportioning profits. The upstream participant may have differing views of how these choices are made, depending on whether it participates in the downstream as well.

9. Conclusion

A qualitative assessment of African fiscal regimes and their economic impact shows many differences in detail, despite a preponderance of regimes using production sharing and including a minority carried interest for the state or its NOC. In assessing the economics of particular opportunities, the behaviour of the economics resulting from changing prices should be assessed, both directly and also with regard to whether or not the fiscal terms can be changed without the contractor's agreement. Recent changes include various responses to the perception that host governments are missing out when direct or indirect transfers occur that involve significant oil fields prior to production start-up and hence first government revenues. The emergence of additional regions where gas can be monetised suggests a need for flexibility in structuring appropriate fiscal systems for such potentially integrated projects.

Oil and gas mergers and acquisitions in Africa

Adam Blythe
Bracewell & Giuliani (UK) LLP
Ben Donovan
DLA Piper

1. Introduction

Ukitaka kuoga, usiogope baridi
Swahili proverb: *if you want to take a bath, you should not be afraid of the cold*

Oil and gas-related mergers and acquisitions (M&A) activity across Africa remains buoyant. As exploration and production work continues apace and new frontiers for petroleum operations are identified and harnessed, this has created new acquisition opportunities that are well supported by fundamental M&A rationale. Deals are available, commercially justifiable and are being realised. Throughout the continent, governments view the exploitation of oil and gas as a route to economic and social development, causing external investment and expertise to be ever more welcomed and facilitated.

Reported M&A activity in the region bears out this macro view. In 2013, transaction volumes maintained the high levels seen in previous years; the aggregate value of these deals continued on its upward trend, with a reported cumulative amount of $22.2 billion.[1] Exploration and production in the continent has moved from promise to performance: Africa now holds 7.7% of the world's proven oil reserves and a 10.1% share of global production volumes.[2] What is increasingly clear is not only the significance of Africa as a global oil and gas reserve holder and production source, but also its place now as a forum for M&A activity. In 2013, Africa was the third largest global region for reported upstream transaction value[3] (it was sixth in 2012). This trend was driven by a small number of world-class M&A transactions with multi-billion dollar tickets. This is well illustrated by examples such as CNPC's $4.2 billion acquisition of an indirect 20% participating interest in Area 4 in Mozambique, or Oando's $1.9 billion purchase of ConocoPhillips' entire upstream position in Nigeria. These indicate the scale of transactions possible in Africa. They are also key bellwethers for the direction of the region, a matter explored further in this chapter.

While the sub-surface story for many African countries continues only to improve, the same cannot always be said at ground level. Many profound legal, commercial and operational challenges still remain for oil and gas companies working

1 Ernst & Young, *Global oil and gas transactions review 2013*, p X.
2 BP, *Statistical Review of World Energy 2014*, p X.
3 Ernst & Young, *op cit* (note 1 above), p X.

on the continent, and these have implications for M&A transactions. In many African countries, the legislative framework for oil and gas is being reviewed and reappraised, often contemporaneously with major discoveries. This means that the long-term regulatory, health and safety, environmental and fiscal requirements of a country cannot always be forecast. In a number of jurisdictions, there may also be wider questions about the country's political stability. Increased local 'content' and industry participation is now a common and ever-developing feature. In a sector that requires stability in its fiscal and regulatory environment in order to evaluate the application of the sizeable capital demands and the resulting returns, these shifting scenes represent a difficult challenge when deciding on where to place future investment.

An understanding of the nuances of each jurisdiction's legal regime, its particular vagaries and any applicable 'risk' factors is vital to ensure a successful M&A transaction. Such an analysis will inform the approach taken when conducting due diligence on an opportunity. It is also essential for the transaction documents and for determining the warranties and other investment protection required by a purchaser. This, of course, works both ways, and sellers will not accept buyer positions that attempt simply to parcel all potential or unknown risk to the seller; a more educated and sophisticated view is required. In an increasingly competitive market, buyers must now do their homework in order to understand what constitutes a real and appreciable risk factor, and then give careful thought to how to resolve this (potentially through pricing or through protection in the sale and purchase agreement).

One further introductory point worth noting is the true extent of an 'African' M&A environment. The vast diversity of the continent, through its differing political and regulatory environments, the contrasting anglophone, francophone and lusophone backgrounds, and the shifting maturity of its legal and banking systems can, when taken all together, mean (at least in the context of this chapter) that the African label must cover a great deal of ground. It is both difficult and unwise to draw broad generalisations: what is done and accepted in Lagos may not be so in Dar es Salaam. The nascent attempts at regional integration, such as the East African Community or the OHADA system of laws do not (as yet) offer close continental harmony and the depth of this integration appears shallow, with little consequence for oil and gas-related M&A work. Africa remains heterogeneous: each jurisdiction has its unique features and surprises.

This chapter explores how much of the above commentary translates into actual practice, as well as exploring some of the significant challenges and issues that remain and how the industry and its M&A advisers are responding to these obstacles.

2. African M&A trends

In recent years, some clear patterns within the region have been discernible. These help to explain the sustained M&A activity and offer indicators about how this will continue and evolve. Material trends include the following matters.

2.1 Active portfolio management by IOCs

Demands to deliver ever better returns for shareholders have seen international oil companies (IOCs) optimising their focus to projects that can provide enhanced revenues or best utilise their financial and technical muscle. They may also be seeking shelter from areas most at risk from legal and fiscal re-evaluation. This is most clearly seen in Nigeria, where major divestiture programmes continue to be made by IOCs of their onshore/shallow water positions, while they migrate to the challenging deep water opportunities. The prospective effects of Nigeria's long-awaited Petroleum Industry Bill can also be seen at play here, with the expected fiscal terms set to favour deep water exploration and production at the expense of onshore projects.

2.2 New buyer/operator parties

As and where the IOCs leave the stage, there are many emergent actors who are ready to fill their vacant parts, or pursue opportunities ignored by (or unpalatable to) the IOCs. Asian national oil companies (principally Chinese state-owned companies) have become active investors in Africa, seeking assets with proven reserves in order to satisfy their countries' oil and gas demands. CNPC's acquisition of a significant stake in Area 4 of Mozambique (following significant investments in upstream assets in other African countries, such as Chad and South Sudan) demonstrates how far these investors are willing to participate, given the expected multi-billion dollar funding requirements needed in the planned LNG onshore/offshore projects.

Other Asian energy companies have followed this trend, as shown by Pavilion Energy's farm-in to a 20% interest in Blocks 1, 3 and 4 offshore Tanzania from Ophir. These companies are looking to African upstream opportunities in order to diversify their sources of LNG supply so as to be ready to meet growing Asian gas demands.

The retreat of the IOCs in Nigeria, alongside a changing legal/regulatory regime now geared to promote local content and participation, has seen indigenous companies like Oando and Seplat emerge as national champions. These new contenders are now capable of acquiring (and funding) the sizeable onshore positions put up for sale by the IOCs. The 2014 ConocoPhillips acquisition by Oando saw it increase its production tenfold overnight, to 50,000 barrels per day, and extend its operator role to cover some of Nigeria's largest onshore fields. That transaction, alongside its multi-source international and domestic financing, is expected to serve as a pathfinder for other Nigerian companies in exploiting subsequent IOC divestitures. These companies seem unlikely to stand still and may soon look beyond Nigeria to become regional players, heralding a new class of African IOCs.

Investment banks and private equity firms have also become active in the African upstream market and provide another new source for M&A activity.

2.3 East African gas

This region has quickly established itself as the continent's new energy frontier. Alongside the oil finds in Uganda and Kenya, the offshore gas discoveries in Mozambique (proven reserves of over 100 TCF as at the time of writing) and Tanzania (estimated reserves of over 46 TCF as at the time of writing) have created the potential for a number of LNG hubs to be constructed in a series of mega-projects. The capital demands to fund these developments have caused participants to sell down and spread their exposure. As the US looks inwards for its gas supply (and ever closer as an export market), Asia and India represent the likely future markets for East African LNG, which has led to increased interest from Asian gas consumers/sellers to participate in the source upstream position.

2.4 New locales for major project development

As more African countries become viewed as sufficiently stable jurisdictions within which to locate high-investment projects, this has in turn caused high levels of farm-out activity in order to seek funding and partners with deep pockets for this scale of development and production.

3. Structuring M&A transactions

The same fundamental factors that apply anywhere in the world when determining a suitable transaction structure are also relevant to an African deal. In addition, however, there are a range of local considerations and complications that may have a bearing on making an appropriate choice of structure and help to eliminate potential risks to deal certainty. These are explored below. This option analysis will also be driven by fiscal considerations, namely the tax consequences for both buyer and seller on completion of the sale, and thus will require the involvement of commercial and financial advisers to assess the position.

3.1 Structural options: a sale of shares or the 'asset'?

There are two fundamental routes when seeking to transfer an upstream oil and gas interest.

- *An asset sale.* In an upstream M&A context, this will be a transfer of a particular share in the interests (this constituting rights, liabilities and obligations) arising under the relevant production sharing agreement (PSA)/licence, joint operating agreement (JOA) and any other relevant petroleum/upstream-related agreement. That 'share' in those interests is commonly referred to as the 'participating interest' and will express (as a percentage) the participation of a party in the rights and obligations arising from the particular concession and its related agreements.
- *A share sale.* In an upstream M&A context, this will be a transfer of the shares in a company that holds the asset, ie, the participating interest in the relevant PSA/licence, JOA and any other relevant petroleum/upstream-related agreement. This is effectively an indirect transfer of the participating interest.

As a very general rule of thumb, a share sale will tend to offer greater simplicity in terms of deal process and analysis than an asset sale, which may require complex arrangements to ensure all the expected interests and assets actually transfer to the purchaser, and at the same time. It does not, however, follow that a share sale will always be the most appropriate approach to take; a share purchase might include liabilities that may be avoided by purchasing the assets alone, and there are myriad commercial, legal, fiscal and regulatory factors that will determine the optimal structure.

3.2 Sale and purchase agreement or a farm-in/farm-out?

While a detailed consideration of the differences in approach and use (as well as the many similarities) of sale and purchase agreements and farm-out agreements lies beyond the scope of this chapter, it is worth noting that farm-out agreements are commonly used across Africa, with the Association of International Petroleum Negotiators (AIPN) model form often serving as the base document. Farm-outs tend to be typically employed by African explorers in the early exploration/appraisal life of a field and are used to reduce their participation in a concession, to raise funds for other opportunities, and also to pass over exploration work and costs commitments until production commences (which the explorer may not have been able to fund), while maintaining participation in the concession for the eventual production revenues and profits. While they may not be suitable to more mature fields or complex sale arrangements, the farm-out agreement approach does tend to allow for flexibility in the commercial terms of a deal and the consideration for the transfer (though it is worth noting that the base AIPN document does not include a comprehensive list of warranties about the seller/target, nor does it have a developed liability limitation regime).

3.3 Use of assignment instruments and other transfer documents

A common feature in many oil and gas regimes in Africa (and elsewhere) is the use of a separate instrument to convey the transfer of the participating interest in the asset: a deed of assignment. These tend to be simple instruments with the sole purpose of effecting the transfer of the petroleum interests (whereas the sale and purchase agreement establishes the terms and conditions for that transfer to take place). Care must be taken, however, in reviewing how the assignment purports to pass liabilities and obligations. This is to ensure that its provisions do not contradict those in the negotiated sale and purchase agreement (as the assignment instrument will often attempt to pass all past, present and future liabilities to the incoming transferee). These instruments often have a locally prescribed form and will be presented to the relevant government ministry in order to obtain its consent to the transaction. They can be helpful to sellers and purchasers, in that it is only the assignment instrument that need be publicly disclosed to the government, while the commercially sensitive terms of the sale and purchase agreement can remain confidential between the parties to it.

Where the relevant upstream interest also involves a JOA, it will be necessary also to consider how the rights/obligations under that agreement will pass to the purchaser. In the case of a share sale, this should be reasonably straightforward: upon completion of the sale, the target company should continue to hold the interest under the JOA (though there may be separate requirements to obtain consent from the other parties to the JOA, or pre-emption rights for those parties, as described at 5.3 below). With an asset sale, it will be necessary to have a separate agreement to effect the transfer of the seller's interest in the JOA. In African countries that follow the English law system or where the JOA is otherwise governed by English law, this will be achieved through a novation agreement (though this is commonly described as an assignment agreement) and will require all the parties to the JOA to be a party (along with the seller and purchaser). This is because the transfer of the obligations under the JOA can only occur with the consent and acquiescence of all the parties to the agreement. The effect of the novation agreement will be that the purchaser becomes a party to the JOA and will assume all the obligations and liabilities, along with the rights and benefits, that the seller had under the agreement.

3.4 Legal factors in determining the structure

There will be a range of considerations for both seller and purchaser when establishing the transaction structure. The following matters are of particular relevance.

- *Applicability of consents and pre-emption rights.* As is explained at 5.1 below, any arrangement to transfer an upstream interest will raise the question of what consents may be required to allow the sale, along with the applicability of any 'first-refusal' or 'right-to-match'-type rights that the other existing upstream participants may enjoy. These matters can have serious implications for the transfer: they can introduce risk that the deal will not proceed, or can allow third parties to impose new terms in return for their consent (which may affect the commercial aspects of the sale). They can also materially alter the expected deal timetable and bring the risk of significant delays to completion. Thus, any structure that avoids the need to seek such consents (and avoids the possibility of a refusal or delay) may be advantageous to seller and buyer.

  In an asset sale structure, the transfer represents a direct change in the identity of the legal person holding the participating interest. In a share sale, the same person will continue to own the participating interest (ie, the target company); there is, however, a change in the shareholding of that person, commonly referred to as a 'change in control'. This concept recognises the fact that any change in a company's ultimate shareholders can have implications for its future prospects (in terms of its management and its financial support), particularly when the company is a thinly-capitalised shell company, as will often be the case in the corporate structures used to hold oil and gas interests by foreign investors in Africa.

  Governments have a legitimate concern to monitor and regulate the persons that hold interests in the upstream space. The initial award of the PSA or licence to a contractor will have been made pursuant to an evaluation process. The contractor will have been selected by the government as an entity with sufficient technical and financial wherewithal to undertake the exploration and production works required under that concession. The government will want to ensure that any person who subsequently seeks to obtain an interest in the concession can meet these same requirements. Accordingly, petroleum legislation throughout Africa tends to afford governments wide latitude in requiring their consent before any transfer of an upstream interest can be made. The involvement of a national oil company (NOC) in the concession can complicate this further and, in such circumstances, may mean that the NOC enjoys a right to pre-empt the sale under the terms of the PSA/licence.

  Petroleum legislation (and the terms of PSAs or licences) throughout

Africa generally requires a selling contractor seeking to transfer its participating interest (ie, an asset sale) to obtain prior government consent. This same legislation can be imperfectly worded and it is unclear in many African jurisdictions whether these consent requirements apply to share sales that operate as an indirect transfer of the participating interest. Accordingly, it may sometimes be the case that a share sale does not trigger the legislative need for government consent (though some of the problems that can arise in these circumstances are noted at 5.1 below).

Similar consent rights will commonly exist for the other participants that comprise the PSA/licence 'contractor' interest. These parties have a proper interest in knowing who is, and will be, their counterparty. JOAs tend to address this position through various ways, which include:

- restricting a party from transferring its PSA/licence interest without its accompanying JOA interest;
- requiring all parties to consent before a transfer of JOA and concession interest can be made; and
- providing the non-transferring parties with pre-emption rights to intervene to acquire the interest that has been made available for sale.

Once again, the precise terms of the language used in the JOA must be considered in order to assess whether the consent or pre-emption provisions apply to the proposed sale transaction and whether they restrict changes in control resulting from a share sale process.

- *Allocation of liabilities.* One obvious distinction between the two forms of structure is that, under a share sale, the purchaser will acquire both all the rights and all the liabilities and obligations that may exist (even if unknown to the purchaser) for the target company. This is typically not the case with an asset sale, where only the rights, obligations and liabilities that are expressly transferred pursuant to the sale agreement will pass to the purchaser. Care must be taken, however, when making this assumption with regard to liabilities associated with oil and gas assets/interests. Environmental and decommissioning liabilities can, under various local laws or the terms of PSAs utilised across Africa, either attach to the asset (and may therefore pass to a purchaser on an asset sale, even where they are not specifically transferred under the asset sale agreement) or to the responsible person, ie, they will remain with the person who undertook the activities or caused any pollution or other environmental damage (and may therefore remain with a selling company that has sold an asset with the intention of disposing of all liabilities relating to that asset, or which could potentially apply to the seller shareholders of a company). It is therefore important that a careful legal analysis of the relevant local laws on such matters is undertaken, so as to ensure that the actual post-transaction liability allocation reflects the terms of the deal the parties think they have made.

  Such matters will often be a critical concern for divesting companies, who will want absolute certainty as between buyer and seller about who assumes any latent environmental or decommissioning liabilities (irrespective of what the domestic law may say) that may become due following completion of the acquisition. Recent IOC divestiture programmes in Africa have seen IOC sellers seek to impose 'clean-break' provisions on their purchasers. These require the purchaser to assume all past, present and future liability for environmental and decommissioning liabilities, irrespective of when the event triggering the liability occurred. These are often supported by indemnities in favour of the seller against any such losses for which it could become liable as a result of the application of the local law. The seller may also require the buyer to provide payment security or guarantees in support of this indemnity obligation. The willingness of the buyer to assume such a position (even in circumstances where it may not be possible to undertake sufficient due diligence in order to understand properly the likely extent of the exposure) may become a critical deal matter (and in an auction bidding process, will be a material factor in bid evaluation). Outside of such 'clean-break' mechanics, establishing and agreeing the baseline and timing for when such environmental and decommissioning liabilities are assumed by either buyer or seller can be an important matter in the sale and purchase documents and negotiations.

As stated previously, when purchasing a company, the buyer will assume all the liabilities and obligations that have been acquired by that target company throughout its life (whether known or not). This has the potential to cause a real due diligence concern in African M&A matters, given the difficulties that a purchaser may face when conducting its corporate investigations and its questionable ability to verify independently the past life of the target company (as to which, see 4.2 below).

3.5 Domestic ownership

Many African petroleum regimes contain mandatory requirements about the identity and domicile of persons holding upstream interests that can have implications for the transaction structure: this will affect both the sale structure and also the purchaser's proposed corporate structure post-completion. These issues need careful assessment at the initial stage of the deal, in order to ensure that it is achievable under the relevant local law and to assess the taxation position (with regard to both transfer taxes and taxes applicable to the target's future profits). For example, a common requirement across Africa is that the company holding the upstream interest must be a domestic company. As the authors will explore at 6.2 below, many legal systems now have more complex local participation requirements that can include a minimum mandatory domestic 'ownership' component. Ensuring compliance with these requirements may raise challenging issues for international investors.

4. Considerations for the M&A process

4.1 Form of the deal

A common feature of the divestiture programmes made by the IOCs, in Nigeria and elsewhere across Africa, is the seller's use of an 'auction-style' competitive bid process. This will usually involve a qualifying stage, where only limited information is made available about the target, and potentially interested parties are asked to submit indicative bids. Those bidders selected by the seller (with some consideration having been paid to their respective financial resources and their capability to close the deal) then proceed to the next stage, where they are given access to an electronic data room (often containing a voluminous quantity of documents) and a draft sale and purchase agreement. The bidders are then given a period of time within which they can conduct due diligence and pose questions to the seller's team. Bidders who wish to proceed must submit a purchase price and a marked-up copy of the sale and purchase documents. Participants may also be asked to pay a deposit in advance of being confirmed as the winning bidder and may even be required to submit funding commitments to support their purchase price, along with security for payment of the deposit/purchase price.

The bidders are evaluated through both a consideration of their proposed purchase price and their mark-up of the sale and purchase agreement, among a range of other qualitative factors. A bidder's approach to certain matters in the sale and purchase agreement can often be a determining factor. Matters such as the purchaser's assumption of environmental/decommissioning liability, an ability to rely only on a limited set of warranties (and to accept wide disclosures against such warranties, as to which, see 4.2 below) or a willingness to reduce the conditions to closing the deal and to eliminate deal uncertainty, may often sway a seller where the financial terms are similar as between competing bidders. There may also be other relevant local factors to consider: in jurisdictions such as Nigeria, where local content can have important legal and political consequences, an indigenous company may gain a special advantage. Indeed, certain marginal fields in Nigeria can only be held by, and transferred to, buyers with the requisite Nigerian ownership.

More orthodox bilateral sales processes are also commonplace, particularly in African jurisdictions with less well-developed hydrocarbon and/or public procurement legislation.

4.2 Due diligence

While African-related transactions do not depart from the usual requirements for a due diligence exercise, they can raise some novel considerations. Due diligence (legal, technical and financial) still remains a vital part of the transaction process and is essential for a buyer to perform in order to ensure that it understands the business of the target and to assist in gathering sufficient information with which to undertake this analysis. The results of this exercise then allow the buyer to assess the potential risks and liabilities and respond to these findings, and to determine whether to continue with the sale or to negotiate specific warranties and indemnities, or address these matters in the target's valuation. Given that each jurisdiction can have unique features within its petroleum and company laws, the involvement of local legal experts can be essential to ensuring that the proper legal context and framework is understood (and that local risks/issues do not remain Rumsfeldian 'unknown unknowns').

The approach taken in the IOC divestiture processes in Africa has been to make available sizeable electronic data rooms. The contents of a data room are deemed to be 'disclosed' to the buyer under the terms of the sale and purchase agreement (though sellers will often simultaneously seek to exclude any form of warranty or assurance from being offered or implied by the contents of the data room, or in certain circumstances even as to the accuracy and/or completeness of the data room contents). The purpose of this disclosure is to qualify the warranties given in the sale and purchase agreement (ie, to prevent the buyer from having any claim or remedy for a breach of a warranty that is due to any circumstance that has been set out in the data room). This offers the seller a broad protection against potential warranty claims and shifts the onus onto the purchaser to perform an onerous review of the data room. This exercise is necessary in order to ensure that the apparent protection offered by the warranties in the sale and purchase agreement has not been unknowingly compromised. In return, buyers may often request that sellers should warrant the accuracy and completeness of the data room. This will, however, be met with strong resistance from sellers and cannot be said to represent a market norm.

One area of potential due diligence concern for buyers is the limited ability to undertake public searches to verify information. Company registries and petroleum registries in many African jurisdictions may not contain accurate or complete information and it can be unwise to rely on registry results alone with regard to shareholdings or encumbrances. These are matters that should also be specifically addressed in the sale and purchase agreement through warranties. Few jurisdictions will have registers that verify the PSA/licence holders and participants and fewer still will provide that the petroleum register itself demonstrates title to such matters, or that it is valid and subsisting. Again, warranty protection is therefore essential for such matters; alongside conducting a forensic 'chain of title' due diligence exercise. This will track the validity of the transfers made from the award of the PSA/licence through to the seller (along with evidence of receipt of requisite approvals and consents for such transfers).

4.3 Choice of law

As one would expect, PSAs and licences in African countries tend to be governed by their domestic systems of law.[4] It may also be a requirement that the associated joint operating agreement is governed by the same national law, though this is matter more open to challenge by contractors. As stated previously, many countries require PSA/licence participants to hold this interest in a locally incorporated company. When it comes, however, to the question of which system of law should govern the terms of the sale and purchase agreement to transfer these interests, and in jurisdictions where the governing law of the JOA can be chosen by the contractors, the laws of England and Wales tend to be the default choice and commonly feature in many transactions across Africa.

This may be the case despite the fact that England and Wales have no connection with the assets or the domicile of the parties, or the governing law of the contractual

4 One exception to this principle recently seen by the authors was a PSA in Somaliland, in which English law was, due to a lack of local laws, stated to govern the agreement.

interests being transferred. A justification for this position lies somewhat beyond the scope of this chapter, though it is trite to say that English law offers the parties a developed, settled and commercially-minded system of laws, with few impositions on the freedom of the parties to make binding agreements, and is supported by a depth of precedent and practice. Given the use of English as the international *lingua franca* of commercial arrangements, it also follows that English law is well suited to determining the meaning of contracts written in English. Given the history of many oil and gas countries in Africa, the role of English law, both as the foundation for their domestic legal systems and as a source of statute and precedent, means that it can also be well placed to work alongside many conventions and precedents found in certain local jurisdictions. The fund-raising process for the acquisition and demands of international lenders may also dictate choice of law considerations. It is also the case, given the likely mix of nationalities involved in an African M&A deal and the potential jurisdictions that could claim some connection to the transaction, that the law of England and Wales offers a suitable, neutral and market-standard position upon which the parties may easily agree.

This is, of course, not always the case, and is worthy of fresh appraisal on each transaction. In francophone jurisdictions, there may be good reasons to prefer French law as the system that should govern the transaction. The laws of New York are also employed as another system of neutral and internationally recognised law in the African oil and gas sector, though far less commonly than the law of England and Wales. There may also be no need and no desire to move away from the local laws that already govern the underlying target interest/asset.

5. Common material issues affecting the ability to transfer and deal certainty

Nearly all oil and gas M&A transactions in Africa will be structured as a split exchange and completion. This is because there will be a number of conditions (legal requirements and often also other commercial considerations) that must be satisfied before the legal interest in the target can properly pass to the buyer. If these conditions are not satisfied (usually before a contractually-prescribed long stop date), then the transaction will terminate before completion; the target interests will not pass; any deposit paid may or may not be forfeit; and the planned commercial intentions of the parties will have been defeated. Given the significant investment of money, time and resources which must often be employed in such sale processes, this is not a welcome occurrence and deal certainty has become a matter of clear concern for many sellers (and buyers) trying to complete transactions in Africa. This part of the chapter considers some of the material challenges that sellers/buyers may face and how they try to address those matters in their sale agreements.

5.1 Requirement for government consent

It is a standard and uniform requirement that any change in the identity of the PSA/licence participant will trigger a requirement to obtain prior governmental consent. This principle will be enshrined either in the terms of the concession, or in national petroleum laws, or in both. The rationale behind this approach has already been explained. As a result, almost all sales that are structured as an asset sale will require such consent before the transaction can complete and the interests lawfully pass to the buyer. Depending on the precise wording of the requirement for consent (as well as the nature of the transaction), a share sale will also, more often than not, trigger this approval requirement. Attempting to proceed with the sale, without satisfying any consent requirement, will likely lead to the transfer not being lawfully and validly made, thus making it liable to being unwound or set aside. Such a breach of the terms of the production sharing agreement/licence may also provide the government with a right to terminate the underlying petroleum agreement.

This is a matter that can sometimes require careful local due diligence. For example, until recently, the position in Nigeria was well understood: asset sales would trigger a need to obtain ministerial consent, whereas share sales did not. A decision of the Federal High Court of Nigeria in May 2012[5] changed this settled understanding, when court reinterpreted paragraph 14 of the First Schedule to the Petroleum Act to require prior ministerial consent before a controlling shareholding in a company holding an oil mining lease could be transferred. This had implications for a number of upstream transactions, not least the previously-mentioned Oando/ConocoPhillips deal, which saw its proposed transaction schedule severely delayed, owing to the need to obtain a consent which traditionally had not been required (exacerbated by the fact that the ministry was now compelled to issue a consent on grounds that were less than certain or settled, due to pending appeals against the High Court decision).

Seeking governmental consent can, in some jurisdictions, bring the potential for unforeseen consequences. Notwithstanding the prospect that the consent may be withheld (and, under the petroleum laws of many African jurisdictions, the government or a minister may enjoy wide discretion to refuse approval), it may also provide the government with the opportunity to seek concessions in return for a positive outcome to this process. These could include amending the terms of the PSA/licence, or altering the fiscal, royalty or production sharing take. Sizeable fees may also be payable for the making of any such application.

Understanding the formal requirements for the necessary consents is a critical matter that should be analysed and agreed between the parties at the earliest opportunity. Both the buyer and the seller have a proper interest not only in getting this right, but also in ensuring a common approach, in terms of addressing who is primarily responsible for seeking that consent and how they may go about obtaining it (for example, if the seller is the party responsible under local law for applying for the consent, then the buyer has a legitimate interest in ensuring that the process of obtaining the consent does not lead to any material change in the terms of the PSA/licence).

5.2 The need for competition/regulatory approval

Alongside the requirements of national petroleum laws for governmental consent, there may be additional merger/competition requirements to satisfy, as well as the

5 *Moni Pulo v Brass Exploration Limited et al*, FHC/L/CS/835/2011.

potential need to obtain wider regulatory permissions and consents (eg, relating to the particular activities that may be carried out by the transferee after closing the deal). This chapter does not purport to give a detailed analysis of the position across the continent as to competition, and local law advice should always be taken on the position. Generally speaking, for many jurisdictions across Africa, the competition/merger regime is relatively under-developed and has few formal requirements for consents (usually there is merely a notification requirement and a filing fee). Many of the controls that do exist are largely calibrated to prevent cartels or abuse of a dominant position. Accordingly, this is something that does not commonly pose a material issue for buyer/seller and the sale and purchase agreement may often be silent on this point.

There is a developing common market-based competition system in east and southern Africa that may become increasingly relevant to oil and gas M&A in this region. The Common Market for Eastern and Southern Africa (COMESA) is an African free trade bloc comprising 19 countries.[6] It has supranational competition laws and a recently established Competition Commission, located in Malawi with effect from January 14 2013). While the Competition Commission is in its infancy, it is already in the process of reviewing its rules and guidelines. Standard practice with regard to the competition notification has yet to be established in the market: COMESA reports that 18 notifications were made to it in the first half of 2014 (which, of course, cannot be said to be reflective of the number of mergers and acquisitions in the region).

On the face of it, the Competition Commission places an easily-triggered hurdle for any M&A or joint venture transaction in the COMESA region. The requirement to notify a transaction is stated to apply when one of more of the relevant parties have operations in two or more COMESA countries. There is no threshold value for the deal to require a notification. This establishes, therefore, very wide scope in the notification of deals, even where there may be minimal involvement or activity within the COMESA region. Another significant concern with the scheme is the notification fee: it is set at 0.5% of the merging parties' combined annual turnover or the combined value of their assets in the COMESA region (whichever is higher) and is capped at $500,000. The COMESA competition laws state that any failure to notify an applicable transaction can mean that it would be unenforceable in the COMESA region (though it is unclear how this would have direct consequence in all COMESA member states) and fines may be imposed of up to 10% of the parties' combined turnover in the COMESA region.

Given its relatively recent introduction, along with the limited resources of the COMESA Competition Commission to carry out investigations in such a large region (or even be aware of merger activity), the COMESA competition notification requirements have not, as yet, come to be reflected in everyday practice. To date, it appears as though there have been no public examples of fines being imposed by the

6 At the time of writing, the COMESA member states are: Angola, Burundi, Comoros Islands, Democratic Republic of Congo, Djibouti, Egypt, Eritrea, Ethiopia, Kenya, Libya, Madagascar, Malawi, Mauritius, Namibia, Rwanda, Seychelles, Sudan, Swaziland, Uganda, Zambia and Zimbabwe.

Competition Commission or of transactions set aside. Its provisions and practices will, however, need constant consideration (particularly as they evolve) and parties should consider whether their transactions in the region could and should be notified.

5.3 Participants' rights to consent and pre-emption

The participants in a JOA will nearly always enjoy rights to consent to any proposed transfer of the participating interest (though their ability to refuse consent is typically restricted to being dissatisfied with the technical and financial capability of the incoming transferee); they may also have a first right of refusal or pre-emption, affording them the option to acquire the target interest. These will most commonly apply to asset-structured sales, but may also be relevant to share sales and changes in control of a participating interest holder. Any upstream M&A deal will therefore need to take account of these positions. Clearly, this is a matter that will primarily concern a buyer: will its purchase be defeated due to the exercise of such a right? It also has consequences for sellers. The existence of such rights may limit the marketability of the potential target, so sellers will often work to provide advance comfort to potential buyers that these consents will be forthcoming and that pre-emption rights will be waived.

5.4 Approaches to addressing these issues in M&A agreements

- *Conditions and the process of obtaining consents.* Many of the above-mentioned matters are mandatory features of local laws or express contractual requirements. This means they will often be addressed in the sale and purchase agreement as conditions to be satisfied before the transaction can complete and title to the target interest transfers. The parties will allocate primary responsibility for satisfying the condition (usually to the seller) but require all sides to work collaboratively to achieve this. Given the possible risk of such matters affording government or third parties the opportunity to impose new terms (or, to the extent there is any applicable competition law, the potential that the competition authority may impose conditions to its approval), buyers may introduce requirements that they should either be involved in the process of seeking consent or have an opportunity to review and accept the terms of any conditions for granting a consent.

  Another related issue is the prospect of uncertainty over the tax consequences that might arise upon the completion of an M&A transaction. The amicable resolution of such matters in advance of a sale can help achieve the timely delivery of the necessary governmental consents. Many African countries have unclear taxation provisions about how and when capital gains liabilities are triggered on petroleum-related sales, which can lead to disputes over whether any such taxes have become due and who is liable to pay them (with the example of Heritage and Tullow in Uganda being a well-known case where the obligation to pay is disputed between the seller and the buyer). The government's ability to withhold consents (either for the transaction or for contemplated projects or activities) is a strong weapon in its arsenal.

Sellers and buyers have aligned interests in preventing such an outcome. The recent Ophir farm-out to Pavilion Energy in Tanzania is reflective of how parties can gain deal certainty by addressing such concerns. In that example, the payment of a capital gains liability was very quickly addressed with the revenue authority during the sale process. Flushed with the certainty of a sizeable tax payment becoming due and payable on the completion of the sale, the Tanzanian government was prompt in issuing the necessary consent to allow the transaction to close.

- *Allowing for delays.* It is a common reality of navigating the process of governmental consent in many countries in Africa that there is potential for significant delay to an expected transaction schedule. Parties should therefore prepare for this possibility within their transaction documents and process. One common approach (though one also driven by other commercial and legal factors) is to structure the transaction on an 'effective-date' basis, ie, a specific (past) date is selected as the point in time from which the purchaser is to assume the financial and operational position of the company (supported by various covenants and warranties from the seller), and the positions of seller and buyer are reconciled to that date once closing of the deal actually occurs. The buyer and seller will also need to consider carefully the interim operating regime for the target interests (ie, as between signing and completion) and ensure that this can practicably work over a long period of time (though there may be a tension between the seller's desire not overly to constrain its ability to run the business and the buyer's wish to preserve value and not become subject to new conditions arising post-signing). Another consequence arising from delays to the schedule for closing can be a difficulty in obtaining external financing for the transaction. Lenders may be reluctant to commit funds until the consent position is clear and the timing for closing of the sale has been fixed. The effects of this can also further defer the ability of the buyer to close matters. The parties may also wish to address the time period within which the conditions must be satisfied, and allow for the potential to renew this long stop, or to address the consequences flowing from any failure to satisfy the conditions (most significantly, the treatment of any deposit paid by the buyer).
- *Payment security.* As has been explained previously, 'deal certainty' is often a paramount concern for sellers in the African context, particularly given the strong possibility for delay as described in the previous section. One method commonly employed to help cement the transaction at the signing stage is the payment of a deposit by the buyer. The terms of the sale and purchase agreement will establish the circumstances in which that deposit may be retained by the seller if the transaction does not proceed.

The divestiture programmes in Nigeria provide an example of how sellers are evaluating these risks. Many of the previous sale processes have not run to the timetable expected by the selling IOCs, nor have they all led to concluded sales. In response to this, the terms of recent sale offers have hardened. Buyers may now be required to provide security for the deposit payment as part of their bid. The size of the deposit demanded may exceed the typical 10% requirement. Buyers may also be asked to provide (at signing) liquid forms of security for payment of the completion monies. The terms on which either the deposit can be retained, or the seller is entitled to claim under the payment security, also appear to be shifting. This reflects a philosophy of passing the risk of obtaining the requisite consents to the buyer and helping to secure some financial outcome for the seller in most circumstances. Whether buyers will be willing to accept such positions is, of course, another matter, though it may present opportunities for indigenous companies who feel comfortable in assuming such risks and in their ability to influence and accelerate the consent granting process.

6. Other regulatory factors affecting M&A activity in Africa

6.1 Shifting regulatory frameworks

Many countries in Africa are considering their legislative regimes for oil and gas activities. This is true for countries with long histories of oil and production, such as Nigeria, where wholesale changes to the institutional and regulatory structure, along with new fiscal terms for certain upstream operations, have been looming over the industry since 2008. At the time of writing, the Petroleum Industry Bill remains locked in stasis. This is also the case in emergent oil and gas countries with newly found reserves. Mozambique has very recently enacted new petroleum legislation, designed in part to address offshore gas reserves and proposed LNG projects, and in part to impose stricter obligations on industry participants (though the terms of the prior concessions appear to be grandfathered). Tanzania has released a number of draft policies with regard to its gas position and local participation, though the precise terms of the legislation are yet to be settled. Alongside changes to the statutory framework, concession terms for new contractors are constantly evolving. This was the case with the latest 2014 Tanzanian PSA bid round, which imposed more onerous terms for contractors, particularly in terms of production sharing. The prospect of revisiting the terms of subsisting PSAs/licences is often raised by governments, albeit the process for doing so is not always clear. Another critical consideration within this regulatory framework is the stability of the fiscal terms and their application by the revenue authority.

A fluid regulatory position has an inhibitive effect for M&A transactions, as well as for wider industry participation and operations, and introduces issues that cannot always be foreseen, with effects that cannot always be addressed as between buyer and seller.

6.2 Local content requirements

Engendering domestic participation in the oil and gas industry has become a priority for governments across Africa. While no clear model for this approach has yet been established, the scope of 'local content' can include a wide variety of factors, ranging from the development of working capacity within the country (through training and education measures and mandatory employment requirements) through to the use of local materials and contractors in the performance of petroleum operations. These requirements may be prescribed in the PSA/licence or in the petroleum legislation, or increasingly through separate local content-focused legislation, such as the Black Economic Empowerment (BEE) legislation in South Africa.

A considered review and discussion of local content requirements across the continent lies beyond the scope of this chapter. Such requirements will, however, be a central matter when undertaking due diligence for any M&A activity in Africa. It is essential to ensure that there is an understanding of a particular jurisdiction's requirements and for this to form part of the commercial/legal analysis of the opportunity.

Local content in certain African jurisdictions may extend to mandatory ownership/equity positions for local persons in the upstream interest. Examples include Nigeria's Oil and Gas Industry Content Development Act, which affords priority to Nigerian companies and operators for the award of new oil field licences[7] and prescribes levels of Nigerian content for various upstream activities. Namibia has established policies (though currently short of introducing full legal requirements) to assist previously disadvantaged citizens in a manner similar to the South African BEE regime, which is a statutory requirement for investors wishing to do business with the government in South Africa. It should also be noted that these local content regimes are in addition to any required participation by, or carried interest to, the relevant NOC. Satisfying such requirements can have a bearing on the transaction and corporate ownership structures. One reaction in Nigeria to this shift has been the development of complex shareholder/joint venture arrangements with local partners. These structures often separate the economic, voting and ownership rights of the participants, sometimes relegating the local component to mere bare 'ownership', with limited economic and controlling rights over the company or asset. The veracity and regulatory compliance of this approach has not been tested.

'Local content' and domestic preference requirements may not only concern the upstream participating interest position. It is also necessary to consider wider requirements about related-midstream activities and how production can be disposed. One developing trend across the continent is for governments to promote or restrict the sale of gas to the power sector, in a bid to obtain reliable and economic fuel sources for electricity generation in order to serve developmental aims. Nigeria serves as a good example once again, its National Gas Supply and Pricing Policy and the National Gas Supply and Pricing Regulations establishing a requirement for gas producers to allocate a certain proportion of their reserves for supply to the domestic market, these reserves then being sold at a regulated price to a national gas aggregator. Tanzania appears to be adopting a similar model, as was set out in its (draft) National Natural Gas Policy[8] and the recent establishment of its own national gas aggregator. Putting the developmental reasons for such a structure to one side,

7 See section 3(1) of the act.

8 By way of example, one of the express policy statements is "[ensuring] that the domestic market is given first priority over the export market in gas supply". The draft Policy also states that one of the country's aims is to ensure a "reasonable share of the resource for domestic applications as a necessary measure to ensure diversification of the gas economy before export market".

matters such as this may have obvious consequences for the economics of gas-related projects, in that they can limit the sales price available to the producer, as well as raise questions about the performance risk of the aggregator. It can also frustrate the ability of the gas producer to sell any or all of its gas to other industries or to export, which may offer improved prices and payment arrangements. Clearly, such regulatory controls can have implications for the long-term success of any M&A deal from a buyer's perspective; it is therefore important that this position is well understood as part of the due diligence process.

6.3 Approaches to addressing these issues in the M&A process

An obvious first step for any buyer is to ensure that it is informed about, and aware of, the regulatory regime to which it is about to become subject and of the potential for this to change. Forewarned is forearmed. Another relevant and critical area of due diligence will be to understand the extent of any stabilisation protection – primarily, protections from government action in respect of changes in tax or law, capital and dividend expatriation support, and undertakings relating to the nationalisation or confiscation of assets – that might exist under the PSA/licence and to assess how the target interest could avail itself of these provisions, though care must always be taken when considering the effectiveness and enforceability of such measures. If such provisions do not exist as part of the existing legislative or contract structure, as is the case in some of the emergent African countries which have only commenced the licensing of exploration areas relatively recently, then consideration must be given by the contractor as to whether a separate government support agreement containing such provisions will be a condition precedent to investment. There may also be international investor protection (through bilateral investment treaties, which are common for many African jurisdictions) that can offer comfort to incoming buyers.

The sale and purchase agreement may specifically address the risk and consequences of changes in the law. On the buyer's side, this can be achieved through conditions to the transaction becoming effective, or through the terms of material adverse change protection (which can be creatively drafted to include political risk matters or new legislation). Sellers may expressly try to exclude any such risks. For example, a common limitation on a seller's liability is the exacerbating effect of any change in the law arising post-signature of the sale and purchase agreement. Sellers may force the buyer to accept risk for the domestic regulatory position from the date the deal is signed. Such matters may prove a controversial topic in negotiations, as each side tries to push the consequences of this political risk onto the other, when ultimately this lies beyond the control of either of them.

7. Conclusion

Because of the incalculable variety of scenarios that can occur in over fifty widely disparate jurisdictions, each with its own distinctive laws, customs and requirements, it is not possible to provide an exhaustive treatise on 'African' oil & gas M&A. As discussed in this chapter, however, there are some common issues that can be identified across most transactions (including issues that are common to other developing markets). Understanding critical matters such as 'Africa time' and the timeframes compared with transactions in other markets, government and PSA/JOA counterparty consent requirements, stabilisation provisions available (and required), local content requirements, and the laws of the jurisdiction and (if different) those governing the transaction documents, is the key to the success of oil & gas transactions in Africa.

State participation and local participation in oil and gas in Africa

John C LaMaster
Caroline-Lucy Moran
Akin Gump Strauss Hauer & Feld LLP

1. Introduction

There has been a marked intensification in recent years of international oil and gas industry activity across African regions, including recent focus on the potential of the east coast (eg, Mozambique, Kenya, Tanzania and Somalia) and the pre-salt plays of west Africa (eg, Angola, Gabon and the Republic of Congo). There has also been increased activity in 'frontier' states (eg, Namibia and Liberia) and those seeing revival following periods of political instability (eg, Ivory Coast and Egypt).

This upswing in international oil company (IOC) interest brings into renewed focus the means by which African governments may seek, through legislative and regulatory regimes, to maximise the benefits of oil and gas investment to their host states. These efforts take several forms, including government-imposed requirements for 'state participation' and 'local participation'.

State participation in the oil and gas industry is the legislated or otherwise mandatory requirement that the state or a state-owned entity, such as the national oil company (NOC), participate in oil and gas activities as a working interest or participating interest owner. Local participation is the requirement that local persons or entities that are not state-owned participate in oil and gas activities as direct or indirect working interest or participating interest owners.

The public policies underlying state participation and local participation in the African context are different. State participation is ideologically driven by resource nationalism, which is a global phenomenon and is embedded in the wider oil and gas industry. It is inherently linked to international politics. Approximately $2 billion a day of petroleum is traded worldwide, making it the largest single item in the balance of payments and exchanges between nations.[1] In this context, it is unsurprising that "many producing and importing countries have, at least at some point during the course of history, opted for direct state intervention rather than more liberal governance regimes."[2] Local participation has developed more uniquely in the African oil and gas industry in the light of wider political policies, such as economic empowerment.

1 Silvana Tordo with Brandon S Tracy & Noora Arfaa, *National Oil Companies and Value Creation*, World Bank paper no 28 (2011), at p xi.
2 *Ibid.*

Both state participation and local participation have similar consequences for IOCs, in that they reduce the levels of IOC participation and control in oil and gas activities. Both also raise certain challenges for host states as well as IOCs. For IOCs, these challenges are part of the wider risks associated with doing business in Africa. For example, both state participation and local participation regimes are subject to the risk of political instability and regulatory uncertainty. In addition, local participation in particular may give rise to anti-bribery and corruption issues.

This chapter will consider the historic origins of state participation and local participation, their prevalence in the African oil and gas industry and the resulting challenges faced by host states and IOCs. Finally, this chapter will suggest means of addressing these challenges in the legal context with a view to risk mitigation.

2. State 'take' under petroleum agreements

In a chapter examining state participation, it is important to consider briefly the wider fiscal environment of host state/IOC interaction. Across the global oil and gas industry, the concept of financial or commercial benefit accruing to the host state is fundamental. This has been a feature since the royalty provisions of the earliest petroleum agreements (which originally took the form of concessions) between host states and IOCs, albeit historically the commercial and financial benefits to the state were limited. In addition to royalties, provisions concerning taxation, bonus payments and/or rental payments are other examples of the traditional mechanisms comprising the state's 'take' under an upstream petroleum agreement.

Nowadays, the fiscal framework varies between different types of petroleum agreements, being primarily concessions, risk service agreements and, most commonly in developing states, production sharing contracts (PSCs). Under the PSC model, the government's primary financial benefit derives from 'profit oil'. This is the amount of oil or gas production that is divided between the IOC participating parties and the host state under the petroleum agreement, after deducting the amount of oil and gas production that has been allocated to reimbursement of exploration and development costs and expenses. This concept of production sharing under petroleum agreements began in the 1950s, thereby preceding the introduction of PSCs (which were first introduced in Indonesia in 1966), but it is nonetheless the PSC that best illustrates this fiscal structure.

The modern legal framework for state participation progressed in tandem with the evolution of production sharing and PSCs. PSCs were the first host state agreements to provide that the ownership of and right to exploit oil and gas remain with the host state or its NOC, with the IOC being, in legal terms, a contractor hired to perform the operations.[3] As will be discussed, however, state participation as a concept pre-dates both production sharing and the PSC and goes beyond mere financial 'take'. The challenges for the host state of balancing fiscal concerns with the wider political and social aspects of state participation will also be discussed later in this chapter.

---

3 Claude Duval, Honoré Le Leuch, André Pertuzio & Jacqueline Lang Weaver, *International Petroleum Exploration and Exploitation Agreements: Legal, Economic and Policy Aspects* (2009, Barrows, New York), at p 71.

It should be noted that fiscal aspects and state participation interact in different ways across different petroleum agreements, often creating a 'hybrid' approach. For example, many modern PSCs retain a royalty payment, and since the 1960s and 1970s many old-style concession agreements have also included an element of profit oil and/or state participation.[4]

3. State participation – the historical context

State participation in the oil and gas industry was first seen at the beginning of the last century. The first NOC was founded in Argentina in 1922, prior to which Russia had already nationalised its oil and gas industry (in 1918), with NOCs to follow there in the 1930s.[5] It was not, however, until the 1950s that state participation in the oil and gas industry advanced significantly. This occurred at the same time as the principle of state sovereignty over national resources was formally recognised by the United Nations (UN) as part of the New International Economic Order, which was "a comprehensive package of multilateral policy options that aimed to improve the position of Third World countries in the world economy relative to the richest states."[6]

By the time of the UN General Assembly's 'Permanent sovereignty over natural resources' resolution in 1962, the concept of state participation already had widespread application and significant momentum under international law.[7] The resolution stated, among other things:

> *The right of peoples and nations to permanent sovereignty over their natural wealth and resources must be exercised in the interest of their national development and of the well-being of the people of the State concerned. The exploration, development and disposition of such resources, as well as the import of the foreign capital required for these purposes, should be in conformity with the rules and conditions which the peoples and nations freely consider to be necessary or desirable with regard to the authorization, restriction or prohibition of such activities.*[8]

The ideological and public policy driver for direct state participation in the oil and gas industry was therefore the notion that it could secure crucial national interests more effectively than market forces and private initiative.[9] Simply put, sovereignty needed a 'tool'.[10] Also important (and which remains the case) was the 'strategic' nature of oil, principally realised by way of the oil revenues generated for national treasuries.[11] As a result of these and a range of other (always context-specific)

4 *Ibid*, at p 68.

5 Charalambos Constantinou, 'State Petroleum Enterprises in Developing Countries', in *Natural Resources Forum*, Vol 3, Issue 1 (1978) at pp 73-82.

6 Adam Sneyd, *New International Economic Order (NIEO)*, Globalization and Autonomy Online Compendium McMaster University, available at http://globalautonomy.ca/global1/index.jsp (accessed January 2015).

7 Professor Dr Erica-Irene A Daes, *Indigenous Peoples' Permanent Sovereignty Over Natural Resources*, UN Commission on Human Rights (2004), at p 6.

8 UN General Assembly resolution 1803 (XVII) of December 14 1962, *Permanent sovereignty over natural resources*, available at www.ohchr.org/EN/ProfessionalInterest/Pages/NaturalResources.aspx.

9 O Noreng, *Oil and Islam: Social and Economic Issues*, (1997, John Wiley & Sons, Chichester), as cited by Miranda Ferrell Wainburg, Dr Michelle Michot Foss *et al* in their 2007 working paper, *Commercial Frameworks for National Oil Companies* (University of Texas at Austin), at p 4.

10 Professor Paul Stevens, *An Overview of NOC Experience*, paper delivered at a workshop for the World Bank (2003).

11 Wainburg *et al*, *op cit* (note 9 above), at p 4.

factors, state participation became a key component of the public policy of petroleum states.

A prime example is that of Iran. In 1951, the Mossadegh government took the then radical step of nationalising the oil and gas industry, and the National Iranian Oil Company (NIOC) was formed. This move was not only contested unsuccessfully by the British government at the International Court of Justice at The Hague, but also led to a worldwide embargo on Iranian oil. Despite this political upheaval, petroleum nationalisation pushed forward.[12] The NIOC first entered into an arrangement with an American and French consortium of IOCs and, in 1957, a 50/50 joint venture with Italy's own NOC, AGIP, to hold one offshore area in the Persian Gulf and two onshore in Iran.[13] It has been noted that, "somewhat ironically, it was the arrangement between a national oil company of a Western nation and the national oil company of a developing [host state] that led to the advent of... state participation" in the oil and gas industry.[14]

State participation became prominent again as a global trend during the 1970s. For example, in the North Sea, Norway, the United Kingdom and Denmark introduced state participation in the award of offshore licences. During the same period, a number of nationalisations took place in both OPEC and non-OPEC countries. Saudi Arabia presents perhaps the most extreme example of that era. In 1976, the Saudi government assumed 100% control of what is now Saudi Aramco and, by royal decree, obtained ownership of all Saudi petroleum assets. Today, oil and natural gas operations remain dominated by Saudi Aramco, which is the world's largest oil company in terms of production.[15]

Following the expansion of state participation and nationalisation during the 1970s and 1980s, the 1990s brought in an era of privatisation that saw many state oil companies morph into investor-owned IOCs. This was seen across both developing and more mature petroleum economies. For example, by 1999 previously state-owned NOC YPF-Argentina had become 100% privatised, as had the UK's British National Oil Corporation and France's Elf and Total.[16] In other states, governments sought significant IOC investment in their NOCs, often retaining an ownership interest, as was seen in the case of, for example, Petro-Canada, Petrobras (Brazil) and Eni (Italy).

There were a variety of complex contributing factors to these privatisations, one of which, in developing countries, was the expanding role of the NOCs. As one commentator explains, looking back to the 1990s, the wider political and social roles of NOCs had:

> *expanded rapidly based on perceptions of almost limitless cash available to the NOCs... and their near monopoly on local technical and commercial talent. At the same time, NOCs were expected to emulate the IOCs in the areas of technical and managerial skill*

---

12 Duval *et al*, *op cit* (note 3 above), at p 45.

13 Eni online summary, *History of Eni's Operations in Iran*, available at www.eni.com/en_IT/world-eni/iran/history-eni-presence/history-eni-presence.shtml (accessed January 2015).

14 Duval *et al*, *op cit* (note 3 above), at p 46.

15 US Energy Information Administration, online *Country Analysis Brief: Saudi Arabia*, available at www.eia.gov/countries/analysisbriefs/Saudi_Arabia/saudi_arabia.pdf (accessed January 2015).

16 Wainburg *et al*, *op cit* (note 9 above), at p 7.

and the ability to generate profits, with the aim of either effectively counter-balancing the local influence of the IOCs, or of replacing the IOCs altogether... Politics, however, meant that priority was assigned to the achievement of social, economic and political goals, and the cracks that began to emerge with respect to attainment of commercial goals were ignored, papered over by massive cash flows. The oil crisis of 1986, the dramatic revenue drops associated with it, and continued lower real oil prices, exposed these cracks and the incompatibility of the dual roles the NOCs were expected to play.[17]

Today, NOCs are considered crucial to economic development for many states. Nonetheless, there are many criticisms of NOCs, including with regard to their commercial inefficiencies, non-commercial agendas (eg, job creation, income redistribution, state borrowing), weak governance and significant budgetary requirements (notwithstanding their potential to generate income).[18] These issues can be seen as particularly significant for African states, each of which generally faces a unique and diverse range of developmental challenges.

Notwithstanding these issues, state participation in the global oil and gas industry today remains hugely influential and is embedded in the regimes of numerous developed petroleum economies. As a result, NOCs rank significantly among the global top ten oil and gas companies, based on production. These are: Saudi Aramco (ranked 1); National Iranian Oil Company (ranked 3); PetroChina (ranked 7); Pemex (ranked 8); and Kuwait Petroleum Corporation (ranked 10).[19] The influence of state entities often now extends significantly beyond the geographic boundaries of the state itself, as NOCs invest in petroleum ventures abroad. For example, Chinese NOCs now hold significant oil and gas interests throughout Africa.

4. State participation in the African oil and gas industry

Across African states, constitutions or petroleum legislation make clear the governing rule that all petroleum resources within state boundaries, whether onshore or offshore, are the exclusive property of the state, reiterating the overriding principle of permanent sovereignty over natural resources. For example, the Nigerian constitution provides:

Notwithstanding the foregoing provisions of this section, the entire property in and control of all minerals, mineral oils and natural gas in, under or upon the territorial waters and the Exclusive Economic Zone of Nigeria shall vest in the Government of the Federation and shall be managed in such manner as may be prescribed by the National Assembly.[20]

State participation in the oil and gas industry can be seen as a logical extension of this fundamental principle. As will be seen from the examples that follow, many African states mandate state participation by a NOC from the outset of any arrangement with an IOC, either in legislation or in the 'model' form of petroleum

---

17 Charles McPherson, lecture *National Oil Companies: Evolution, Issues, Outlook*, World Bank National Oil Companies Workshop, May 27 2003, at p 2.

18 *Ibid*, at pp 4-8.

19 Based on BOE (barrels of oil equivalent) per day. See Forbes *2013 Ranking of the World's Biggest Oil Companies*, November 17 2013, available at www.forbes.com/sites/christopherhelman/2013/ 11/17/the-worlds-biggest-oil-companies-2013/ (accessed January 2015).

20 Constitution of the Federal Republic of Nigeria, section 44(3).

agreement. The extent of such participation, in terms of percentage participating interest under the petroleum agreement, varies across African jurisdictions.

In Nigeria, the government participates in the oil and gas industry through the wholly-owned Nigerian National Petroleum Corporation (NNPC), founded in 1971. Today, IOC investment in Nigerian upstream petroleum assets is structured using multiple contractual methods, including PSCs, joint venture arrangements and risk service contracts. While this provides a somewhat complex environment for comparative analysis, common to all arrangements is the majority participation (55%-60%) of the NNPC.

Certain aspects of the history of state participation in Nigeria's oil and gas industry are particularly notable for their interaction with wider principles of indigenisation and Africa-specific politics. In July 1979, the government issued a decree which by law nationalised Shell-BP and British Petroleum (Nigeria) by way of the NNPC acquiring 100% of their Nigerian-held oil and gas assets.[21] While commentators have attributed several factors to this move, there is a widely held belief that it was, in part, a reaction to wider African politics, such as British Petroleum's violation of the Nigerian government's oil embargo against South Africa during the latter's apartheid regime.[22]

Nigeria's culture of economic empowerment through local participation (discussed below) was also a factor in this nationalisation, particularly against the backdrop of the Nigerian-Biafran civil war. The Biafran war is said to have provoked distrust and resentment of IOCs, which were perceived to have failed to co-operate effectively with the Nigerian government during that war.[23] Notable also was the Nigerian government's interest at that time in increasing participation in the industry in the light of OPEC requirements.

In Angola, the Petroleum Activities Law 2004 (PAL) requires that any IOC carrying out petroleum operations must do so in association with wholly-owned NOC Sociedade Nacional de Combustíveis de Angola (Sonangol), founded in 1976. Participation may be by way of consortium or joint venture but, since the enactment of PAL and associated regulations, has primarily taken the form of a PSC (based on a model form) entered into between Sonangol and the IOC(s). Sonangol must take a significant interest (commonly, 20%-50%) in any venture unless a special dispensation is granted by the government, which has not happened so far.[24] While this presents commercial inflexibility for IOCs, the clear-cut regime has been stable and consistent in its application and is therefore valued by IOCs.[25] At the time of writing, Sonangol operates its petroleum assets with a range of IOCs, including BP, ExxonMobil, Chevron, Petrobras, Statoil and Total.

---

21 Ann Genova, 'Nigeria's Nationalization of British Petroleum', *The International Journal of African Historical Studies*, Vol 43, No 1 (2010), pp 115-136.

22 Uchenna Jerome Orji, 'Towards sustainable local content development in the Nigerian oil and gas industry: an appraisal of the legal framework and challenges – Part 1', (2014) *International Energy Law Review* Vol 1, pp 30-42.

23 Genova, *op cit* (note 21 above).

24 Eduardo Vera-Cruz Advogados and FCB & AF Castelo Branco & Associados, *Angola Oil and Gas Report* (2013), available at www.fcblegal.com/xms/files/Angola_oil_and_gas.pdf (accessed January 2015).

25 'Sonangol: An economic octopus', *Financial Times*, July 18 2012.

In Namibia, the Namibian Petroleum Act 1998 and 'model' PSC do not include any mandatory requirement for the participation of the National Petroleum Corporation of Namibia (NAMCOR). In reality, however, it is standard practice that the Namibian Ministry of Mines and Energy requires NAMCOR to hold a minority (eg, 10%) participating interest from the outset. The ambiguity here between the lack of legislative requirements and the reality of government requirements is a notable challenge for IOCs, as will be discussed later in this chapter.

Elsewhere, by way of further example, Libya's NOC, the National Oil Corporation, historically holds a 51% participating interest under concession agreements,[26] and Ghana's NOC, the Ghana National Petroleum Corporation, has an initial participating interest of 10% in all petroleum operations under the model petroleum agreement.[27]

These examples highlight instances of mandated state participation, through a NOC, from the commencement of petroleum arrangements with an IOC. It is, however, also important to recognise that the vast majority of modern PSCs provide that the state has the option to participate in the event of a commercial discovery. This provision commonly arises whether or not the government has any initial participating interest, and is familiar both across Africa and worldwide.

5. Challenges for the host state with regard to state participation

State participation in the oil and gas industry is therefore complex and has a long history. It also raises a variety of challenges for both host states and IOCs. This section briefly examines the issues for host states. The challenges faced by IOCs will be examined later in this chapter, as several such challenges are common to both state participation and local participation.

As previously discussed, the host state 'take' under an upstream petroleum agreement comprises multiple elements. From the fiscal perspective, state participation may not lead to the most optimal or efficient form of 'take' for several reasons. Firstly, the NOC, as a participating interest owner, is subject to its proportionate share of all risks and liabilities associated with oil and gas operations. Traditionally, the host state granting a PSC or other upstream petroleum agreement is shielded against such risks and liabilities through the joint and several liability of the participating interest owners under that agreement, but this shield is at least partially defeated by the participation of the NOC, which essentially participates on the same terms as an IOC.

Secondly, while the NOC is typically carried by the IOCs through the exploration phase, the NOC is typically obliged to pay its participating interest share of the costs of development and eventually of abandonment and decommissioning. This can create cash flow issues for the NOC. Even if this cash flow problem is averted by the NOC paying its share of development costs out of production, the NOC may nevertheless also have to pay interest for the time value of money in circumstances where the other participating interest owners are funding their shares in advance by

26 Deutsche Bank industry update, *Oil & Gas for Beginners* (2014), at p 378.
27 Model Petroleum Agreement of Ghana, clause 2.4.

means of cash calls. The host state could obtain the same fiscal results of state participation, without the corresponding increased risks or obligations, by providing in the PSC for a larger host state share of profit oil.

As previously discussed in the context of the privatisations of the 1990s, the dichotomy in the framework and goals of NOCs is also a challenge for the host state. Particularly in developing countries, NOCs are typically established with oil and gas sector-specific commercial goals, but once oil and gas revenues start flowing, the NOCs are often expected to take on weighty and wider economic, political and social objectives. For example, Angola's Sonangol has been referred to as an "octopus enveloping the economy" due to its "growing portfolio... in infrastructure, banking and real estate, the literary prize it offers and Petro, the football team it owns".[28]

This inherent conflict often results in commercial shortcomings, including a loss of focus and an increased level of inefficiency, that can eventually undermine the NOC's operation or, at worst, its very existence. The wider developmental goals of the NOC may also be compromised as a result. State participation is intended, for example, to give the NOC access to the technical capabilities of the participating IOCs and to provide training opportunities for NOC personnel, but it may be that such goals are better obtained by other means, rather than as a secondary focus of the NOC. For example, the relevant national petroleum law may require contributions from IOCs towards training. Similarly, training can be provided for through contractual commitments in the relevant PSC, concession or other upstream petroleum agreement.

Finally, state participation may create legal ambiguity. For example, where a NOC is the grantor of a PSC and is also a participant or co-contractor under that PSC, the NOC legally becomes its own contractor. This has the potential to create confusion with regard to not only to the precise role of the NOC but also the division of responsibilities between the NOC and the IOC(s). This legal ambiguity can be addressed by adopting different contractual structures, such as having the host state rather than the NOC grant the PSC, or by using a different form of upstream petroleum agreement altogether, such as a concession.[29]

6. Local participation

For the purposes of this analysis, the term 'local participation' refers to the concept of local persons or entities that are not state-owned, having direct or indirect working interests or participating interests in the relevant PSC, concession or other upstream petroleum agreement. This may be in addition to, or in substitution for, the state participating interest.

Local participation falls within the ambit of empowerment or indigenisation (the latter being adopted particularly by Nigerian policy) and can be seen to concern broadly local benefits for local people. This wider concept impacts upon several other aspects of the African oil and gas industry, most notably the 'local content' requirements with regard to employment, training and service providers. Local

28 *Financial Times*, *op cit* (note 25 above).
29 Duval et al, *op cit* (note 3 above), at pp 82 and 121.

content is dealt with only in the sense of local participation in the ownership of upstream petroleum assets.

Local participation in Africa is not unique to the oil and gas industry, but is one aspect of a wider ongoing policy movement, across Africa, in response to colonial history. Common to all local participation policies is the need to redress significant and highly ingrained socio-economic imbalances, which are often primarily (although by no means exclusively) based on racial lines. As one commentary states:

> *Historically the basic objectives of indigenisation have formed the fundamental issues of national economic policies in many countries.... In order to be completely freed of the past colonial rule, indigenisation of the national economy has become an important objective of national policy in almost all independent African countries.*[30]

In the case of Nigeria, the government introduced significant local participation legislation throughout the 1970s, commencing with the Nigerian Enterprises Act of 1972. As has been noted, "the net effect of the policies embodied in these statutes was to encourage and enable Nigerians to have prioritised access to ownership, management and control of the economy as against foreign investors."[31] There is a view that this local participation policy may be considered a precursor to Nigeria's oil and gas industry nationalisation (as previously discussed), but other commentators point out that the concept of nationalisation "does not... equate with the continuous part-ownership and control of private business", whether by Nigerians or otherwise.[32]

Modern local participation requirements specific to the oil and gas industry can be seen to have originated from the government's Indigenous Concession Programme (ICP) of the 1990s, which was aimed at expanding the scope of local participation and led to the emergence of 'indigenous oil companies' in oil and gas exploration and production.[33] Under the ICP, indigenous oil companies were entitled to enter into ventures with IOCs, provided that they retained at least a 60% participating interest.[34] The ICP did not require the NNPC to have a participating interest in such ventures and thus represented a policy whereby local participation was substituted for state participation. The same structure for local participation prevails today under the Marginal Fields Development Programme. Under this programme, fields on existing blocks that have had reserves booked for 10 years but which remain unexploited are farmed out on a periodic basis, by way of a competitive bid process, to indigenous oil companies, which are required to hold a minimum 51% participating interest.[35]

Notably, the 'indigenous blocks' granted under the ICP have seen the interests of state participation and local participation come into conflict in Nigeria. In particular,

---

30 Wilfred A Ndongko, 'Indigenisation Policy and the Development of Private Enterprise in Nigeria', *Africa Spectrum*, Vol 15, No 1 (1980), at p 53.

31 Vincent Akpotaire, 'The Nigerian Indigenisation Laws as Disincentives to Foreign Investment: The End of an Era', *Business Law Review*, Vol 26, Issue 3 (2005), at p 62.

32 Akpotaire, *op cit* (note 31 above), at p 62.

33 Uchenna Jerome Orj, *op cit* (note 22 above), at p 5.

34 Adepetun Caxton-Martins & Segun, online newsletter (March 2013), available at www.acas-law.com/cipxprobe/publications/The_Famfa_Case_-_Indigenous_Petroleum_Companies_-_Petroleum_Equalisation_fund_-_march_20131.pdf (accessed January 2015), at p 2.

35 Nigeria Ministry of Petroleum, *Guidelines for Farmout and Operation of Marginal Fields 2013.*

the government has sought to 'back-in' to indigenous blocks under the Deep Water Blocks Allocations to Companies (Back-in-Rights) Regulations 2003. This was met with controversy in the case of the government's multiple attempts to acquire compulsorily, without negotiation, a majority stake in a local participant's initial oil prospecting lease and subsequent oil mining lease.[36] The asset in question had been granted under the ICP to wholly-Nigerian-owned Famfa Oil Limited, together with a wholly-owned subsidiary of ChevronTexaco (which had a 32% participating interest) and Petrobras (which had a 8% participating interest). Famfa took the case to the Nigerian courts, on the ground that the government's purported participation was "pre-emptive, therefore illegal, null and void."[37] On appeal to the Supreme Court, it was held that the back-in was indeed unlawful. The case affirmed that Nigerian petroleum rights can be protected against arbitrary and/or compulsory acquisition by the government, especially without compensation.[38] It also indicated the increased convergent interests of state participation and local participation in the case of a developed oil and gas industry.

Nowadays, industry-specific local participation is primarily prescribed by the Nigerian Oil and Gas Industry Content Development Act 2010 (NCDA), which provides that:

> *Nigerian independent operators shall be given first consideration in the award of oil blocks, oil field licences, oil lifting licences and all projects for which [a] contract is to be awarded in the Nigerian oil and gas industry subject to the fulfilment of such conditions as may be specified by the Minister.*[39]

For present purposes, a 'Nigerian Company' under the NCDA is a "company formed and registered in Nigeria... with not less than 51% equity shares [held] by Nigerians."[40]

In terms of present impact on IOC strategy, it is clear that, in order for a bidder entity to qualify for the award of a petroleum contract or lease, a minimum of 51% of its shares must be held by Nigerians. This is most commonly achieved by the IOC, together with a one or more Nigerian companies, forming a special purpose vehicle with a majority Nigerian shareholding. In order for a bid to be competitive, an IOC may consider increasing the representative Nigerian shareholding beyond the 51% qualification. The formal arrangements that may be entered into between the IOC and Nigerian 'strategic partners' in this scenario are discussed later in this chapter.

It is likely that local participation requirements in Nigeria will become increasingly stringent. The Petroleum Industry Bill (PIB), originally tabled before the Nigerian National Assembly in December 2008, is designed to supersede pre-existing legislation but has not yet been enacted. The PIB further enshrines the requirements of the local participation policy described above. Of particular interest for the purposes of structuring oil and gas transactions will be the PIB's final definition of an indigenous petroleum company. It has been speculated that the PIB may be more

36 *NNPC v Famfa Oil Limited* (2012) 17 NWLR 148.
37 Adepetun Caxton-Martins & Segun, *op cit* (note 34 above), at p 2.
38 *Ibid.*
39 NCDA, section 3(1).
40 *Ibid*, section 106.

stringent than the NCDA by stipulating a higher percentage level of equity to be held by Nigerians (which currently stands at 51%).

This would align with the approach taken by the Indigenous Oil Companies Bill 2011 (IOCB), which is also being considered by the Nigerian National Assembly. The objective of the IOCB is to set out a structure for the operation of indigenous oil companies.[41] Under the IOCB, an indigenous oil company is:

> *a company incorporated under the laws of the Federal Government of Nigeria for the purpose of exploration for and production of crude oil and natural gas, of which 60% or more of its shares are beneficially owned by citizens of Nigeria and/or associations of such citizens.*[42]

It is presently unclear how the IOCB may interact with the PIB for purposes of dictating the minimum Nigerian equity ownership of entities seeking to qualify as local participants in the Nigerian oil and gas industry.

While the Nigeria regime is perhaps the most prominent with regard to the oil and gas industry, there are a number of other examples of local participation policies across Africa. A policy of significant influence on the wider continent is South Africa's Broad-Based Black Economic Empowerment (B-BBEE), which has existed in various forms since the abolition of apartheid in 1994. B-BBEE was introduced primarily to enhance the participation of historically disadvantaged South Africans (HDSAs) in the economy, in order to redress the inequalities perpetuated by apartheid. In South Africa, "the country's past racism was not purely a matter of attitudes and beliefs of white superiority, it was intrinsically linked to the acquisition of economic resources"[43] and also, crucially, the availability of economic and educational opportunities. Under apartheid, discrimination by segregation dominated the political and economic agenda, with legislation and policies seeking to establish and enforce white/non-white separation in respect of residence, property and business ownership.

A key objective of B-BBEE is to increase the level of business ownership by HDSAs. With regard to the oil and gas industry, this objective was detailed firstly in the Petroleum and Liquid Fuels Industry Charter 2000 (the LFC) and subsequently in several B-BBEE codes of practice. Pursuant to the LFC, the government may make conditional the granting of exploration and production rights on the reservation of a 9% participating interest for an HDSA buy-in (in addition to a 10% participating interest reserved for state participation by the NOC). In practice, the government requires that a 10% participating interest is reserved for a buy-in by HDSAs, which may occur at any time.[44]

The LFC was enacted as an agreement between the then Department of Minerals and Energy and key oil and gas industry participants, including IOCs. Signatories to the LFC agreed the wider objective of the transfer of 25% of the ownership and

---

41 KPMG, online *Nigeria Oil and Gas Industry Brief* (June 2014), available at www.kpmg.com/NG/en/IssuesAndInsights/ArticlesPublications/Documents/Nigerian%20oil%20and%20gas%20Industry%20brief.pdf (accessed January 2015), at p 17.

42 IOCB, section 16.

43 Heather Deegan, *The Politics of New South Africa: Apartheid and After* (2001, Longman, London).

44 Lizel Oberholzer, 'South Africa' chapter, in *Getting the Deal Through – Oil Regulation 2013*, at p 192.

control of oil and gas entities operating in South Africa to HDSAs over a 10-year period. The ownership target for this purpose was defined as 25% of the aggregate value of equity based on the asset values set out in the audited accounts of the entities concerned. As at 2011, the average effective ownership by HDSAs in the oil and gas industry was approximately 19%.[45] This has been achieved primarily through the transfer of ownership from IOCs to HDSAs in the downstream sector, commonly by way of a share sale or joint venture transaction.[46]

Namibia (formerly South-West Africa) has also imposed local participation in the oil and gas industry in a form significantly influenced by the B-BBEE system. This policy also stems from a long history of German and subsequently South African settler rule in Namibia and in the wake of apartheid, which was enforced in Namibia until 1990.

The New Equitable Economic Empowerment Framework (NEEEF), introduced in 2012, is the local participation initiative presently impacting upon the oil and gas sector in Namibia. While the Petroleum (Exploration and Production) Act 1991 is silent on local participation, the Namibian model PSC suggests that the holder must be a company incorporated in Namibia,[47] and in practice the Ministry of Mines and Energy has required that both NAMCOR and a local company become a party to the PSC. Recent indications are that Namibia will require only minority local participation, for example at 5-10%. The local company is in practice commonly required to be an entity incorporated in line with the NEEEF. Notably, the NEEEF has been enacted as a 'framework' rather than a law, and the Namibian government's implementation of the NEEEF has to date been flexible. While beneficial in a sense, this also raises a number of challenges for IOCs, as further discussed later in this chapter.

Elsewhere, local participation in the African oil and gas industry is becoming increasingly prevalent. It is now seen, for example, in the oil and gas regimes of Ghana and Mozambique. Ghana's Petroleum (Local Content and Local Participation) Regulations 2013 provide that "an indigenous Ghanaian company shall be given first preference in the grant of a petroleum agreement or a license with respect to petroleum activities."[48] The regulations also set out the requirement for a minimum 5% Ghanaian equity ownership in any petroleum agreement or license, in addition to that held by the Ghana National Petroleum Corporation.[49] For these purposes, an 'indigenous Ghanaian company' is defined as a company incorporated under local law that both:

- has at least 51% of its equity owned by a Ghanaian citizen; and
- has Ghanaian citizens holding at least 80% of executive and senior management positions and 100% of non-managerial and other positions.[50]

---

45 Department of Energy, Republic of South Africa, *Petroleum and Liquid Fuels Industry Charter Final Audit Report* (August 5 2011), at p 118.

46 Shell online summary, *Black Economic Empowerment Embracing The Process of Black Economic Empowerment In Shell*, available at www.shell.com/zaf/aboutshell/who-we-are/our-values-and-principles/bee/ index-bak.html (accessed January 2015).

47 Namibia Model Petroleum Agreement 2007, clause 2.1.

48 Ghana Petroleum (Local Content and Local Participation) Regulations 2013, regulation 4(1).

49 *Ibid*, regulation 4(2).

50 *Ibid*, regulation 49.

This definition notably employs criteria that go further than mere equity ownership and control. The requirement that the local participant employs solely Ghanaian citizens in non-managerial and other positions applies to asset equity ownership as well as local content provisions. It seems likely that this definition will be difficult to satisfy, given the limited availability of local specialist skills and experience necessary for most roles.

In Mozambique, the Petroleum Law 2014 provides, in relation to 'national entrepreneurship', that oil and gas companies must be listed on the Mozambican Stock Exchange, although it is not yet clear what this specifically requires. It may imply the listing of certain qualifying local participant entities only. Alternatively, it may require that all oil and gas companies, including the special purpose vehicles used by IOCs, must list a specific percentage of their equity. It is anticipated that this will be clarified in future regulations.

7. Challenges for IOCs with regard to state participation and local participation

State participation and local participation raise a myriad of challenges for IOCs. These include reduced levels of control, negative impacts on investment economics, regulatory uncertainty and increased risk of corruption. Particular to local participation, also, are 'fronting' issues. This section will address each of these challenges in turn.

7.1 Investment economics challenges

The extent of mandatory state participation and/or local participation is a commercial feature which must be evaluated by an IOC in line with the wider fiscal terms of the contractual relationship between government, or the NOC, and participating IOCs. State and/or local participation can have a significant negative effect on the IOC's economics; for example, the requirement that an IOC carry a NOC or local participant during the exploration phase certainly increases the IOC's overall costs of that phase. It is a feature of the modern oil and gas industry that different jurisdictions around the world are competing for foreign investment. IOCs must decide where to invest their limited capital, and this involves a risk/reward calculation that considers, among other things, the political stability of the host state, security issues and, perhaps most fundamentally, economics. In this regard, overly favourable terms for state and/or local participation can be one of the factors that drives foreign investment from one host state to another.

7.2 Regulatory uncertainty challenges

One of the greatest challenges facing a prospective IOC investor seeking to accommodate state participation and/or local participation is the risk of regulatory uncertainty. This risk, which pervades the African oil and gas industry, was identified in July 2014 above all other factors, including corruption, as the greatest constraint to IOC development.[51] It has been noted that:

---

51 PWC report, *On the brink of a boom: Africa oil and gas review* (July 2014), at p 8.

> *regulatory uncertainty and delays in passing law[s] are severely inhibiting sector development in many countries… [and] key players have delayed or cancelled projects until further clarity can be obtained… as they simply cannot move forward with doubts given the long-term nature of the needed investments.*[52]

Interestingly, Nigeria, which remains a regime in flux due to the outstanding ratification of the PIB, has been found to be one of few countries in which the regulatory framework is not a top-three challenge to development. While this is an anomaly, it may just be evidence that IOC participants have built the long-standing uncertainty regarding the PIB into their internal risk models.[53] Nigeria also has a well-established and stringent legal framework with regard to state participation, which again has most likely been accepted by IOCs as a risk.

Regulatory uncertainty is a concern with regard to many countries that are in the process of developing or revising their petroleum regimes. This is seen, for example, in South Africa, where the oil and gas industry is expected to see accelerated growth, given its significant shale reserves, which are thought to be among the top ten largest worldwide.[54] At the time of writing, there remains uncertainty with regard to the level of state participation in oil and gas projects in the future. The Mineral and Petroleum Resources Development Act Amendment Bill, which was passed in March 2014, has not yet received final parliamentary approval. In its current form, the bill would enable the government to have a 20% 'free carry' in oil and gas projects, with an uncapped participation clause enabling the state to acquire up to a further 80% at an agreed price.[55] It is predicted that, if passed, the bill would have a "chilling effect on investment".[56]

Host government legislative or other legal requirements for local participation are also often unclear or uncertain. For example, in Namibia the NEEEF has been enacted as a framework rather than a law. The intention is that this would allow broader interpretation and consultation than may be the case with a more prescriptive law. The result is, however, a level of uncertainty over certain aspects of the framework. For example, the term 'previously disadvantaged' is broadly defined to mean 'victims of Apartheid policies', which is somewhat vague and potentially very wide-reaching. Furthermore, given that the NEEEF is only a framework, it is not always clear what specific requirements may apply to foreign investors such as IOCs, and governmental agencies appear to have wide latitude to make requirements of foreign companies like IOCs. This is evidenced by the terms of the NEEEF itself, which provides that the "Government will use all the legitimate market mechanisms at its disposal, in the form of its procurement programmes and licensing regimes, to promote transformation and empowerment."[57]

---

52 *Ibid*, at p 6.
53 *Ibid*, at p 8.
54 'South Africa to review mineral resources law', *Financial Times*, June 18 2014.
55 *Ibid*.
56 Offshore Petroleum Association of South Africa, cited by Mike Cohen, 'South African Oil Law to Choke Investment, Industry Group Says', *Bloomberg*, 10 March 2014.
57 NEEEF, Government of the Republic of Namibia, at 6.

7.3 Corruption challenges

Local participation and, to a lesser extent, state participation also raise the risk of corruption. The introduction of a NOC as an additional participant increases an IOC's interaction with the government and with government officials. This may not ordinarily be a concern, but may become problematic in the case of newly established or ambiguous regulatory requirements that raise questions surrounding the nature or structure of payment arrangements. Notably, officers of NOCs are considered to be "foreign public officials" for the purposes of the United Kingdom Bribery Act 2010 (the 'Bribery Act'),[58] because that term includes persons exercising "public function for any public agency or public enterprise of that country or territory (or subdivision)", which includes those exercising public functions in state-owned enterprises.[59] This is similarly the case under the United States Foreign Corrupt Practices Act 1977 ('FCPA'),[60] as official commentary on the application of the FCPA has indicated.[61]

In the case of local participation requirements, the risk of corruption is more pronounced. A common fact scenario faced by IOCs is where the IOC is attempting to acquire a PSC, concession or other upstream petroleum agreement, and the government requires local participation as a condition of granting such an agreement. This local participation requirement could be in the form of a requirement that the IOC must include indigenous persons or entities as joint venture partners. Alternatively, the requirement could be that the IOC conducts its operations through a local subsidiary which includes local shareholders, directors and/or management. The risks are magnified where the government designates (or at least 'recommends') the specific local persons that are to be involved. There are often also requirements that the IOC make certain payments to those local persons, such as signature bonuses, and/or carry the local persons by paying their shares of exploration costs and expenses.

In such a scenario, an IOC that gives economic benefits to persons designated or recommended by a government agency or official, in return for the granting of an upstream petroleum agreement by that government agency or official, could clearly be in violation of anti-bribery legislation such as the FCPA and the Bribery Act. For example, it has been observed that historically, since 1991 and across successive governments, the award of petroleum assets to indigenous oil companies in Nigeria "appears to have been largely influenced by the extent to which prominent shareholders have been connected to the government" rather than on technical competence and expertise.[62]

There are other legal risks associated with governmental requirements for local participation of this type, including the risk of 'fronting'. Fronting is an abuse of empowerment legislation by using qualifying local persons to meet the literal

58 Bribery Act 2010, section 5.

59 Ministry of Justice, *The Bribery Act 2010: Guidance about procedures which relevant commercial organisations can put into place to prevent persons associated with them from bribing* (2011), at p 11 ('Ministry of Justice Guidance').

60 US Foreign Corrupt Practices Act 1977, section 30A(f)(1)(A).

61 US Department of Justice, *A Resource Guide to the US Foreign Corrupt Practices Act*, at p 20.

62 Orj, *op cit* (note 22 above), at p 5.

requirements of the legislation while circumventing the purpose, spirit and goals of that legislation. This can occur, for example, where the indigenous persons identified as shareholders of an enterprise in fact have no meaningful economic interest in that enterprise, or where the indigenous persons identified as directors or managers of an enterprise in fact have no authority over the activities of that enterprise. Fronting has been identified by the South African Department of Trade and Industry as a fraudulent violation of the B-BBEE, and it is likely that the same approach would be taken with regard to the NEEEF and similar local participation initiatives.

Recent progress has been made by African states in addressing these perceived risks, as evidenced by many states signing up to the global Extractive Industries Transparency Initiative. This is a global coalition of governments and companies "working together to improve openness and accountable management of revenues from natural resources," including, for example, by promoting a standard of disclosure of taxes and other payments made by oil and gas companies to governments.[63]

8. Risk mitigation for IOCs with regard to state participation and local participation

The foregoing risks would appear to present an almost insurmountable challenge to an IOC attempting to do business in Africa. In many cases, however, it is possible to take careful steps to address the risks in a manner that may allow the transaction of business in compliance with state and local participation legislation as well as with anti-bribery and corruption legislation and other laws. The following is an analysis of some, but certainly not all, of the steps that can be taken to address these risks. It should be noted, however, that the risks presented to an IOC will depend on the facts and circumstances of each matter. There is no 'one size fits all' solution. Furthermore, in analysing the risks and the steps that can be taken to mitigate them in a chapter such as this, the issues will often appear to be clear-cut and straightforward, whereas in real life the facts and circumstances are rarely unequivocal.

IOCs may generally mitigate the risks discussed above to some extent through due diligence, contractual mechanisms, such as stabilization clauses and strong dispute resolution provisions, and reliance on bilateral investment treaties (BITs). IOCs can also mitigate these risks to some extent through the way they conduct their business in host jurisdictions.

8.1 Mitigation of regulatory uncertainty

In an environment of regulatory uncertainty, IOCs face the political risk of a change in law. This is always a risk with respect to PSCs, concessions and other upstream petroleum agreements because of their long-term nature, but the risk is intensified where there is regulatory uncertainty. This risk is exacerbated when oil commodity prices are high or rising, which can give rise to a situation in which a host government perceives that an IOC has received too sweet a deal and looks to redress the economic balance through a change in law. Sovereign nations always have the

63 Extractive Industries Transparency Initiative website, https://eiti.org/ (accessed January 2015).

right to change their laws, so it is not possible to craft contractual provisions to prevent such changes. It is, however, possible to address and mitigate the consequences of changes in law through stabilisation clauses.

There are two main types of stabilisation clause: 'freezing provisions' and 'economic equilibrium provisions'.[64] Freezing provisions provide that only those laws, rules, regulations etc, in force at the date of the PSC, concession or other upstream petroleum agreement shall have effect with respect to such agreement and its participants. These types of stabilisation clause raise a couple of issues. First, they arguably deprive the IOC participants of any change in the law that is beneficial to the IOC. Secondly, these types of stabilisation clause raise issues of enforceability; that is, can a current government agree to a contractual provision that effectively prevents a future government from passing a law that will have effect with respect to the relevant contract or IOC? Partly as a consequence of these issues, the more modern form of stabilisation clause is the economic equilibrium clause. This type of clause provides that, in the event of a change in the law that in turn changes the economics under the agreement for the IOC, then the government and the IOC agree to negotiate amendments to the agreement that will restore the economic equilibrium of the original agreement. In this regard, an economic equilibrium clause is similar to a hardship clause. Stabilisation clauses are now commonly included in upstream petroleum agreements.

Some of the risks of state participation and local participation, including the risk of regulatory uncertainty, can be mitigated through a strong dispute resolution regime in the relevant PSC, concession or other upstream petroleum agreement. Although an upstream petroleum agreement will almost uniformly be governed by the law of the host state, it is nevertheless possible to provide for dispute resolution in a manner other than in the local courts. For example, it is common to provide in an upstream petroleum agreement for arbitration under international rules and in a neutral forum.

In the event of a dispute between an IOC on the one hand and a host government or NOC on the other, it is also beneficial for the IOC to rely on BITs. Most countries in Africa are parties to BITs. These treaties provide IOCs with certain protections for their local investments, including access to international arbitration if these investments are threatened.

8.2 Mitigation of corruption risks

IOCs can generally mitigate certain corruption risks posed by state participation and local participation by carefully managing the way in which they conduct their business in the host state. Most fundamentally, the IOC should be familiar with the restrictions imposed by the FCPA and the Bribery Act, and have implemented adequate internal procedures in order to prevent bribery. It is then important for the IOC to conduct business, including all relations with the host state, the NOC and local participants, in a completely transparent manner, and with evidence of due consideration having been given to anti-bribery and corruption principles. IOCs can

64 Duval *et al*, *op cit* (note 3 above), at pp 340-347.

also take actions to develop and maintain good political connections without running afoul of anti-bribery and corruption laws. There are additional specific mitigation practices that should be implemented with regard to local participation.

If a government official, such as a minister, requires local participation through the participation of indigenous persons designated or recommended by that minister, compliance with that request could, in and of itself, constitute an indirect bribe of that person. The definition of a foreign official under the FCPA and the Bribery Act is interpreted broadly, so that a minister in charge of oil and gas will certainly be a 'foreign official' for the purposes of that legislation. This does not mean, however, that complying with that minister's requirement to include local participation will necessarily constitute a violation of the FCPA and the Bribery Act.

All of the facts and circumstances must be analysed. In the first instance, the existence of the empowerment legislation giving rise to the local participation requirement helps to show that legislative legitimacy underlies the requirement. Similarly, it is helpful if it can be demonstrated that similar requests are being made of other similarly situated IOCs. The purpose of the economic empowerment legislation is to level the playing field, and similar requirements addressed to other IOCs would indicate that the playing field is somewhat level. It is also recommended to obtain an official written request for the local participation from the minister concerned, which would make it more transparent and not a 'secret' like a classic bribe. All of these factors should be documented. Based on the foregoing discussion, it may be possible to conclude that the request by the minister and compliance with that request by the IOC does not have the corrupt intent required to constitute a violation of anti-bribery or corruption laws.

One of the most important ways for an IOC to protect itself is to conduct a thorough due diligence investigation of the persons proposed to be included in the local participation. This is essential in order to identify the presence of any government officials as well as to ensure that the IOC is forming a business relationship with reputable and qualified persons. If the local participation includes companies, partnerships, trusts or other entities, then each of the shareholders, directors, officers, partners, trustees and beneficiaries should also be individually investigated.

The scope of the due diligence investigation should include background checks to determine whether the relevant persons are themselves "foreign officials" or "foreign public officials" under the FCPA or the Bribery Act respectively, or whether they have personal or professional ties to such persons or to the government. This is important, given the wide ambit of such definitions. In the United Kingdom legislation, for example, this catches a person who works at any branch of the national, local or municipal government or who exercises a public function for any public agency (eg, a public health agency, local port authority or local power utility). It also catches those officials or agents of a public international organisation, such as the United Nations or the World Bank. Further, the due diligence investigation should also consider the reputation of the relevant persons among the business community and their history of corruption. It may also be useful to know if the relevant persons have experience in the oil and gas industry, which means that they could contribute to the project in its early stages, unlike other participants who may need initial training.

The due diligence investigation can be conducted internally by the IOC or by external consultants. There are, however, at least two reasons why it is recommended to use external consultants. Firstly, given the relatively high risk involved in matters involving anti-bribery and corruption, it is worthwhile to involve persons or companies who are specialists in these types of investigations. Secondly, local companies, partnerships, trusts or other entities in Africa can have opaque ownership, and this risk is exacerbated by poor public records that make it more difficult to conduct thorough due diligence. Specialists with in-country experience can be best placed to produce the most thorough due diligence report.

Regardless of who conducts the due diligence investigation, it should include a variety of sources. These include background checks based on public records, completion of questionnaires by the relevant persons, and interviews not only with the relevant persons but also with other persons who are tangentially involved.

The due diligence investigation may disclose that a person proposed to be included in the local participation (whether as a direct or indirect shareholder, for example) is a "foreign official" or "foreign public official" under the FCPA or the Bribery Act respectively. Participation by such persons certainly raises red flags and makes matters more complicated, but is not necessarily insurmountable. It is important to consider the role of the relevant persons and all of the other facts and circumstances. What is prohibited under the FCPA and the Bribery Act is payments to government officials to induce them to do something improper in their official capacities. If the relevant persons are not involved in, and have no influence over, the granting of upstream petroleum agreements, then including them in the local participation may not be an improper attempt to influence them in their capacity as public officials.

The general bribery provisions of the Bribery Act also prohibit payments to persons who are not foreign public officials. Thus, even if the persons included in the local participation requirement do not fall under the definition of "foreign public official", issues could still arise under the Bribery Act. A payment is, however, only prohibited if it is intended to induce the recipient to perform some function or activity improperly. Again, it is important to analyse all facts and circumstances.

A recent case highlights the need to conduct a thorough due diligence investigation. On June 28 2010, the US Securities and Exchange Commission (SEC) announced a settlement with Technip for multiple violations of the FCPA.[65] The SEC alleged that Technip, a global engineering, construction and services company based in Paris, was part of a four-company joint venture that bribed Nigerian government officials over a ten-year period in order to win construction contracts worth more than $6 billion, including the Bonny Island LNG project. The SEC was particularly critical of the due diligence procedures adopted by Technip. It stated that Technip's due diligence procedures were not adequate to detect, deter or prevent the payment

65 US Securities and Exchange Commission press release, 'SEC Charges Technip with FCPA Violations' (June 28 2010), available at www.sec.gov/news/press/2010/2010-11 0.htm.

of bribes. For example, Technip only required that potential agents respond to a written questionnaire, seeking minimal background information about them. No additional due diligence was conducted, such as an interview with the agent or a background check. The SEC concluded that Technip's due diligence was a "perfunctory exercise" conducted so that Technip would have some documentation in its files as evidence of purported due diligence.[66]

In the context of corruption mitigation, and general good practice, it is also recommended that the IOC enter into an agreement with its local partners (a 'participation agreement'). If the local partners are organised as companies, partnerships, trusts or other entities, then each of the shareholders, directors, officers, partners, trustees and beneficiaries should also be a party to the agreement. The participation agreement should include a variety of warranties, representations and covenants from the local participants. It may be an insurmountable red flag if any local party refuses to provide any of these warranties, representations and covenants.

The types of warranties and representations from the local parties that should be included in the participation agreement include, for example:

- identification of all direct and indirect legal and beneficial owners of any companies, partnerships, trusts and other entities included in the local participation;
- confirmation that the local person is not a "foreign public official" or "foreign official" (as defined under the relevant legislation), a member of the immediate family of any such person, or otherwise closely connected with any such person;
- compliance with all applicable anti-bribery and corruption laws, including the FCPA, the Bribery Act and those of the host jurisdiction;
- confirmation that the local person has not been charged with or convicted of, or has pleaded guilty to any offence involving bribery, corruption or other relevant crimes; and
- all the usual and customary representations regarding matters such as due authorisation and due execution.

The participation agreement should also include covenants from the local participants regarding, among other things:

- ongoing compliance with all applicable anti-bribery and corruption laws, including the FCPA, the Bribery Act and those of the host jurisdiction;
- an obligation to notify the other parties in the event that any of the participant's warranties or representations are shown to be untrue;
- an obligation to notify the other parties if the participant receives a request for a bribe;
- an obligation to notify the other parties if the participant becomes subject to an investigation or proceeding under any applicable anti-bribery or corruption laws;

66 *Ibid*; SEC complaint at paragraph 31: see *SEC v Technip*, Incv-02289 (SD Tex, 2010).

- the establishment and maintenance of adequate internal controls regarding anti-bribery and corruption; and
- the maintenance of books and records that properly reflect transactions and are otherwise in compliance with applicable generally accepted accounting practices.

The local participants may also be asked to indemnify and hold harmless the other parties from and against any damages and other losses arising from the local participant's breach of any of its warranties, representations or covenants. Given the importance of compliance with anti-bribery and corruption laws, this may be appropriate even in an agreement governed by English law, where it is not customary for warranties and representations to be given 'on an indemnity basis'. Breach of warranties, representations or covenants regarding anti-bribery and corruption should be deemed to be a material breach that could lead to termination of the breaching party's participating interests or other similarly significant consequences.

If the local partners are intended to be direct holders of participating interests in an upstream petroleum agreement such as a PSC, then the IOC and such local partners would in any case enter into a joint operating agreement (JOA). The form of JOA most commonly used in Africa is the 2012 Model Form of JOA (Model Form) prepared by the Association of International Petroleum Negotiators (AIPN). Article 20.1 of the Model Form includes some comprehensive representations and covenants regarding anti-bribery and corruption (including alternative provisions). It provides as follows:

"20.1 – Conduct of the Parties

"20.1.A – Each Party with regard to operations and/or activities under this Agreement (i) warrants that such Party and its Affiliates and their respective directors, officers, employees and personnel have not made, offered, or authorized, and (ii) covenants that such Party and its Affiliates and their respective directors, officers, employees, and personnel will not make, offer, or authorize, any payment, gift, promise or other advantage, whether directly or through any other person or entity, to or for the use or benefit of any Public Official, any political party, political party official, or candidate for office,

"OPTIONAL PROVISION, CHOOSE, IF DESIRED.
or any other individual or entity,
where such payment, gift, promise or advantage would violate the Anti-Bribery Laws and Obligations applicable to such Party.
"OPTIONAL PROVISION, CHOOSE, IF DESIRED.
In addition each Party with regard to operations and/or activities under this Agreement (i) warrants that such Party and its Affiliates and their respective directors, officers, employees and personnel have complied with, and (ii) covenants that such Party and its Affiliates and their respective directors, officers, employees, and personnel will comply with the Anti-Bribery Laws and Obligations applicable to such Party.
"20.1.B – Each Party shall as soon as possible notify the other Parties of any investigation or proceeding initiated by a governmental authority relating to an alleged

violation of applicable Anti-Bribery Laws and Obligations by such Party, or its Affiliates, or any of their directors, officers, employees, personnel, or any service providers of such Party or its Affiliates, concerning operations and activities under this Agreement. Such Party shall use reasonable efforts to keep the other Parties informed as to the progress and disposition of such investigation or proceeding, except that such Party shall not be obligated to disclose to the other Parties any information that would be considered legally privileged.

"20.1.C – Each Party shall indemnify the other Parties for any damages, losses, penalties, costs (including reasonable legal costs and attorneys' fees), and liabilities arising from, or related to the events underlying:

20.1.C.1 – such Party's admission of allegations made by a governmental authority concerning operations and/or activities under this Agreement that such Party or its Affiliates or their directors, officers, employees and personnel have violated Anti-Bribery Laws and Obligations applicable to such Party; or

20.1.C.2 – the final adjudication concerning operations and/or activities under this Agreement that such Party or its Affiliates or their directors, officers, employees and personnel have violated Anti-Bribery Laws and Obligations applicable to such Party[.] Such indemnity obligations shall survive termination or expiration of this Agreement.

"20.1.D – Each Party shall concerning matters that are the subject of this Agreement:

20.1.D.1 – Devise and maintain adequate internal controls concerning such Party's undertakings under Article 20.1.A;

20.1.D.2 – Establish and prepare its books and records in accordance with generally accepted accounting practices applicable to such Party;

20.1.D.3 – Properly record and report such Party's transactions in a manner that accurately and fairly reflects in reasonable detail such Party's assets and liabilities;

20.1.D.4 – Retain such books and records for a period of at least __ Calendar Years; and

20.1.D.5 – Comply with the laws applicable to such Party.

"20.1.E – Each Party must be able to rely on the adequacy of the other Parties' system of internal controls, and on the adequacy of full disclosure of the facts, and of financial and other information concerning operations and/or activities under this Agreement.

"20.1.F – Each Party shall promptly respond in reasonable detail to any reasonable request from any other Party concerning a notice sent by such Party under Article 20.1.B and shall furnish applicable documentary support for such Party's response, including showing such Party's compliance with the undertakings set out in Article 20.1.A and Article 20.1.D, except that such Party shall not be obligated to disclose to the other Parties any information that would be considered legally privileged.

"OPTIONAL PROVISION, CHOOSE, IF DESIRED.

"20.1.G – In addition each Party shall on the written request of any Party furnish to the other Parties a written certification in a form substantially similar to Exhibit F and signed by an authorized representative to the effect that such Party has complied with Article 20.1.A, subject to any notices given under Article 20.1.B."

Notwithstanding that these are thorough and well-drafted provisions, there are at least two reasons why it is not advisable to rely solely on the provisions of the

Model Form JOA. Firstly, it is an approximately 100-page agreement (not including complicated attachments such as the Accounting Procedure). The relevant anti-bribery and corruption provisions can easily be 'lost' among the many other provisions of the JOA and thus may not receive the level of attention that is necessary or appropriate. Secondly, and most importantly, the only parties to the JOA will be the direct holders of participating interests in the upstream petroleum agreement, so that the shareholders, directors, officers and other relevant individuals will not be giving the relevant warranties, representations or covenants in the JOA. Although the parties to the JOA give warranties, representations and covenants regarding their affiliates and their directors, officers, employees and personnel, it is recommended also to obtain direct warranties, representations and covenants from such persons in the participation agreement discussed above.

As previously discussed, an appropriate due diligence investigation will include background checks on the relevant persons. It should be noted, however, that background checks exist as snapshots as at the time they are conducted. It is not sufficient to conduct a background check, put it in the file and consider the matter completed. Compliance with anti-bribery and corruption laws must be viewed as an ongoing process. The AIPN Model Form JOA addresses this in two usual and customary ways. Firstly, under Article 20.1.F, each party agrees to respond promptly and in reasonable detail to any reasonable request from any other party concerning any notice sent by such party regarding an anti-bribery or corruption investigation or proceeding, and agrees to provide documentary support for its response. Secondly, under Article 20.1.G, each party to the JOA shall, on the written request of any other party, provide to the other parties a written certificate in a form attached to the JOA evidencing ongoing compliance with the relevant anti-bribery and corruption laws. Such ongoing compliance verification mechanisms should also be included in the participation agreement.

Payments to persons included in local participation raise a host of additional issues. In some cases, the government agency or official who makes the local participation requirement will also require that certain payments be made to the local participants. These can range from a signature bonus to the carrying of costs of oil and gas exploration activities. As previously advised, an official written request for any payment from the relevant government agency or official should be obtained, thus making the request more transparent and not secret. A request for a signature bonus is particularly troublesome, as there does not appear to be an ongoing business purpose for the payment. If possible, it is desirable to require that such consideration should constitute payment for services rendered by the local participant, such as:

- providing periodic written updates on local legal and political developments;
- providing local administrative and logistical support;
- participating in meetings with government officials; and/or
- assisting in identifying local suppliers of goods and services.

Such payments could also be structured for specific purposes, such as allowing the local participants to establish a valid company with proper accounting and record-keeping practices, and to open a physical office. In each case the amount, source and use of any such payment should be documented. Any payments should, to the extent possible, be made by direct electronic bank transfer. It should be verified, as part of the due diligence investigation, which bank accounts are to be used and who is the owner of each such bank account. This should be documented by warranties, representations and covenants in the participation agreement. Cash payments should be avoided if at all possible.

The IOC may also require audit rights in respect of the local participants. This is not an unreasonable request in most cases, considering that the IOC and the local participants are entering into a long-term relationship. Thus, where funds are designated for specific uses, as suggested above, the IOC can verify that those funds have been applied for such uses. These types of audit right are supported, for example, by Namibia's NEEEF, which provides that "businesses that need to comply with the NEEEF will be expected to provide audited proof that they have achieved NEEEF targets."[67] Having audit rights with respect to the NEEEF company will support the IOC's 'audited proof' of compliance.

It is a possible defence to any claim of an anti-bribery or corruption offence that a company had in place adequate procedures to prevent persons associated with it from committing bribery.[68] The procedures discussed above, combined with a robust internal policy and a zero tolerance approach to bribery and corruption, will help bolster this defence.

9. Conclusion

This chapter has explained the unique historical origins of state participation and local participation in the African oil and gas industry, and the main features of these regimes. While state participation has long been embedded in the African, and indeed global, oil and gas industry, local participation is also becoming increasingly prevalent.

This chapter has also examined the challenges that state participation and local participation present, both for host states and IOCs seeking to invest in Africa. For a host state, these include potential fiscal inefficiencies and the conflict between a NOC's economic and social goals, while an IOC must consider a potential negative impact on investment economics, regulatory uncertainty and an increased risk of corruption.

An IOC must employ a robust procedural and contractual framework in order best to address and mitigate these challenges in a legal context. The nature and scope of due diligence and documentation must be tailored to the relevant jurisdiction and, crucially, must be forward-looking, in order to accommodate both present and potential risk. By employing this approach, most IOCs will likely find the challenges of state participation and local participation to be manageable opportunity costs, rather than barriers, to doing business in Africa.

---

67 NEEEF, at 22.

68 Bribery Act, section 7(2); Ministry of Justice Guidance, paragraphs 1, and 33.

Ohada: the organisation for harmonisation of business law in Africa

Olivier Chambord
Allison Soilihi
Morgan, Lewis & Bockius UK LLP

1. Introduction

In the years following the decolonizations of the 1960s, the view took hold that domestic legislation in various African states was unsuitable to meet the challenges of globalization, leading increasingly to legal uncertainty. Several African countries therefore decided to address this issue collectively. A steering committee was accordingly constituted with a view to drafting an international treaty and identifying areas of business law that most needed to be harmonised.

The result of these deliberations was the Organization for the Harmonization of Business Law in Africa (*Organisation pour l'Harmonisation en Afrique du Droit des Affaires*), most commonly known by its French acronym, OHADA. The organisation was created on October 17 1993 by the adoption in Port Louis, Mauritius of the original OHADA Treaty. OHADA, an international organisation with legal personality, has played a crucial role in harmonising the business law framework applicable in a number of African countries, initially only in Francophone Africa, but since also encompassing non-Francophone countries.

This chapter gives an overview of OHADA and its institutions and provides key information on OHADA legislation that may be particularly relevant to mergers and acquisitions in OHADA member states.

2. A brief overview of OHADA

The original 1993 OHADA Treaty[1] was subsequently revised by a second treaty adopted in Quebec on October 17 2008.[2] The Revised Treaty provided that it would enter into force once ratified by eight OHADA member states.[3] Following ratification by the eighth member state, Senegal, the Revised Treaty entered into force on March 21 2010.

Accession to OHADA is governed by article 53 of the OHADA Treaty and is open to any member state of the African Union (AU) or any state that is not an AU member state but has been invited to join OHADA by unanimous agreement of the

1 Treaty Creating the Organization for the Harmonization of Business Law in Africa (Port Louis, Mauritius, October 17 1993) ('the OHADA Treaty').

2 Revised Treaty on the Harmonization of Business Law in Africa (Quebec, October 17 2008) ('the Revised Treaty').

3 Article 2 of the Revised Treaty.

OHADA member states. Seventeen member states have joined OHADA to date. They are: Benin, Burkina Faso, Cameroon, the Central African Republic, Chad, Comoros, Congo, Equatorial Guinea, Gabon, Guinea, Guinea-Bissau, Ivory Coast, Mali, Niger, Senegal, Togo and the most recent member, the Democratic Republic of Congo.

OHADA is headquartered in the Cameroon capital, Yaoundé. Prior to the Revised Treaty of 2008, its sole working language was French. English, Spanish and Portuguese were added as working languages by the Revised Treaty.

The stated objectives of the OHADA Treaty are:

the harmonization of business laws in the Contracting States by the elaboration and adoption of simple modern common rules adapted to their economies, by setting up appropriate judicial procedures, and by encouraging arbitration for the settlement of contractual disputes.[4]

The various pieces of legislation promulgated by OHADA in order to apply these common rules across the member states are named uniform acts. By virtue of article 10 of the OHADA Treaty, these uniform acts are directly applicable in each member state and override local laws.[5] A Common Court of Justice and Arbitration seeks to ensure that the provisions of the uniform acts and other OHADA instruments and decisions are construed and applied consistently throughout all member states.

3. An introduction to the institutions of OHADA

3.1 The Council of Ministers

Article 27 of the OHADA Treaty provides for the setting up of a Council of Ministers, which is the supreme decision-making body of the organisation. In accordance with the treaty's provisions, the Council of Ministers comprises the ministers of justice and ministers of finance of each OHADA member state. The council is chaired by each member state on a rotating basis for a term of one year and meetings are held at least once a year upon the giving of notice by its president.

The powers of the Council of Ministers are wide-ranging and may, in summary, be divided into two categories: legislative and executive.

- Legislative powers essentially comprise the power to adopt uniform acts and to further integration by approving programmes for the harmonisation of business laws.
- Executive powers include powers to:
  - adopt the annual budgets of the Permanent Secretariat (3.3 below) and of the Common Court of Justice and Arbitration (CCJA) (3.4 below);
  - elect members of the CCJA;
  - promulgate the procedural rules of the CCJA;
  - approve the organisation's accounts and appoint statutory auditors to review them; and, more generally,
  - adopt regulations to implement the OHADA Treaty.

---

4 Article 1 of OHADA Treaty.

5 Article 10 of the OHADA Treaty states: "Uniform Acts are directly applicable and overriding in the Contracting States notwithstanding any conflict they may give rise to in respect of previous or subsequent enactment of municipal laws." (Free translation from the original French text.)

3.2 The Heads of the State and Governments Conference

The Conference, which was introduced by the Revised Treaty, comprises the heads of state and governments of the OHADA member states. The Conference is chaired by the head of state or government that chairs the Council of Ministers and meets, as and when required, upon notice being given by the President of the Council. The Conference deals with any matter relating to the OHADA Treaty and is the authority entitled to change the location of OHADA's headquarters.

3.3 The Permanent Secretariat

The Permanent Secretariat is the administrative body of the organisation and is headquartered in Yaoundé, Cameroon. It is chaired by a Permanent Secretary who is appointed by the Council of Ministers for a term of four years, renewable once. The Permanent Secretary represents OHADA, pursuant to article 40 of the Revised Treaty.

The powers of the Permanent Secretariat are administrative in nature and its main role is to assist the Council of Ministers with regard to the exercise of the latter's legislative powers. In particular, the Permanent Secretariat has a key role in preparing and drafting new uniform acts that are submitted to the Council of Ministers for approval. The Permanent Secretariat also has an important liaison role in seeking feedback from OHADA member states and the CCJA when preparing draft uniform acts. Once uniform acts have been adopted by the Council of Ministers, the Permanent Secretariat is responsible for publishing them in the OHADA Official Journal. Uniform acts become applicable 90 days after they are published in the *Official Journal*, unless provided otherwise in the uniform acts.[6]

3.4 The Common Court of Justice and Arbitration

Disputes arising in connection with the application of the uniform acts are settled at first instance and on appeal by the national courts of the OHADA member states. The CCJA, which is a creation of the OHADA Treaty, is responsible for making final decisions with regard to the interpretation and application of the OHADA Treaty and the Revised Treaty, regulations implementing them, uniform acts and decisions of OHADA organs. The CCJA, which is seated in Abidjan, the economic capital of the Ivory Coast, comprises nine judges elected by the Council of Ministers for a non-renewable term of seven years.

The CCJA has a consultative role in respect of any matter falling within the scope of its powers and may be consulted directly by any OHADA member state, the Council of Ministers or a national court. In addition to its consultative role, the CCJA exercises judicial powers and an arbitration role.

The judicial role and powers of the CCJA are aimed primarily at construing the uniform acts. The CCJA is a supranational court. Its aim is to avoid conflicting interpretations of the OHADA Treaty and the uniform acts by the courts of each member state and to ensure a cohesive and consistent construction and application of these instruments by all member states.

The CCJA is a court of last resort, which means that, in accordance with the

6 Article 9 of the Revised Treaty.

OHADA Treaty,[7] it can rule finally on decisions rendered by the courts of appeal of the member states in respect of any matters relating to the application of the uniform acts and regulations made under the treaty, with the exception of decisions applying criminal sanctions. In addition, the CCJA can rule on decisions rendered by the courts of any member state in respect of the same matters, where no appeal is possible.

With regard to procedure, proceedings may be initiated before the CCJA by a party to a dispute, either for a ruling as to an alleged lack of jurisdiction on the part of a court of a member state, or to resolve a dispute as the court of final appeal. Courts of the member states may also initiate proceedings in order to confirm whether or not they have jurisdiction.

Finally, the CCJA acts as an arbitration centre. Any party to an arbitration clause or agreement may refer a dispute arising under or in connection with it to the CCJA. Such an application may be made either if one of the parties to the agreement has its usual residence in one of the OHADA member states or if the agreement is (or is to be) performed wholly or partly in the territory of one or more member states.[8] The CCJA does not arbitrate the referred case itself but appoints or confirms arbitrators, is informed of the status of the proceedings and examines the drafts of arbitral awards as to matters of form. The arbitration rules of the CCJA are set by the Council of Ministers.

3.5 Superior Regional School of Magistrature[9]

The School is headquartered in Porto Novo, Benin. Its main purpose is to train judges, lawyers and staff of the courts of the member states in OHADA law.

4. The OHADA business law framework

Under the OHADA Treaty's umbrella of supranational norms for member states, nine uniform acts have been passed to date. These are as follows:

- (Revised) Uniform Act relating to General Commercial Law;[10]
- (Revised) Uniform Act relating to Commercial Companies and Economic Interest Group Law ('UACC');[11]
- (Revised) Uniform Act relating to Security;[12]
- Uniform Act relating to Simplified Recovery Procedures and Measures of Execution;[13]
- Uniform Act relating to Collective Proceedings for the Clearance of Debts;[14]

---

7 *Ibid*, article 13.

8 *Ibid*, article 21.

9 Translation of the French acronym 'ERSUMA', which stands for *Ecole Régionale Supérieure de la Magistrature.*

10 *Acte Uniforme Révisé portant sur le Droit Commercial Général* (dated December 15 2010), which entered into force on May 16 2011.

11 *Acte Uniforme Révisé relatif au Droit des Sociétés Commerciales et du Groupement d'Intérêt Economique* (dated January 30 2014), which entered into force on May 5 2014.

12 *Acte Uniforme Révisé portant Organisation des Sûretés* (dated December 15 2010), which entered into force on May 16 2011.

13 *Acte Uniforme portant Organisation des Procédures Simplifiées de Recouvrement et des Voies d'Exécution* (dated April 10 1998), which entered into force on July 10 1998.

14 *Acte Uniforme portant Organisation des Procédures Collectives d'Apurement du Passif* (dated April 10 1998), which entered into force on January 1 1999. Revision of this instrument is currently under discussion.

- Uniform Act relating to Arbitration;[15]
- Uniform Act relating to the Organisation and Harmonisation of the Accounting Systems of Enterprises;[16]
- Uniform Act relating to Contracts for the Transport of Goods by Road;[17] and
- Uniform Act relating to Co-operative Companies.[18]

As mentioned previously, the provisions of these acts are directly applicable in each of the OHADA member states. Preliminary drafts of new uniform acts are currently under discussion in respect of a number of other areas of law, including labour law and special contracts (eg, construction sub-contracting, franchises and public-private partnerships).

5. The relevance of OHADA to mergers and acquisitions

As the provisions of the uniform acts harmonise the subject matter with which they deal across the OHADA member states, they are directly relevant to a number of legal issues relating to mergers and acquisitions (M&A).

From a legal standpoint, differences in legal systems between African countries can make due diligence and execution of M&A transactions (particularly in relation to multi-jurisdictional transactions) challenging on the African continent. The harmonisation that results from the OHADA Treaty and legislation made under it facilitates due diligence by improving the legal and regulatory framework applicable to these transactions and by providing, in OHADA member states, clear and common rules that are relevant to most transactions. For example, as companies within OHADA member states are all governed by the same corporate law set out in the UACC (see 4 above), conducting due diligence on a target company and effectuating transactions in one or more OHADA member states will be facilitated.

The purpose of this part of this chapter is not to explain comprehensively the content of all of the uniform acts listed at 4 above, but rather to provide a brief overview of the legal framework instituted by OHADA with regard to:

- corporations and the taking of securities over assets that are often relevant to M&A transactions entered into by petroleum companies, and
- the operation of companies and assets acquired.

Further details can be found in the texts of the relevant uniform acts.

5.1 OHADA corporate law

OHADA corporate law was initially created by the original version of the UACC that was adopted on April 17 1997. The Council of Ministers adopted a revised version of

---

15 *Acte Uniforme relatif au Droit de l'Arbitrage* (dated March 11 1999), which entered into force on June 11 1999.

16 *Acte Uniforme portant Organisation et Harmonisation des Comptabilités des Entreprises* (dated March 24 2000), the revision of which is currently under discussion.

17 *Acte Uniforme relatif aux Contrats de Transport de Marchandises par route* (dated March 22 2003), which entered into force on January 1 2004.

18 *Acte Uniforme relative au Droit des Sociétés Coopératives* (dated December 15 2010), which entered into force on May 16 2011.

the UACC on January 30 2014, amending the original Uniform Act. The current UACC was published in the OHADA Official Journal on February 4 2014 and entered into force on May 5 2014.

In summary, the main changes made by the revised UACC include the following:

- the introduction of a new form of corporation: the simplified joint stock company (*société par actions simplifiée*), which provides more flexibility in the drafting of articles of association than the SA[19] and the SARL;[20]
- the introduction of new provisions to enable the issuance of preferred shares, hybrid securities or free shares;
- clarification of the legal framework applicable to company branches within the OHADA area;
- the reinforcement of corporate governance rules; and
- reform of the conditions for holding general shareholders' meetings and other corporate meetings.

(a) The joint stock company: the Société Anonyme ('SA')

The SA is one of the most commonly used types of companies in OHADA member states. It is a company in which the shareholders' liability is limited to their contributions and their rights are represented by shares.[21] There is no minimum required number of shareholders, so the SA may comprise only one shareholder (a sole shareholder company).

The minimum share capital of an SA is CFA Francs 10 million (where there is no public call for capital). The share capital is divided into shares with a par value minimum amount that may be freely set by the company's articles of association.[22] Shares are negotiable instruments or registered securities; the form of registered securities may, however, be specified by the provisions of the UACC or the articles of association.

The management structure[23] of an SA may take the form of either:

- a board of directors comprising between three and twelve directors,[24] or
- a sole managing director (*administrateur unique*) for companies that have, at most, three shareholders.[25]

Where the SA is managed by a board of directors, the company may appoint either:

- a single chairman of the board and general manager (*Président Directeur-Général*), or
- a separate chairman of the board (*Président du Conseil d'Administration*) and a general manager (*Directeur Général*).

---

19 See further commentary on the SA at 5.1(a) below.
20 See further commentary on the SARL at 5.1(b) below.
21 Article 385 of the UACC.
22 *Ibid*, article 387.
23 *Ibid*, articles 414 *et seq*.
24 *Ibid*, article 416.
25 *Ibid*, article 494.

The chairman of the board is appointed by the board of directors from among its members for a term that cannot exceed the duration of his/her office as a director. The chairmanship of the board may be revoked at any time by the board of directors. The chairman of the board chairs meetings of the board of directors. In addition, when the chairman of the board is also general manager, s/he has wide powers to bind the company *vis-à-vis* third parties. While these powers may be limited by the articles of association, such limitations are not binding against *bona fide* third parties. In case of the breach of such limitations, any remedy for the company normally stems from the liability to it of the chairman and general manager.

As mentioned previously, the office of chairman of the board and the office of general manager may be held by different persons. In such a case, the general manager may be appointed by the board of directors, either from among its members or from outside. The general manager (but not the chairman of the board) will then exercise general management powers and will bind the company *vis-à-vis* third parties. Where one person exercises the offices of chairman and general manager, the articles of association may limit the powers of the general manager, but such limitations will not be binding on *bona fide* third parties provided that, in the event of breach of limitations set out in the articles of association, the company may seek to invoke the general manager's liability.

Shareholder meetings must be held at least once a year. Decisions are normally passed by a simple majority, except for decisions that entail a change to the articles of association, which can only be passed with a two-thirds majority.

(b) Société à Responsabilité Limitée *(SARL)*

The SARL is also customarily used in OHADA member states. As with the SA, the SARL is a company in which the shareholders' liability is limited to their contributions and whose rights are represented by shares.[26] There is no minimum required number of shareholders, so the SARL may comprise only one shareholder (a sole shareholder company).

The minimum share capital of a SARL is CFA Francs 1 million. This is divided into shares with a par value of at least CFA Francs 5,000.[27] Assignments of shares of a SARL must be made in writing and are only effective *vis-à-vis* third parties once certain formalities have been observed.[28] The articles of association may stipulate the terms and conditions of the assignment of shares to other shareholders. In the absence of specific provisions in the articles of association, shares may be transferred to other shareholders without restriction.[29] The articles of association may also stipulate specific terms and conditions of an assignment of shares to third parties. In the absence of such provisions, shares may be transferred to third parties, subject to compliance with specific terms, conditions and procedures set out in the UACC.[30]

The SARL may be managed by either:

---

26 *Ibid*, article 309.
27 *Ibid*, article 311.
28 *Ibid*, article 317.
29 *Ibid*, article 318.
30 *Ibid*, articles 319 *et seq*.

- several managers (*gérants*), or
- a single manager.

General meetings must be held at least once a year to approve the annual accounts of the company.

(c) Société par Actions Simplifiée *(SAS)*

The introduction of the SAS type of company is one of the major innovations of the revised UACC. This type of company may be set up by one or several partners. As with the SA and SARL, the liability of the shareholders will be limited to their contributions and their rights are represented by shares.

One of the main advantages of this type of company, the introduction of which was inspired by the *Société par Actions Simplifiée* under French law, is that it offers greater flexibility and freedom in drafting the articles of association. By contrast with the SA and SARL, the management and administrative structure may, subject to several exceptions, be freely stipulated in the articles of association and is not constrained by the type of mandatory provisions that apply to SAs or SARLs with regard to these matters. A very limited number of mandatory provisions will, however, still need to be included in the articles of association: certain powers are reserved to shareholders (eg, approval of end-of-year accounts, increases and reductions in share capital, mergers) and the company must be represented by a president, who may be either an individual (natural) or a corporate (legal) person.

The amount of the company's capital, as well as that of the par value of shares, may be freely fixed in the articles of association. The company may also issue a variety of securities, including preference shares.

This new type of company will undoubtedly be used increasingly in OHADA member states, especially in joint venture (JV) situations, where partners need to be able to work with as much flexibility as possible under the articles of association of the JV company. One of the main advantages of this type of company, for example, is that it should also be possible to obtain enforcement and specific performance of provisions of the articles of association for matters such as restrictions on the sale of shares (pre-emption rights, tag along and drag along rights, etc) rather than seeking enforcement of similar provisions in shareholder agreements. The transfer of shares made in breach of shareholder agreement restrictions in OHADA member states often traditionally gives rise only to a right to damages rather than annulment of the transfer. Including bespoke share transfer restrictions in the articles of association of an SAS should, however, normally permit the annulment of transfers of shares made in breach of provisions of the articles of association, which is often considered a more desirable remedy than damages.

(d) Société en Nom Collectif *(SNC)*

In this type of company, members are jointly and severally liable without limitation for the debts of the company (instead of their liability being limited to their contributions, as with the SA, SARL and SAS).

The share capital of the SNC is divided into shares with a par value. Such shares may, however, only be assigned with the unanimous consent of all of the shareholders and any assignment that is carried out without such consent is null and void.[31] The assignment must be made in writing and will only be effective *vis-à-vis* third parties after certain formalities have been observed.[32]

The management of the SNC is stipulated in the articles of association of the company, which may be managed by one or several managers (*gérants*) appointed in the articles of association or by a subsequent decision of the shareholders. The managers have wide powers to represent the company *vis-à-vis* third parties and to bind the company in its relations with those parties. The articles of association may restrict the powers of the managers, but such restrictions are not enforceable *vis-à-vis* third parties unless those parties were aware of the restrictions.

Collective decisions are, in principle, taken unanimously, unless the articles of association provide otherwise.[33] Shareholder meetings are held at least once a year to approve the accounts.[34] Rules as to the convening of meetings and the majorities required to pass votes are set out in the articles of association.[35]

(e) Société en Commandite Simple (SCS)

The SCS type of company is analogous to a sleeping partnership.[36] Under this structure, some partners are indefinitely, jointly and severally liable without limitation for the company's debts, referred to as *associés commandités* (ie, they are akin to active partners), whereas other partners are only liable for the company's debts up to the limit of their shares, referred to as *associés commanditaires* (ie, they are akin to sleeping partners).[37] This type of company, although it exists under the UACC, is rarely used in OHADA member states.

The share capital of the SCS is divided into shares. There is no requirement with regard to the minimum amount of registered share capital.

The articles of association of the company must set out the amount or value of all shareholders' contributions, each shareholder's share in the said amount or value, and the global share of active partners and sleeping partners in the allocation of profits and in any liquidation surplus.

A sleeping partnership may be managed by all the active partners, unless otherwise provided by the articles of association, which may appoint one or more managers from among the active partners, or provide for the appointment of such manager(s) by a subsequent instrument, under the same conditions and with the same powers as in a SNC.[38] A sleeping partner may not perform any act of external management, even pursuant to a power of attorney.

---

31 *Ibid*, article 274.
32 *Ibid*, article 275.
33 *Ibid*, article 283.
34 *Ibid*, article 286.
35 *Ibid*, article 285.
36 It should, however, be noted that the concept of 'partnership' as understood under the common law does not exist *per se* under the OHADA law.
37 Article 293 of the UACC.
38 See further commentary on the SNC at 5.1(d) above.

(f) ***Overview of new types of securities***

With the introduction of the SAS, the introduction of new types of securities is one other major innovation under the revised UACC.

- *Introduction of preference shares.* Companies may, either on incorporation or in the course of operations, create preference shares. These include, for example, shares with or without voting rights, or shares to which are attached certain specific rights and advantages (such as a right to a priority dividend or special rights of information), whether temporary or permanent.
- *Introduction of hybrid securities.* SAs and SASs may issue a variety of hybrid securities, such as bonds convertible into shares, bonds redeemable in shares and bonds with share subscription warrants. This should facilitate the structuring of complex financial operations that comprise mezzanine and subordinated debt, as seen in more mature markets, and permit the establishment of priorities between different hybrid securities, for example, in cases of insolvency or prepayment events.
- *Introduction of free shares.* SAs and SASs may issue free shares to employees and/or managers. The total amount of free shares issued cannot, however, exceed 10% of the share capital of the company.

(g) ***Reform of rules on the holding of meetings***

Video conferencing and other communication technologies may be used to convene meetings and hold and vote at shareholder and board meetings, if the articles of association so permit and subject to certain restrictions.

Formalities for the setting up of companies may, in principle, be completed online, though the implementation of this reform will depend on the computerisation of the registers of commerce and credit in each of the member states. The use of notaries remains mandatory for the preparation and amendment of the initial articles of association.

(h) ***Treatment of foreign-owned branches***

Another of the key amendments made by the revised UACC is the amendment of article 120, which relates to branches of foreign corporations operating in OHADA member states.

Under the original version of the UACC, article 120 provided that a foreign-owned branch should, no later than two years after it was set up in an OHADA member state, be attached to a company in existence or a company to be created that is governed by the laws of one of the OHADA member states. This applied unless an exemption was obtained from the minister for trade in the relevant member state. No limitation was imposed with regard to the duration of such exemptions or the number of exemptions that could be obtained. It therefore became customary for petroleum companies (among others) to operate in some OHADA countries through branches for more than four years, rather than through locally incorporated subsidiaries, by obtaining successive exemptions.

Under the revised version of article 120 of the UACC, exemptions are now limited to a one-time, non-renewable exemption for a maximum period of two years, subject to special rules (which are not defined in the UACC, thus resulting in some uncertainty). The maximum time period for operating as a foreign-owned branch in an OHADA member state will consequently be four years if an exemption is granted, or two years without an exemption. Any branch so registered will thereafter need to be attached to a company governed by the laws of an OHADA member state.

Failure to comply with these new provisions may lead to the branch being struck from the trade and personal property credit register (*registre du commerce et du crédit mobilier*, better known by the French initialism RCCM). This would have potentially adverse consequences and effectively make it impossible to carry out business legally in an OHADA member state.

In practice, the transaction required to achieve such an attachment may take the form of the business and assets of the branch being contributed to a local subsidiary in exchange for the issuance of shares of that subsidiary, or the sale of assets to a pre-existing or newly incorporated subsidiary. The contribution of the business and assets will need to be carefully prepared and a host of issues will need to be addressed, such as obtaining required regulatory and contractual approvals for such transfers. In the case of petroleum companies, such transfers of business and assets will necessitate the transfer of petroleum agreements, host government agreements, permits and authorisations, various assets connected with the carrying out of petroleum operations and third party contracts that will raise prior approval issues. Consequently, if an audit of a target petroleum company is carried out in an OHADA member state, particular attention will need to be paid to:

- the target's compliance with article 120 of the UACC, and
- if a transfer of business and assets has been carried out, compliance with applicable rules as to consents.

The tax implications of such an attachment will also need to be managed through careful tax planning and structuring in order to minimise taxation (in particular, possible liabilities to capital gains or transfer taxes), and to maximise favourable tax regimes, such as those usually applicable to petroleum companies.

5.2 The main types of security that can be taken over assets in OHADA countries

Historically and prior to the implementation of OHADA, the types of security that could be taken over assets in the countries now constituting the OHADA member states were inherited from French law, in particular from the provisions of the French Civil Code that applied to these countries prior to their independence. Post-independence, these provisions soon became outdated, but few countries proceeded to update their laws on the taking of security.

The adoption of the original version of the Uniform Act on Securities (UAS) of April 17 1997 was thus a welcome change, harmonising and updating the laws of OHADA member states at the time. This version entered into force on January 1 1998.

In summary, the original UAS covered the types of security that are commonplace in civil law countries, with a distinction being drawn between guarantees *in personam* (*sûretés personelles*), where the guarantee is constituted by an undertaking made by a guarantor, and security *in rem* (*sûretés réelles*) that are granted over either movable or immovable property. Guarantees *in personam* comprise personal guarantees (*cautionnements*) and autonomous guarantees (*garanties autonomes*). The autonomous guarantee introduced by the UAS differs from the traditional civil law personal guarantee in the form of a caution, as the latter is not autonomous from the debt it guarantees. Guarantees *in rem* comprise security over movables (*sûretés mobilières*) and security over immovable property, such as mortgages (*hypothèques*). Security over movables included, under the original UAS, several types of guarantee, such as the right of retention, pledges over claims (*gages de créances*), pledges over shares (*nantissement d'actions et parts sociales*) and pledges over inventory (*nantissement de stocks*).

Ten years after its initial adoption, it was considered that the UAS needed improvement and updating. In particular, it was felt that the regimes introduced by the UAS were still overly rigid and did not permit the taking of security and guarantees over all types of obligation (in particular over future or conditional obligations). It was suggested that the taking of security be permitted over all types of goods, whether future or current, and whether or not with a right of dispossession, in order to facilitate the taking of credit, financing and investment in OHADA member states. Another stated objective of the reform was to reduce the formalism and costs related to the taking of security in OHADA member states.

After consultation with a variety of experts from the private sector, the World Bank and France and the setting up of working groups to identify issues with and shortcomings in the original UAS, a revised Uniform Act relating to Security (the revised UAS) was prepared and submitted to and adopted by the Council of Ministers in December 2010. The revised UAS was published in the OHADA Official Journal of February 15 2011 and entered into force on May 16 2011. As from this date, any new security taken in an OHADA member state would be governed by the revised UAS.

The revised UAS introduced several new types of guarantee, such as pledges over financial security accounts (*nantissement de compte de titres financiers*, which was inspired by reforms under French law that introduced the same type of security), the assignment of claims as a guarantee (*cession de créance titre de garantie*) and the fiduciary transfer of sums of money (*transfert fiduciaire de somme d'argent*). The revised UAS made new provision as to security agents[39] (which was inspired by a French law of February 19 2007) to govern investments made by pools of investors and banks.

The comments made below are only a brief overview of the variety of securities that exist under the revised UAS. Practitioners should refer to the statute for further details on such securities and their enforcement.

(a) Guarantees in personam (sûretés personelles)

- *Personal guarantee (cautionnement).* The personal guarantee is defined in the UAS as the contract by which the guarantor (*caution*) undertakes, for the benefit of the creditor, the performance of an obligation (whether current or future) contracted by the debtor if the latter does not perform it him/herself.

---

39 Articles 5-11 of the UAS.

This type of non-autonomous personal guarantee, the performance of which is subject to the non-performance of an underlying obligation by a debtor, already existed prior to the revised UAS. The innovation lies in the express extension of the scope of this guarantee by the revised UAS to future obligations. The guarantee must be evidenced by a written agreement, signed by the guarantor and the creditor and including the maximum amount that is guaranteed (principal, interest and other costs), expressed both alphabetically and and numerically and hand-written by the guarantor.[40]

- *Autonomous guarantee (garantie autonome).* The autonomous guarantee and the autonomous counter-guarantee are defined in the UAS as undertakings by which the guarantor or the counter-guarantor bear an obligation to pay the beneficiary in respect of an obligation of the instructing party (*donneur d'ordre*) and pursuant to instructions from the instructing party, at first demand or pursuant to the terms agreed.[41] Contrary to the previously discussed *cautionnement* type of guarantee, this type is, in principle, independent from the underlying obligations of an instructing party[42] and can be exercised in principle at first demand or according to terms agreed between the parties, thus providing flexibility to adapt this type of guarantee on a case-by-case basis. The autonomous guarantee and counter-guarantee must be in writing and contain certain information in order to be valid (including the maximum amount of the autonomous guarantee or counter-guarantee). It should be noted that individuals cannot issue an autonomous guarantee.[43]

(b) *Guarantees in rem (sûretés réelles)*

Security over movables (*sûretés mobilières*) are defined by the revised UAS as the right of retention (*droit de rétention*), ownership rights retained or assigned as security (*propriété retenue ou cédée à titre de garantie*), pledge over tangible assets (*gage de meubles corporels*), pledges over intangible assets (*nantissements de meubles incorporels*) and liens (*privilèges*). Except as otherwise provided, securities over movables are subject to registration with the RCCM.[44] Under the revised UAS, rules relating to registration formalities for the different types of security are set out in articles 51-66. These include territorial jurisdiction to register the security, information to be included in the registration form, procedure for registration with the RCCM, and renewal or modification of a registration.

- *Right of retention of goods.* Subject to certain conditions, the beneficiary of this right is entitled to retain or keep (movable) goods in his/her possession until such beneficiary has been repaid in full by its debtor. This effectively creates an exclusive right for the beneficiary over goods retained and thus prohibits

40 *Ibid*, article 14.
41 *Ibid*, article 39.
42 *Ibid*, article 40.
43 *Ibid*.
44 See 4.1(h) above for the meaning of this initialism.

any other creditor from exercising rights over such goods (insofar as they do not hold prior perfected security over those goods). The right of retention is not a right to be paid through the proceeds of sale of the goods (except in limited circumstances set out by the revised UAS). The right of retention can only apply if the debt of the beneficiary is unquestionable, due and payable, if there exists a connection between the origin of the debt and the retained movable goods and if the movable goods have not been attached before being retained by the beneficiary.[45]

- *Ownership rights retained as security or assigned as security.*[46] The ownership of a movable asset can be retained through a retention of title clause (*clause de réserve de propriété*) in order to guarantee an obligation. The retention of title clause suspends the transfer of ownership of goods until full payment of the obligation. The retention of the ownership must be agreed in writing at the latest on the day of delivery of the goods. The retention can be agreed in a document governing current or future operations between the parties. In order to be enforceable *vis-à-vis* third parties, the retention must be validly registered with the RCCM.[47]

  Article 79 of the revised UAS provides that ownership rights over current or future goods can also be assigned as a guarantee of payment of current or future debts in accordance with the terms of the statute. Although this provision sets out a general principle, the only types of mechanism for the assignment of ownership rights that are referred to in the revised UAS are:
  - an assignment of a claim as a security,[48] and
  - the fiduciary transfer of monies.[49]

  A claim against a third party may be assigned as a security for a credit granted by a national or a foreign corporate entity carrying out banking or credit operations as its usual business.[50] Such an assignment of claim as a security must be in writing and include certain information: the name of the assignor and of the assignee, the date of assignment and the designation of the guaranteed debts and of the assigned claims, failing which the assignment is null and void.[51] In case of future claims, the assignment agreement must enable the identification of the claims or include such information as will enable identification of the claims, such as the debtor, the place of payment, the amount (or assessed amount) of the claims and their due date. The assignment agreement is effective immediately between the parties on the date on which the agreement is entered into, but becomes enforceable *vis-à-vis* third parties as from its registration with the RCCM.[52]

  The fiduciary transfer of monies is the agreement by which a person

---

45 Article 68 of the UAS.
46 *Propriété cédée à titre de garantie.*
47 Articles 72 and 73 of the UAS.
48 *Cession de créance à titre de garantie.*
49 *Transfert fiduciaire d'une somme d'argent.*
50 Article 80 of the UAS.
51 *Ibid*, article 81.
52 *Ibid*, article 82.

transfers monies as a guarantee of the performance of its obligation.[53] Such a mechanism is a new type of security introduced by the revised UAS. The monies that are the subject of the fiduciary transfer are kept in an account under the name of the creditor of the obligation in a credit institution entitled to receive such monies. The agreement sets out the guaranteed debt(s) and the amount of the monies transferred as a guarantee, as well as the identification of the account. The fiduciary transfer becomes enforceable *vis-à-vis* third parties on the date of its notification to the institution holding the account, provided that the monies are deposited in that account. Unless the parties agree otherwise, the interest generated, if any, is credited to the account. On the due date, in the event the guaranteed debt is fully paid, the monies deposited in the account are returned to the person who provided the guarantee. In the case of a default by the debtor and eight days after notification to the person who provided the guarantee, the creditor can be provided with the transferred monies within the limit of the amount of the guaranteed debts unpaid.[54]

- *Pledge over tangible assets.*[55] A pledge is defined by article 92 of the revised UAS as a contract by which the grantor grants the creditor the right to be paid by priority on a tangible movable asset or a series of such assets, whether current or future. The pledge must comply with certain conditions, including as to form. Under certain conditions, the assets that have been pledged can be sold and the proceeds of the sale allocated to the beneficiary of the pledge for payment of the underlying debt. The ownership of the goods can also, subject to certain conditions, be transferred to the beneficiary by a court decision or by contractual terms agreed (*pacte commissoire*) in certain cases. The revised UAS sets out detailed rules governing a variety of pledges over certain types of assets: these include, for example, pledges over professional materials,[56] pledges over vehicles[57] and pledges over inventory.[58]
- *Pledge over intangible assets.*[59] A pledge over intangible assets is defined in article 125 of the revised UAS as the allocation of intangible goods or a series of intangible goods, whether current or future, as a guarantee for one or several claims, current or future, on condition that these claims are determined or determinable. Article 126 of the UAS provides a list of the types of intangible asset that can be pledged. These include, for example, claims (*créances*), other intangible goods, bank accounts in credit (*solde créditeur de compte bancaire*), businesses as a going concern (*fonds de commerce*), shareholder rights (*droits d'associés*), securities and financial instrument accounts (*valeurs mobilières et comptes d'instrument financiers*) and intellectual property rights. This list is not intended to be exhaustive. The

53 *Ibid*, article 87.
54 *Ibid*, article 91.
55 *Gage de meubles corporels.*
56 Article 118 of the UAS.
57 *Ibid.*
58 *Ibid*, article 120.
59 *Nantissement de meubles incorporels.*

above-mentioned categories of pledge over goods are, however, governed by specific rules in the revised UAS for each type of pledge. The rules applicable to pledges that are not included in one of the above-mentioned categories remains unclear, however.

- *Liens*. The revised UAS distinguishes between general and special liens. General liens (*privileges généraux*) grant a preferential right exercised by their holders. Specific national legislation of OHADA member states may provide for general liens, provided that such legislation refers to the priority ranking of these general liens over the general liens otherwise provided for by article 180 of the UAS.[60]

  The revised UAS confers a special lien on movable assets to certain holders, the list of which is provided in articles 183-189 (for instance, the seller of movable goods or the lessor).

(c) ***Mortgage***[61]

Pursuant to article 190 of the revised UAS, a mortgage is defined as the allocation of immovable property (*immeuble*) that is or can be determined as belonging to the mortgage provider as a guarantee for one or several debts, current or future, provided that the said debts are or can be determined.[62] Under the revised UAS, a mortgage may be legal, conventional or judicial. The mortgage gives a preferential right to the beneficiary creditor and a right of resale, which means that the right of the mortgagee follows the mortgaged property even if that property is detained by a third party other than the debtor.

The document constituting the mortgage, whether conventional or judicial, must be registered in accordance with the registration rules of the member state where the mortgaged asset is located.[63] Whether or not the mortgage is granted for a limited period of time, its registration is only valid for a limited period of time set as set out in the mortgage convention or the court decision and for a maximum period of thirty years, subject to any contrary provisions in the national legislation of a member state. The registration may, however, be renewed for a further limited period of time.

Article 203 of the revised UAS provides that a contractual mortgage may only be granted by the holder of immovable property validly registered and entitled to dispose of it. An exception to this rule is that a mortgage may be granted over a future immovable property, subject to certain conditions set out in article 203 of the revised UAS. The contractual mortgage is granted, in accordance with the national law of the place of location of the property, pursuant to a notarised act (or an act by

---

60 Examples of such liens include:
- monies owed to workers and apprentices for the performance and termination of their contracts during the last year prior to the death of the debtor;
- monies owed to the authors of intellectual, literary and artistic works during the last three years prior to the death of the debtor; and
- within the amount limits prescribed by law, monies owed to social security and welfare bodies and to tax and customs authorities.

61 *Hypothèque*.

62 Article 190 of the UAS.

63 *Ibid*, articles 195 and 196.

a duly empowered relevant authority) or a private act that follows the form agreed by the national authorities in charge of land ownership and mortgages. So long as the registration has not been carried out, the mortgage contract is not enforceable *vis-à-vis* third parties and constitutes a bilateral commitment between the parties that requires them to proceed with the registration.

(d) Security agent (agent de sûreté)

Articles 5-11 of the revised UAS introduce a legal regime applicable to security agents. Any security (whether *in personam* or *in rem*) in respect of the performance of an obligation may now be created, registered, managed and enforced by a national or foreign financial institution or a credit institution, acting as a security agent to the benefit of the creditors of the guaranteed obligations that appointed it. The creditors are represented by the security agent in their relationship with the debtors, the guarantors and third parties, including for the purpose of legal representation before a court. When it acts to the benefit of the creditors, the security agent must indicate that it acts in its capacity as a 'security agent'.

6. Other harmonisation efforts

In addition to the OHADA harmonisation efforts discussed above, other harmonisation efforts worth mentioning are those of the EMMCA (Economic and Monetary Community of Central Africa, known by its French acronym, CEMAC) and WAEMU (West African Economic and Monetary Union, known by its French acronym, UEMOA), both of which were created in 1994.

The six member states of CEMAC are Cameroon, the Central African Republic, Congo, Gabon, Equatorial Guinea and Chad. The eight members of WAEMU are Benin, Burkina Faso, Ivory Coast, Guinea-Bissau, Mali, Niger, Senegal and Togo.

These two organisations seek to harmonise business and monetary environments between their member states. In particular, all member states have adopted a common currency, the CFA Franc – one for the EMMCA zone and one for the WAEMU zone. This common currency is pegged to the Euro and its conversion is guaranteed by the French treasury. The member states have also set up a central bank and seek to guarantee the free transfer of funds between member states, while also implementing common rules on foreign exchange and the transfer of funds abroad. These rules may have a direct impact on M&A transactions and on the operation of companies and assets acquired.

7. Conclusion

The harmonisation of various areas of law, in particular corporate law and the laws on the taking of security over various assets, is undoubtedly both relevant and extremely useful to practitioners in the context of M&A transactions, by virtue of increasing the clarity, comprehensibility and flexibility of applicable laws, as discussed in this chapter.

Chasing shadows: security of oil and gas projects in Africa

John C LaMaster
Akin Gump Strauss Hauer & Feld LLP

1. Case studies

Case Study 1: Algeria's In Amenas gas facility is operated as a joint venture by BP (46%), Statoil (46%) and Sonatrach (8%). Prior to 2013, the government of Algeria had a strong track record of safeguarding the oil and gas industry,[1] despite occasional attacks by insurgents on soldiers and western nationals. At dawn on January 16 2013, 32 heavily armed terrorists attacked the In Amenas facility. They were led by Makhtar Belmokhtar, an Algerian terrorist associated with al-Qaeda in the Islamic Maghreb (AQIM). AQIM's goals are to oppose what its leaders consider to be illegitimate and corrupt Islamic regimes and to remove foreign presence and influence from Islamic lands.[2] At the time of the attack, there were over 800 persons on the site. The attack took place over four days and resulted in the death of 40 innocent persons from 10 different nations. In an Algerian context, a major terrorist attack by an almost paramilitary army on such a significant oil and gas infrastructure target was unprecedented.

Case Study 2: Nigeria's oil and gas industry has long been the subject of attacks from multiple sources, including the Movement for the Emancipation of the Niger Delta (MEND). Most recently, bunkering, consisting of the sabotage of pipelines and the theft of crude oil, has reached an industrial scale. The process of bunkering often results in considerable amounts of crude oil spilling uncontrollably onto the land and into the waterways. In March 2013, Italian explorer Eni's local subsidiary suspended its activities at oil fields in Bayelsa state after a steep increase in bunkering. Eni stated that it was losing approximately 7,000 barrels of crude production daily to oil thieves out of its typical total production in Bayelsa of 40,000 barrels per day. A statement from Eni said the decision was made because the bunkering had "recently reached unsustainable levels regarding both personal safety and damage to the environment."[3] The bunkering is generally seen as efforts by militants such as MEND to protest that the benefits of oil and gas production are not shared proportionately with the local people in the area where the production

1 *The In Amenas Attack, Report of the Investigation into the Terrorist Attack on In Amenas*, prepared for Statoil ASA's board of directors (September 8 2013), at 4.3.5.
2 Loïc Conan, 'The Trans-Saharan Gas Pipeline: An Overview of the Threats to its Success and the Means to Prevent its Failure', 31 *Utah Environmental Law Review* 205 (2011), at 222.
3 Helen Castell, 'Nigeria Faces Return to the Bad Old Days', *AfrOil 2013 Annual Review* (January 2013), at 8.

occurs, with the result that the local people suffer the direct effects of oil exploration without realising corresponding tangible benefits.

Case Study 3: The Arab Gas Pipeline runs across the Sinai Peninsula from al-Arish, Egypt to Aqaba, Jordan. It is connected to the Arish-Ashkelon submarine pipeline that supplies natural gas to Israel and to other sections in Jordan that carry Egyptian natural gas to Jordan and other countries. Starting in early 2011, mass protests against Egyptian President Hosni Mubarak and the resulting 'Arab Spring' created political instability across Egypt. The first bombing attack on the pipeline occurred in February 2011. It was followed by dozens of attacks over the ensuing years. The attacks were generally blamed on Bedouin Islamists who were taking advantage of the political instability in Egypt to protest that the people living in the Sinai Peninsula had not been benefiting from the wealth generated by oil and gas activities in the peninsula. The attacks resulted in the pipeline being shut down on many occasions, halting the flow of natural gas to Israel and Jordan.

Case Study 4: Piracy in the Arabian Sea and the Indian Ocean off the coast of Somalia has been a threat to shipping for many years. Pirates have typically hijacked vessels and their crews for ransom. Although the rate of pirate attacks has dropped off from its peak in the early 2000s, the London insurance market's Joint War Committee continues to include Somalia in its list of areas of perceived highest risk for shipping. Given the recent lack of oil and gas operations in offshore Somalia, this piracy has not been an issue for the exploration and production side of the oil and gas industry. In August 2013, however, Soma Oil & Gas entered into a Seismic Option Agreement with the federal government of Somalia, whereby Soma agreed to conduct seismic surveying across certain areas of offshore Somalia. Soma engaged seismic acquisition company SeaBird Exploration to acquire 2D seismic data across a 185,000 sq km offshore evaluation and reconnaissance area. SeaBird Exploration engaged the private maritime security contractors Solace Global and Salama Fikira, as well as Somali security personnel from Peace Business Services, to provide security for the operation. Starting in early 2014, two seismic vessels, the *Northern Explorer* and the *Hawk Explorer*, were used to acquire the seismic data. The vessels were accompanied by eight security/support vessels and approximately 40-50 private maritime security personnel on a round the clock operational basis. Soma successfully completed the acquisition of 20,500 km of 2D seismic data in June 2014 without any security incidents.

2. Introduction

These case studies highlight the growing threat to oil and gas infrastructure and to the oil and gas industry throughout Africa. As these threats have increased, international oil companies (IOCs) and governments have had to change their policies, practices and procedures and develop an enhanced focus on the security of their oil and gas infrastructure and personnel. This chapter discusses the sources, means and consequences of the increased level of attacks and other security breaches. It then discusses some of the actions that are recommended to IOCs to enhance security. Finally, it discusses some specific contractual issues affecting IOCs and arising in connection with the attacks and other security breaches.

3. Security breaches: who, why, how and where?

Threats to and attacks on oil and gas infrastructure and personnel are not a new phenomenon. For example, the Trans-Arabian Pipeline Company (Tapline) pipeline was sabotaged in the Golan Heights by the Popular Front for the Liberation of Palestine as early as 1969. Furthermore, IOCs have long been the target of kidnappings and there are many examples of kidnappers of Western oil and gas workers successfully extorting ransoms from IOCs, foreign governments and insurance companies. IOCs have also historically suffered low-level sabotage. The latest surge of terrorist and other attacks in Africa, however, has been unprecedented in its scope and in its consequences.

Any act of violence or other unlawful interference with an oil and gas installation can be considered a security threat. These threats can come from a variety of sources ie, from different types of persons or groups of persons who have a wide variety of motivations. The means of carrying out their threats also vary in their scope and level of violence. The type of threat also varies from state to state.

There are several categories of persons or groups who threaten oil and gas infrastructure in Africa. The highest profile are terrorists, as in the In Amenas attack in Algeria (described in Case Study 1 above). Given the growth of terrorist groups around the world, these persons must continue to be considered one of the highest level threats. Insurgent groups are also responsible for many threats against oil and gas installations. These include groups such as AQIM in Algeria, MEND in Nigeria and the Bedouin Islamists in Egypt (described respectively in Case Studies 1-3 above), who are typically motivated by political struggles. Another group of persons threatening oil and gas installations are pirates (described in Case Study 4 above). For the most part, threats of piracy have historically been levied against shipping targets, but the prospect remains for attacks against offshore installations. Organised crime constitutes another threat to oil and gas installations, through activities such as bunkering, kidnapping, theft of property and other criminal activity. Even civil activists, who typically use non-violent means, constitute threats to the oil and gas installations they target. Any of these persons can work with insiders who provide a threat from within the relevant oil and gas installation or organisation.

These persons or groups have a wide variety of motivations for threatening oil and gas infrastructure. Terrorists can be motivated by religious, political or ideological factors, each of which can lead to the desire to destabilise governments by demonstrating their inability to protect important infrastructure and by depriving them of critical sources of revenue. The attack against the In Amenas gas facility (Case Study 1) was both an attack against the Algerian government's most strategic industry and most important source of revenue, and an attack against western interests. Many insurgent groups are motivated by the desire to achieve a fairer share of the benefits that accrue or should accrue from oil and gas activities in their regions. These include, for example, the MEND group in Nigeria (Case Study 2) and the Bedouin Islamists in Egypt (Case Study 3). Organised crime and pirates can be motivated by financial gain (Case Study 4). Civil activists are motivated by the desire to raise awareness of environmental issues, such as pollution resulting from oil and gas operations. The one thing in common among all of these groups is the desire to create greater publicity for their organisations and their goals. The motivations behind the various threats are important because they can colour the level of violence and other attributes of the resulting threats. For example, if pirates seek financial gain by means of a ransom, then it is in their interests to keep hostages alive and detained vessels in reasonable condition in order to realise the ransom. On the other hand, a terrorist seeking to destabilise a government in order to achieve a religious, political or ideological goal may actively seek a high level of violence and destruction.

Persons or groups posing threats to oil and gas installations also have different means of carrying out those threats. These means will depend on the internal capabilities of the persons as well as the level of security they are up against. The tactics of terrorists and insurgents have included bombings (as in the case of the Arab Gas Pipeline – Case Study 3) and armed attacks and the taking of hostages (as in the case of In Amenas – Case Study 1). Organised crime and pirates carry out their kidnap-for-ransom schemes in increasingly sophisticated ways, as evidenced by the use by Somali pirates of 'mother ships' that launch multiple high speed skiffs for attacks on merchant vessels. Civil activists tend to carry out their protests by unauthorised boarding and occupation of oil and gas installations, such as the incident involving Shell's Brent Spar floating oil storage facility in the North Sea in 1995. In analysing the level of threat to an oil and gas installation, it is important to consider the capabilities and tactics of those who pose the most likely threat to those facilities. Doing so can also help to predict future types of attacks, such as cyber-attacks.

The types of security threat to oil and gas installations in Africa vary from state to state. Nigeria faces the severe threat of bunkering and other criminal activity by insurgents. Algeria has been the site of the most severe terrorist attack to date on oil and gas facilities. The revolution and civil war that overthrew Libyan dictator Colonel Muammar Ghadaffi in 2011 continues to affect the county, with oil and gas production and exports far below historic levels. Similarly, the post-regime change environment in Egypt fosters continued uncertainty and unrest, including threats from terrorists and insurgents. Somalia remains a source of piracy that threatens shipping in the Arabian Sea and the Indian Ocean.

4. Consequences of security breaches

Oil and gas plays a crucial role in the world economy; attacks on its facilities in Africa affect countries outside Africa's borders by disrupting secure energy supplies, which has a knock-on effect on non-African economies. More severe consequences are, however, suffered in the African countries where the attacks occur. They include:

- loss of life and property;
- economic losses;
- loss of foreign investment;
- loss of markets, and
- increased costs of security.

These consequences are discussed in greater detail below.

Oil and gas production and exports from Africa are important to many western countries. For example, Spain, Italy and France are dependent on north African natural gas supplies to meet much of their energy needs. For the European Union as a whole, Algeria is the third largest supplier of natural gas after Russia and Norway. Both Jordan and Israel have suffered significant economic losses as a result of attacks on the Arab Gas Pipeline. Although individual terrorist attacks in Africa cause disruptions to non-African economies, they are more nuisances than major threats to those economies because energy is available from other sources, albeit sometimes at a higher price. It would take co-ordinated and simultaneous attacks on multiple facilities to cause severe consequences to most non-African economies.[4]

The more severe consequences are suffered in Africa. In addition to the loss of African lives and property, the attacks have significant economic consequences for the countries involved. For example, Algeria's economy is heavily dependent on its energy sector, with oil and gas accounting for more than 95% of export earnings, 60% of budget revenues and 30% of the country's gross domestic product (GDP), according to the International Monetary Fund (IMF).[5] The attack on In Amenas is assumed to have deprived Algeria of more than $10 million per day in lost revenue for several months while the facility was totally or partially shut down.[6] Similarly, the Libyan economy is one of the most oil and gas dependent in the world. According to the IMF, oil and gas accounts for roughly 98% of export earnings and 96% of budget revenues. The unrest caused by the civil war has included direct attacks on oil and gas installations, with the result that production has fallen to one-tenth of what it could be. The drop in oil and natural gas production has led to an economic collapse; for example, real GDP contracted by 62% in 2011.[7] In Nigeria, losses of oil production as a result of bunkering are estimated at between 5%[8] and 20%[9] of total production, which is a massive economic blow to a country that relies on crude oil exports for the bulk of its government revenues.

The worsening security situation can also lead to a loss of foreign investment. Algeria had already been struggling to attract new foreign investment; there were disappointing results in its licensing rounds in 2008, 2009 and 2011, with only nine of 34 blocks licensed over that period.[10] The now-precarious security environment will cause additional concern for investors. In Nigeria, IOCs such as Shell, Total and Eni are divesting onshore assets, doubtless (at least in part) as a result of weariness over the difficult security environment. Another example is the Trans-Saharan Gas Pipeline from Nigeria through Niger to Algeria, which has been delayed in part because of security concerns arising from threats by insurgent groups such as MEND.

---

4 Diego Cordano, 'The Terrorist Threat to Energy Infrastructure in North Africa', *Consultancy Africa Intelligence* (May 21 2014), available at www.consultancyafrica.com.

5 US Energy Information Administration (EIA), *Algeria Country Report*, available at www.eia.gov (last updated July 24 2014).

6 Diego Cordano, *op cit* (note 5 above).

7 US Energy Information Administration (EIA), *Libya Country Report*, available at www.eia.gov (last updated October 10 2013).

8 Helen Castell, 'African Woes Hit OPEC Numbers', *AfrOil*, Issue 519 (December 10 2013), at 2.

9 Castell, *op cit* (note 4 above), at 8.

10 *Algeria Country Report* (note 6 above).

Loss of foreign investment could be a significant problem for the many countries in Africa that rely on it to develop their natural resources.

Eventually, continued interruptions of supplies of oil and gas resulting from attacks and other security breaches can result in loss of markets for African countries. For example, following multiple attacks on the Arab Gas Pipeline, both Jordan and Israel took steps to reduce their reliance on Egyptian natural gas. Jordan, which had used Egyptian gas to generate 80% of its electricity, began to use oil and diesel in its Aqaba power plants, despite the higher cost. In the short term, Israel replaced Egyptian gas with more expensive purchases on the spot market, while working to develop its own internal supplies. By 2013, Israel had discovered enough offshore natural gas to become energy self-sufficient and no longer need Egyptian gas at all. Furthermore, Israel had found enough gas to allow it to export to Jordan; it was announced in September 2013 that Israel would supply Jordan with up to $15 billion of natural gas from its Leviathan field over 15 years. Meanwhile, in August 2014, the Arab Gas Pipeline was bombed for the 25th time since the overthrow of the Mubarak regime. The complete loss of the Israeli market and the partial loss of the Jordanian market is certainly a blow to the Egyptian economy.[11]

Increased security risks have also caused both governments and IOCs to review their security arrangements, which will inevitably result in increased costs of security. For example, following the In Amenas attack, the government of Algeria said that it would increase its security presence at oil and gas facilities throughout the country. In Nigeria, new and replacement pipelines are being installed at much greater depths than before, in order to counter pipeline sabotage, vandalism and bunkering. The shipping industry has responded to the threat of piracy in offshore Somalia by hardening and fortifying vessels; this, combined with international naval intervention, has repressed the piracy.

Security breaches have even been blamed for decreased levels of food security. In Nigeria, the theft of oil by bunkering often results in oil spills which impact negatively on agricultural farmland in the Niger Delta. The oil spills trigger "the decomposition and crumbling of community farmlands, causing intense erosion and deforestation by incremental grass wiping, tidal waves, flooding, clearing of mangroves and falling of economic trees, polluting wetlands, creeks, fish ponds, air and rainwater, and obstructing the natural sequence of waterways".[12]

This, in turn, worsens the already bad food security situation for the people of the region.

5. Recommendations for preventing security breaches

The increase in security breaches in Africa has caused governments and IOCs to reassess their security arrangements. This ongoing reassessment has identified several ways in which governments and IOCs can reduce the risk of security breaches. These include further co-operation between the public and private sectors to provide

11 J Millard Burr, *Egypt: Natural Gas, Pipelines, and the Gas Exporting Countries Forum*, American Centre for Democracy (January 25 2012), available at acdemocracy.org.

12 BOG Nwanolue *et al*, 'The Nigerian State and Crude Oil Bunkering in Niger Delta: Examining the Environmental Vulnerability', 3 *African Journal of Social Sciences* 31 (2013), at 36.

multiple layers of security, further engagement and employment of indigenous persons, the development of better risk assessment methodologies, and further education.

Security must be a collaborative effort between the public and private sectors. The security of large oil and gas installations should comprise multiple layers. Certain types of security are the responsibility of governments. These include the prevention of terrorism through border controls, intelligence gathering and area surveillance. Armed military and law enforcement capabilities are also sovereign responsibilities. The level of security provided by the government is often referred to as the 'outer layer' of security. Other types of security are the responsibility of the private sector. These include the 'inner layer' of security at oil and gas installations, such as physical protective barriers, civilian guards, access controls, security plans and procedures, and other measures to protect the joint venture's personnel and assets from security threats.

At In Amenas, the BP/Statoil/Sonatrach joint venture relied on the Algerian military to provide the outer layer of protection against terrorist threats. This was an appropriate allocation of responsibility between the public and the private sectors. It was also understandable for the joint venture to rely on the government to provide such protection, given the latter's history of successfully defending oil and gas installations from major security incidents. The In Amenas attack, however, revealed several gaps between public and private responsibilities. For example, the joint venture did not have detailed knowledge about the outer layer of security. To some extent, the nature of the government's and the military's role in providing the outer layer of security meant that the process could not be transparent and fully known to the joint venture, because some information had to be classified or withheld on national security grounds. Better communication, co-ordination, planning and exercises between the joint venture and the military could, however, have lessened the impacts of the attack. For example, the inner layer of security at the In Amenas facility was designed based on the belief that the military would prevent an armed assault as part of its responsibility to provide the outer layer of security. What this meant, however, was that once the military failed to prevent the terrorist attack at the outer layer of security, the inner layer of security was not adequate to prevent or even substantially delay the attack. Better awareness by the joint venture of the capabilities of the outer layer of security might have resulted in a better designed inner layer of security that could have prevented or at least delayed the attack.[13]

It is important for private sector participants to assess continually the capabilities of the host government and military and not just rely on past experience or assume that the outer layer of protection is adequate. Companies should hold regular meetings with public security forces to discuss and co-ordinate security issues. In some cases, private sector participants may assess that the host government and military are not capable of providing, or are unwilling to provide, the necessary level of outer security. In such cases, private sector participants may need to provide or engage private security to complement the public security. The prospect of armed

13 *The In Amenas Attack* (note 2 above), at 1.5, 8.2, 8.3 and 8.4.

private security capable of using force raises its own set of issues. For example, while armed private security may decrease the risk of an attack or a successful attack, the trade-off is that the presence of armed private security raises the risk of potential escalation in the use of force, which could increase the chances of injury or death to persons. At In Amenas, Statoil had concluded that the risks posed by deploying armed private security outweighed the benefits, due to:

- human rights concerns;
- the risk of having two armed bodies in the same area;
- difficulties in providing training;
- concerns over the adequacy of background checks; and
- the perceived risk that the deployment of armed private security would result in the reduction of military forces in the area.[14]

The risks associated with armed private security are addressed by codes of conduct such as the International Code of Conduct for Private Security Service Providers[15] and by the Voluntary Principles on Security and Human Rights.[16]

The inner layer of security is the responsibility of the private sector. Ideally, an oil and gas installation should be developed as an island site, with clearly defined perimeters. These perimeters should be secured to provide for early detection and deterrence of and delay to any threats. Other physical facilities include access controls and private guards. The inner layer of security should also comprise non-physical items, such as training of personnel and security plans and procedures. At In Amenas, the inner layer of physical security comprised double fences, a ring of concrete vehicle barriers, unarmed civilian guards, chicanes and road blocks to slow down approaching vehicles, and CCTV surveillance and alarm systems. As the attack demonstrated, physical barriers alone are insufficient to stop an attack, but the inner security layer should at least provide a degree of resilience and deterrence that will cause delay and give more time for a military response to arrive.[17]

In the same way that private sector participants should not simply rely on the government's provision of the outer layer of security, non-operators should not simply rely on operators to provide the inner layer of security. Rather, non-operators should take the initiative to assess and verify independently the adequacy of the inner layer of security.

Another way to manage risks associated with oil and gas operations is to use more local workers. This has the benefit of reducing the number of expatriates, which reduces both the attractiveness to terrorists of attacking the relevant installation and the IOC's expatriate exposure. This policy would also be popular with local communities who provide the local workforce. Conversely, relevant local skills may not be adequate, especially in the early days of an operation. Furthermore, the use of local workers potentially increases the exposure of the installation to insider risk.

---

14 *Ibid*, at 5.2.5.
15 *International Code of Conduct for Private Security Service Providers* (2010), available at www.icoc-psp.org.
16 *Voluntary Principles on Security and Human Rights* (2000), available at www.voluntaryprinciples.org.
17 *The In Amenas Attack* (note 2 above), at 5.1 and 8.5.

Insider threats have long been recognised as a serious challenge to the oil and gas industry. Insiders will either perpetrate or assist others in the perpetration of the theft, attack or other security breach. Insiders can be especially dangerous because they may know the weaknesses of the existing security systems. This is one of the reasons why background checks on new employees are standard operating procedure. Background checks alone are not adequate protection, however. It is also necessary to monitor employees after the background checks have been carried out. In some cases, insiders may only become criminals or terrorists once on the job. Similarly, insiders can be subject to coercion, such as blackmail or threats to family members. Disgruntlement, substance abuse, mental health problems or other personal problems can also affect an insider's allegiances.[18] The Statoil team investigating the In Amenas attack considered it likely that the terrorists benefited from insider knowledge in their planning of the attack, but they had no conclusive evidence that this was the case.[19]

The ability to assess risks is a critical component in protecting the security of persons and property. As explained above, it is important to understand the persons or groups who constitute the threat, their motivations and their capabilities. In a continent as diverse as Africa, this will vary from region to region and country to country. As a result, certain persons or assets may be at greater risk than others. It is also important that risk assessments look beyond what has already happened and think about what could happen. The In Amenas attack was unprecedented and therefore unanticipated. The Statoil team investigating the attack referred to the failure to plan for such a scenario as a "failure of imagination".[20] That type of low probability/high impact risk must now be contemplated in any security assessment. Future risks, such as cyber-attacks, must also be assessed.

In the oil and gas industry, the sharing of information about safety incidents and the lessons learned is routine. This level of sharing does not, however, exist with regard to security, which is often treated as a 'need to know' topic. For example, information regarding kidnapping insurance is always closely held. In some cases, however, information should be shared more openly. For example, where IOCs operating in the same region or country have concerns regarding security, they should share those concerns and consider jointly raising them with the relevant government(s).

Many IOCs include security as part of their corporate health, safety and environmental (HSE) function, rather than treating it as a stand-alone function. Given both the increased level of security threats and the specialist knowledge and experience that is required to meet those threats, it makes sense for the security function to be given separate status as a discipline all of its own, with appropriate priorities and resources.[21]

Insurance can be used to bolster security programmes. For example, western expatriate workers should always be covered by insurance against kidnapping.

---

18 Matthew Bunn & Scott D Sagan, *A Worst Practices Guide to Insider Threats: Lessons from Past Mistakes*, American Academy of Arts and Sciences (2014).

19 *The In Amenas Attack* (note 2 above), at 8.7.

20 *Ibid*, at 8.3.

21 *Ibid*, at 1.6.4, 8.9 and 9.1.

Lastly, education regarding security is important. In the same way that environmental safety was reassessed following the Macondo well blow-out in the Gulf of Mexico in 2010, security needs to be reassessed in the wake of the In Amenas attack. In this regard, anyone involved in the security of an oil and gas installation should read the *Report of the Investigation into the Terrorist Attack on In Amenas* prepared for Statoil ASA's board of directors[22] for the many lessons it imparts.

6. Contractual issues

Certain provisions of oil and gas agreements should be reconsidered in the wake of the In Amenas attack, the ongoing issues involving bunkering in Nigeria and in the face of escalating security threats throughout Africa. The primary type of agreement to be considered in this chapter is the joint operating agreement (JOA).

Typically, several IOCs and perhaps the national oil company (NOC) will jointly acquire undivided interests in an upstream petroleum agreement (UPA), such as a licence, concession or production sharing agreement (PSA) with the host country. These participants will then enter into a JOA to govern their relationship and establish the contractual framework for their joint exploration, development and production of oil and gas from the relevant UPA. One of the participants will be designated as the 'Operator' and the other participants will be designated as the 'Non-Operators'. The JOA will establish the rights, obligations and liabilities applicable among the participants, including with regard to security.

Security raises issues with regard to:

- the HSE plan;
- the responsibilities of the Operator; and
- *force majeure*.

The discussion of these issues in this section is based upon the provisions of the 2012 Model Form International Operating Agreement (the Model Form) prepared by the Association of International Petroleum Negotiators (AIPN), as this is the most common form of JOA used in Africa.

6.1 Contractual issues – the HSE Plan

It is sometimes questioned whether the Model Form has provisions that deal with security of the type discussed in this chapter. While the Model Form contains provisions that address financial security, in the sense of security for decommissioning costs or financing, the term 'security' does not appear in any other context in the Model Form.

The relevant provision of the Model Form is Article 6.6, which requires the Operator to prepare an HSE (Health, Safety and the Environment) Plan, and to carry out 'Joint Operations' in a manner consistent with the HSE Plan. Article 6.6, including its alternative provisions, provides as follows:

6.6 HSE Plan

6.6.A Operator shall in the conduct of Joint Operations:

---

22 *Ibid.*

6.6.A.1 Prepare and establish an HSE Plan designed to achieve safe and reliable conduct of operations and activities, to avoid significant and unintended impact on the safety and health of people, on property, and on the environment, and to comply with Laws relating to HSE;
6.6.A.1.1 Carry out the HSE Plan in conformance with Laws relating to HSE and in a manner consistent with standards and procedures generally followed in the international petroleum industry under similar circumstances;
6.6.A.1.2 Plan and conduct Joint Operations consistent with the HSE Plan; and
6.6.A.1.3 Design and operate Joint Property consistent with the HSE Plan.
6.6.B The Operating Committee shall at least annually review and approve:

ALTERNATIVE PROVISION, CHOOSE ONE

ALTERNATIVE #1
the details of the HSE Plan, the implementation of the HSE Plan, and of the effectiveness of the HSE Plan.

ALTERNATIVE #2
an HSE report and letter of assurance from Operator in a form acceptable to the Operating Committee providing adequate evidence that the HSE Plan fulfills the requirements of Article 6.6.A and is in place, that Operator is properly carrying out the HSE Plan, that any major HSE issues have been brought to the attention of the Operating Committee and are being properly managed, and that the HSE Plan as carried out is effective.
6.6.C In the conduct of Joint Operations, Operator shall:

ALTERNATIVE PROVISION, CHOOSE ONE

ALTERNATIVE #1
establish and carry out a program for regular HSE assessments. The purpose of such assessments is to periodically review HSE systems and procedures, including actual practice and performance, to verify that the HSE Plan is in place and fulfills the requirements of Article 6.6.A, that the HSE Plan is being properly carried out and that the HSE Plan as carried out is effective. Operator shall, at a minimum, conduct such an assessment before entering into significant new Joint Operations and before undertaking any major changes to existing Joint Operations. Upon reasonable notice given to Operator, Non-Operators shall have the right to participate in such HSE assessments.

ALTERNATIVE #2
establish an annual audit program in which independent auditors review and verify that the HSE Plan is in place and fulfills the requirements of Article 6.6.A, that the HSE Plan is being properly carried out, and that the HSE Plan as carried out is effective.

6.6.D Operator shall require its contractors, consultants, and agents undertaking activities for the Joint Account to manage HSE risks in a manner consistent with the requirements of HSE Plan.

6.6.E Operator shall establish and enforce rules consistent with those generally followed in the international petroleum industry under similar circumstances that, at a minimum, prohibit within the Contract Area the misuse of prescribed drugs and the possession, use, distribution, or sale of any of the following:
6.6.E.1.1 Firearms, explosives, or other weapons without the prior written approval of Operator's senior management;
6.6.E.1.2 Alcoholic beverages without the prior written approval of Operator's senior management; and
6.6.E.1.3 Illicit or non-prescribed controlled substances.

OPTIONAL PROVISION, CHOOSE IF DESIRED. IF NOT CHOSEN CHECK CROSS-REFERENCES,
6.6.F Without prejudice to a Party's rights under Article 4.2.B.8, with reasonable advance notice, Operator shall permit at all reasonable times during normal business hours each Non-Operator (at its own risk and cost) to conduct an audit of the HSE Plan, its implementation and effectiveness. Where there are two or more Non-Operators, the Non-Operators shall make a reasonable effort to conduct joint or simultaneous HSE audits in a manner that will result in a minimum of inconvenience to Operator.

Although Article 6.6 does not expressly refer to 'security', in the sense discussed in this chapter, the definition of 'HSE Plan' is, in the author's view, broad enough to include it: "achieve safe and reliable conduct of operations and activities, to avoid significant and unintended impact on the safety and health of people, on property, and on the environment".

A drafter who wishes to avoid any doubt on this issue could revise these provisions to refer to a 'HSSE (Health, Safety, Security and the Environment) Plan' and the term 'security' could be expressly included in the definition of 'HSSE Plan'.

In considering which of the alternative provisions to include in a JOA from a security standpoint, the 'best practice' appears to be to choose Alternative #1 in Article 6.6.B, so that the Operating Committee would annually review the details of the HSE Plan and its implementation and effectiveness, rather than merely reviewing a report and a letter of assurance from the Operator. As noted at 5 above, Non-Operators should take the initiative to assess and verify independently the adequacy of the security arrangements.

With regard to article 6.6.C, the 'best practice' from a security standpoint appears to be to choose Alternative #2, so that independent auditors (rather than the Operator) would review and verify that the HSE Plan:

- is in place and fulfils the requirements of Article 6.6.A;
- is being properly carried out; and
- as carried out, is effective.

The participants may also wish to include a provision requiring the Operator to include audit rights in its agreements with contractors and sub-contractors.

Finally, from a security standpoint, it is recommended that alternative provision Article 6.6.F be included, in order to allow Non-Operators to conduct audits of the

HSE Plan and its implementation and effectiveness. This is consistent with the recommendation at 5 above that Non-Operators should be proactive in assessing the adequacy of the security arrangements.

These choices may be somewhat less efficient and more expensive than the alternatives, but security (like safety) is not an area where the lowest cost option should be the default choice.

6.2 Contractual issues – responsibility of the Operator

An important question arises in the wake of experience of the In Amenas attack, bunkering in Nigeria and the other security breaches discussed in this chapter and the unfortunate expectation that security threats will only increase over time: whether this has raised the standard of care owed by an Operator in providing security.

Article 4.2.B.2 of the Model Form JOA states that, in the conduct of Joint Operations, the Operator shall "conduct Joint Operations in a diligent, safe, and efficient manner in accordance with good and prudent petroleum industry practices and field conservation principles generally followed by the international petroleum industry under similar circumstances". This standard is flexible enough to adapt to changing circumstances over time. In the same way that the Macondo oil spill was a 'game changer' in how the oil and gas industry viewed environmental safety, the In Amenas attack and the other security breaches discussed in this chapter should be considered to have raised the bar for the security of oil and gas installations in Africa.

6.3 Contractual issues – *force majeure*

A *force majeure* clause in a contract is typically a means of allocating the risk if performance becomes impracticable or impossible as a result of an event or occurrence that could not have been anticipated or controlled. A *force majeure* clause typically has four elements:

- a definition of the causes or relevant events;
- a requirement that performance be prevented;
- a requirement of a causal link between the cause and the non-performance; and
- consequences where the foregoing three elements are fulfilled.[23]

The *force majeure* provisions in Article 16 of the Model Form JOA state:

If as a result of Force Majeure *any Party is rendered unable, wholly or in part, to carry out its obligations under this Agreement, other than the obligation to pay any amounts due or to furnish Security, then the obligations of the Party giving such notice, so far as and to the extent that the obligations are affected by such* Force Majeure, *shall be suspended during the continuance of any inability so caused and for such reasonable period afterwards as may be necessary for the Party to put itself in the same position that it occupied before the* Force Majeure, *but for no longer period. The Party claiming*

23 Eivind Eriksen, 'Terrorism and Force Majeure in International Contracts', 16 *Bond Law Review* 174 (2004), at 176.

Force Majeure *shall notify the other Parties of the* Force Majeure *within a reasonable time after the occurrence of the facts relied on and shall keep all Parties informed of all significant developments. Such notice shall give reasonably full particulars of the* Force Majeure *and also estimate the period of time that the Party will probably require to remedy the* Force Majeure. *The affected Party shall use all reasonable diligence to remove or overcome the* Force Majeure *situation as quickly as possible in an economic manner but shall not be obligated to settle any labor dispute except on terms acceptable to it, and all such disputes shall be handled within the sole discretion of the affected Party.*

Under English common law, limited relief is available if a *force majeure* event prevents performance. Parties therefore typically provide for contractual relief through a *force majeure* clause.[24] While some civil law jurisdictions address events beyond the control of the parties in their civil codes, it is not uncommon, even in these jurisdictions, for the parties to include contractual *force majeure* provisions.

The issues of terrorism, sabotage and other breaches of security raise many questions with regard to *force majeure*. There is a lack of English case law on the subject, leaving parties with little or no guidance as to whether an act of terrorism, sabotage or other security breach constitutes a *force majeure* event.[25] Furthermore, under English law, a *force majeure* clause is an 'exceptions clause' and so must be construed strictly.[26] If, therefore, contracting parties wish to be certain about their contractual rights and obligations with regard to terrorism, sabotage and other security breaches, they need to be more specific in the drafting of their *force majeure* clauses.

Force majeure is generally considered to be "an event or effect that can be neither anticipated nor controlled".[27] The concept of an event being 'anticipated' raises an issue regarding foreseeability. If an IOC is operating in a country with a notoriously unsafe security situation, is that IOC precluded from claiming *force majeure* because the threat of security breaches could be anticipated?[28] On the one hand, it may be argued that, in countries or regions where terrorism is rampant, the risk of terrorism must be seen as a normal risk. In that case, acts of terrorism are foreseeable and they should not excuse performance or exculpate liability where terrorism occurs.[29] On

24 The common law doctrine of frustration allows a contract to be automatically discharged and the parties excused from their future obligations where performance of the contract has become impossible, due to a major supervening event. The doctrine is applied as narrowly as possible by the English courts and parties face a very high burden of proof to satisfy its requirements. Typically, parties must demonstrate that the frustrating event was not caused by the fault or actions of either party, that further performance has become impossible, illegal or radically different, and that the frustrating event goes both to the 'root of the contract' and beyond what was contemplated by the parties when the contract was entered into. The requirements of the doctrine are harder to satisfy than most contractual *force majeure* provisions and, when considered alongside the question of foreseeability raised by this chapter, it is likely to be incredibly difficult for parties to rely successfully on the doctrine of frustration in the type of situations contemplated herein.

25 Eriksen, *op cit* (note 24 above), at 176.

26 *SHV Gas Supply & Trading SAS v Naftomar Shipping & Trading Co Ltd Inc* [2005] EWHC 2528 (Comm) (November 15 2005).

27 *Black's Law Dictionary* (9th Edn, 2009), at 718.

28 Richard Devine & Paul Neufeld, 'Force Majeure: Risks and Protection', *Petroleum Economist* (June 20 2011).

29 Eriksen, *op cit* (note 24 above), at 193.

the other hand, English courts tend to focus less on the foreseeability of the event than on whether the event was within the control of the affected party.[30]

This issue of foreseeability is highlighted by the Model Form JOA, which offers several alternative versions of the definition of *force majeure*. Under one formulation, a foreseeable event would arguably not constitute *force majeure*. "Force Majeure means for the purposes of this Agreement those circumstances beyond the reasonable control of the Party concerned, that could not have been avoided or mitigated by foresight, planning, and implementation consistent with generally accepted practices of the international petroleum industry." Under an alternative formulation, there is no element of foreseeability "Force Majeure means for the purposes of this Agreement those circumstances beyond the reasonable control of the Party concerned". Drafters of *force majeure* clauses therefore need to consider carefully the use of the concept of foreseeability in a security context.

It is difficult to draft an appropriate definition of 'terrorism'. *Black's Law Dictionary* defines it as "the use or threat of violence to intimidate or cause panic, esp. as a means of affecting political conduct".[31] A party desiring to have the broadest possible *force majeure* protections, such as an IOC in its PSA with the host government, may prefer the use of more general terms such as 'terrorism' or 'acts of terror' that are capable of being interpreted broadly. Conversely, the government or even a counterparty seeking to shift the risk of terrorism to the IOC may wish to specify the exact events and circumstances that will qualify as *force majeure* events.

'Acts of war' are commonly included as specified events of *force majeure*, but do acts of terrorism constitute 'acts of war'? When the 'acts of war' exemption was initially included in *force majeure* clauses, it meant something different from what it means today. Previously, wars were declared and it was clear when a war started and ended. Today, the so-called 'war on terrorism' is a much less clear concept.[32] It is best to avoid this issue altogether by including both 'acts of war' and 'acts of terror' in the *force majeure* clause.

In order to cover circumstances such as bunkering in Nigeria, the definition of *force majeure* should include sabotage, vandalism and criminal damage. Other useful inclusions that implicate security breaches are acts of public enemy, acts of foreign enemy, war (whether declared or undeclared), civil war, threat of war, blockade, revolution, riot, rebellion, civil commotion, insurrection of military or usurped power, and kidnapping. A catch-all may also be useful, such as "any other act, event or circumstance beyond the reasonable control of the affected party, including, without limitation, acts, events or circumstances relating to security situations".

Another issue to consider is whether *force majeure* relief should be granted to a party where the security breach occurs on nearby facilities rather than on the party's own facilities. In this event, it may be the case that the overall security situation is deteriorating, or that the occurrence of the nearby security breach makes it more likely that such a breach will occur at other local facilities. Inclusion of terms such as

30 *Great Elephant Corporation v Trafigura Beheer BV & Ors* [2013] EWCA Civ 905 (July 25 2013).
31 *Black's Law Dictionary* (9th Edn, 2009), at 1611.
32 Eriksen, *op cit* (note 24 above), at 190.

'threat' in the *force majeure* clause is one way to address this; for example, by including the wording "acts of terrorism or the threat of such acts". Another way to address this is to provide *force majeure* relief for events that hinder performance as well as for those that prevent it.

It is also important for contracting parties to consider and review *force majeure* issues across all of their related contracts. It is common in the oil and gas industry to have a series or chain of related agreements, such as a PSA, a JOA, a drilling contract, service agreements, crude oil handling, transportation and sales agreements, and financing agreements. A mismatch in *force majeure* provisions could result in one party having *force majeure* relief in circumstances in which another party must continue to perform, which could lead to disastrous economic results.[33] This risk is recognised in the Model Form JOA, which includes an alternative provision whereby "Force Majeure shall have the same meaning as is set out in the Contract", the Contract being the PSA or other UPA. It is an advisable practice to try to co-ordinate and conform *force majeure* clauses across the entire series or chain of related agreements.

7. Conclusion

It is the responsibility of all participants in the oil and gas industry, including IOCs and host governments, to take further actions to prevent security breaches. Even if IOCs and governments do everything in their power to protect people and property, however, they will still face the threat of terrorism and other attacks. Countering these threats is like chasing shadows, because security in the face of evolving threats is a never-ending quest.

The author would like to thank Kirsty Bell for her valuable assistance in providing research and other input for this chapter. Any views expressed, however, are the author's alone, and any errors are the sole responsibility of the author.

33 Conan, *op cit* (note 3 above), at 236.

Anti-corruption initiatives in Africa

Sarah Banco
Jaelyn Edwards Judelson
Nnedinma C Ifudu Nweke
Tamer Soliman
Akin Gump Strauss Hauer & Feld LLP

1. Introduction

Sub-Saharan Africa[1] provides significant economic opportunities for multinational companies operating in the oil and gas industry. Companies operating in this region may, however, also face significant compliance issues, including the challenges of complying with the requirements of the United States Foreign Corrupt Practices Act (FCPA),[2] the United Kingdom Bribery Act (UKBA)[3] and similar anti-corruption laws.

Enacted in 1977, the FCPA prohibits giving, offering, promising or authorising the provision of anything of value[4] (ie, bribing), directly or indirectly, to a "foreign official"[5] to obtain or retain business, secure an improper advantage, or cause a foreign public official to exercise improperly his or her authority.[6] In addition, the FCPA requires companies to keep accurate books and records and to establish and maintain adequate internal controls.[7] The UKBA generally prohibits the same activity

---

1 The United Nations defines 'sub-Saharan Africa' to refer to all of Africa except Morocco, Algeria, Tunisia, Libya, and Egypt. See UN Statistics Division *Composition of Macro Geographical (Continental) Regions, Geographical Sub-regions, and Selected Economic and Other Groupings* (October 31 2013), available at http://unstats.un.org/unsd/methods/m49/m49regin.htm#ftna.

2 Foreign Corrupt Practices Act of 1977, 15 USC, sections 78dd-1 and 78dd-2 (1994), amended by Pub L No 105-366, 112 Stat 3302 (1998).

3 Bribery Act 2010 (United Kingdom)

4 The phrase "anything of value" is not explicitly defined in the FCPA, but the identical phrase under the domestic United States bribery statute has been broadly construed to include both *tangible* and *intangible* benefits. See, for example, *United States v Moore*, 525 F 3d 1033, at 1048 (11th Cir 2008) (rejecting the defendant's objection to a jury instruction defining sex as a "thing of value", which "unambiguously covers intangible considerations"); *United States v Gorman*, 807 F 2d 1299, at 1304-1305 (6th Cir 1986) (holding that loans and promises of future employment are "things of value"); *United States v Williams*, 705 F 2d 603, at 622-623 (2d Cir 1983) (approving jury instruction that stock could be a "thing of value" if the defendant believed it had value, even though the shares had no commercial value, and noting that "the phrase 'anything of value' in bribery and related statutes has consistently been given a broad meaning".). See US Department of Justice (DoJ), *A Resource Guide to the US Foreign Corrupt Practices, Act*, at 74, note 86 (2012) (DoJ *Resource Guide*), available at www.justice.gov/criminal/fraud/fcpa/ guidance/.

5 The FCPA defines "foreign official" as "any officer or employee of a foreign government or any department, agency, or instrumentality thereof, or of a public international organization, or any person acting in an official capacity for or on behalf of any such government or department, agency, or instrumentality, or for or on behalf of any such public international organization". See Securities Exchange Act of 1934, 15 USC, sections 78dd-1(f)(1)(A) and 30A(f)(1)(A); see also 15 USC, sections 78dd-2(h)(2)(A) and 78dd-3(f)(2)(A).

6 FCPA, note 2 above. The FCPA applies to (1) persons who have issued registered securities in the United States ("issuers"), (2) entities incorporated in the United States and US citizens and permanent residents ("domestic concerns"), (3) foreign nationals or businesses in the United States, and (4) foreign directors, officers, employees, agents, or shareholders acting on behalf of an issuer or domestic concern. See 15 USC, sections 78dd-1, 78dd-2 and 78dd-3.

7 FCPA, note 2 above.

as the FCPA but prohibits additional actions, including receiving a bribe from a foreign public official (ie, passive bribery) and giving or receiving a bribe from a private individual (ie, commercial bribery).[8] In addition, unlike the FCPA, the UKBA creates strict liability for companies that fail to have adequate controls in place to prevent corrupt activity.[9] Local anti-corruption laws must be considered in connection with any potential compliance issue as well, albeit in the context of aggressive enforcement of the FCPA by the United States in sub-Saharan Africa, as well as growing international co-operation in investigations and enforcement activity.

Other national, regional and inter-governmental bodies around the world have established anti-corruption legal frameworks, such as international and regional protocols, since the United States enacted the FCPA in 1977. Notably, the World Bank and the International Monetary Fund (IMF) have used their influence to develop and implement a number of anti-corruption measures focused on fighting corruption at both state government and business levels. Anti-corruption legal frameworks and measures are referred to in this chapter as 'anti-corruption initiatives'.

This chapter discusses the most common anti-corruption challenges[10] that multinational oil and gas companies encounter while operating in sub-Saharan Africa, and assesses the lessons and impact of the major anti-corruption enforcement actions and initiatives designed to respond to those challenges.

2. Anti-corruption challenges for multinational companies operating in the oil and gas industry in sub-Saharan Africa

Multinational companies operating in the oil and gas industry in sub-Saharan Africa generally face some of the highest levels of corruption in any industry in the world. According to Transparency International's 2013 *Corruption Perceptions Index* (CPI), 90% of sub-Saharan African countries scored below 50,[11] making sub-Saharan Africa one of the two most corrupt regions in the world.[12] By comparison, 95% of Eastern Europe and Central Asia and 84% of the Middle East and North Africa scored below 50 on the CPI.[13] The World Bank ranked sub-Saharan Africa's control of corruption in the bottom 30-33% globally between 1996 and 2012, putting it on par with

8 UKBA, note 3 above. Enacted in 2010, the UKBA applies to: (1) British nationals, (2) persons ordinarily resident in the United Kingdom, (3) any entity, wherever formed, which carries on business or part of a business in the United Kingdom, and (4) persons or entities which commit any element of the offence in the United Kingdom. See section 12(4).

9 *Ibid*, section 7.

10 This chapter addresses 'transnational anti-corruption challenges' or anti-corruption challenges arising from laws that address corruption of foreign officials, as opposed to laws that address corruption of domestic officials.

11 A country or territory's score indicates the perceived level of public sector corruption on a scale of 0 to 100. 0 means that a country is perceived as highly corrupt and 100 means that it is perceived as free from corruption. A score of below 50 indicates a high-risk for corruption.

12 See Transparency International, *Corruption Perceptions Index 2013* at 4, available at http://files.transparency.org/content/download/700/3007/file/2013_CPIBrochure_EN.pdf.

13 *Ibid*.

14 See World Bank, *Worldwide Governance Indicators*, available at http://info.worldbank.org/governance/wgi/index.aspx#reports (last visited August 27 2014). The World Bank ranks countries for control of corruption, considering the existence of anticorruption regimes, the quality of enforcement, and the prevalence of common forms of corruption on a country-by-country and a regional basis.

Southeast Asia.[14] In addition, according to Transparency International's 2011 *Bribe Payer's Index*, the oil and gas industry ranks as one of the most likely industries to pay bribes to foreign officials.[15]

The high level of corruption in sub-Saharan Africa, particularly in the oil and gas industry, creates unique challenges for multinational companies in trying to conduct profitable businesses without running afoul of the FCPA, UKBA and similar anti-corruption laws. Some key challenges in this context are discussed below.

2.1 Lack of Information

One common anti-corruption challenge that oil and gas companies face in many parts of sub-Saharan Africa stems from a lack of information that is crucial for compliance. There are several aspects to this problem.

The first aspect is the lack of transparency on local laws, policies and practices, including tax, customs duties and clearance, and immigration laws. This widespread problem is particularly acute in the emerging oil and gas sectors in the region. Many governments are formulating or developing energy policies for newly emerging sectors, and without the benefit of experience. Lack of transparency and clarity can lead to opportunities for bribery in two ways. A lack of clarity regarding legal standards, rights and obligations creates opportunities for abuse of authority through arbitrary delay or onerous interpretations. In some cases, the lack of transparency has also led to a different kind of problem: companies may unknowingly violate the law and come under pressure to make unplanned back payments or to pay penalties to local governments.[16] Under the tight time and budgetary pressure of oil and gas exploration and development projects, employees and agents may be incentivised to pay kickbacks or bribes to local officials in order to resolve quickly any delays caused by demands for back payments or penalties.

The second aspect is the common need to rely on third party middlemen in such an environment. The more opaque the legal and regulatory environment, the greater the need for 'insiders' who can help to navigate the system. Of course, this is not unique to sub-Saharan Africa, and indeed does not necessarily lead to corruption. Reliance on middlemen and insiders, however, creates a particularly acute problem where there is neither a set of laws and standards nor rigorous enforcement of government oversight of conflicts of interest and corruption. In that environment, third party agents and representatives have a strong incentive to abuse influence or engage in corrupt practices to secure business and lucrative success fees. These parties may, in turn, create compliance risks if not carefully managed through compliance mechanisms and controls.

Often compounding this problem is the lack of resources and public records that can be crucial for counterparty and third party due diligence in the anti-corruption context. Companies wishing to ensure compliance face challenges in many parts of

15 See Transparency International, *Bribe Payers Index Report 2011* at 15, available at www.transparency.org/bpi2011/results. The Bribe Payers Index ranks the likelihood of companies from 28 leading economies paying bribes while acquiring or conducting business abroad.

16 See Layne Christensen Company, Cease and Desist Order, Admin Proc File 3-16216 (October 27 2014). See also note 128 below.

sub-Saharan Africa, due to a lack of readily accessible and reliable resources, including information on the background, affiliations, and ultimate ownership, as well as the credentials, capabilities and reputability, of third party agents. Thus, even if a company wishes to hire a legitimate third party to help it navigate local laws, companies often cannot meet FCPA enforcement officials' expectations with regard to due diligence.[17] The short supply of qualified third parties and the increase in FCPA enforcement actions against third parties further complicate the matter.[18] For example, a sophisticated freight forwarding and logistics company withdrew its operations from Nigeria after it pleaded guilty to violating the FCPA, noting that the "ongoing uncertain and hard-to-assess legal environment in Nigeria" made it difficult for the company to provide effective services to its customers without violating anti-corruption laws.[19]

2.2 Local content laws

Local content laws (ie, laws requiring foreign companies to partner with local entities) are prevalent in sub-Saharan Africa, particularly in the oil and gas industry.[20] While these laws are meant to stimulate local economic growth, they also create opportunities for bribes and kickbacks because foreign companies are often required to partner with local entities having direct or indirect government ties and, in some cases, without sufficient capability or incentive to perform in a manner commensurate with their share in a venture. In many cases, local entities in the oil and gas industry in sub-Saharan Africa are state-owned. Even local entities without state ownership may be considered an 'instrumentality' of the state through indirect control (and therefore involve a 'foreign official' for purposes of the FCPA), such as board appointments for government officials or ownership of the local entity by a government official in their individual capacity.

Other laws in sub-Saharan Africa may not require foreign companies to partner with local entities, but may instead require that foreign companies operate through locally-registered subsidiaries.[21] Local subsidiaries are often geographically isolated from parent companies, thus creating additional challenges for anti-corruption monitoring and increased opportunities for bribery.[22] Despite the heightened risks and challenges created by these local partnerships, FCPA enforcement officials still

17 Complaint, paragraphs 31-36, *Securities & Exchange Commission v Halliburton Company and KBR, Inc*, 4:09-cv-00399 (SD Tex 2009).

18 Information, *US v Panalpina, Inc*, 4:10-cr-00765 (SD Tex 2010); see also Information, *US v Panalpina World Transport (Holding) Ltd*, 4:10-cr-00769 (SD Tex 2010).

19 'Panalpina reports dynamic growth in the first half year' (July 30 2008), available at www.panalpina.com/www/global/en/home/news_media/news_archive_folder/08_07_30.html.

20 See Reagan R Demas, 'Doing Business in Africa While Ensuring Compliance with the FCPA', in Baker & McKenzie, *Inside the FCPA: The Corruption & Compliance Quarterly, North America*, Winter 2012, at 1, available at www.bakermckenzie.com/files/Uploads/Documents/Global%20Corporate%20Compliance/nl_na_inside fcpawinter_jan12.pdf; see also PricewaterhouseCoopers, *From Promise to Performance: Africa oil & gas review* (June 2013), at 6, available at https://www.pwc.com/en_NG/ng/pdf/pwc-africa-oil-and-gas-review.pdf.

21 See Demas, *op cit* (note 20 above).

22 See Ernst & Young, *Managing bribery and corruption risks in the oil and gas industry* (2014), at 7, available at www.ey.com/Publication/vwLUAssets/EY-Managing-bribery-and-corruption-risk-in-the-oil-and-gas-industry/$FILE/EY-Managing-bribery-and-corruption-risk-in-the-oil-and-gas-industry.pdf.

expect parent companies to implement effective control mechanisms over their foreign subsidiaries' activities in order adequately to detect, investigate or deter corrupt payments.[23]

2.3 Customs laws

The pressure to meet exploration, development and production timelines in the oil and gas industry also creates incentives for both companies and government officials to engage in bribery in relation to customs laws. For example, companies may have staff and equipment that are mobilised but unable to perform work until critical equipment can be cleared through customs. Understanding this pressure, customs officials often request processing fees to perform routine duties. Between 2007 and 2013, US enforcement officials settled with 12 companies, one freight forwarder and several of its customers, for a scheme involving the bribery of Nigerian Customs Service (NCS) officials.[24]

3. Anti-corruption enforcement efforts in sub-Saharan Africa's oil and gas sector

3.1 Domestic/local anti-corruption law enforcement

A detailed review of the domestic legal and enforcement regimes of each of the countries in sub-Saharan Africa is beyond the scope of this chapter. Companies facing potential corruption issues must, however, carefully weigh and be aware of both the general corruption enforcement environment and the potential impact of applicable local law on their in-country operations and transactions.

In this regard, several points are noteworthy. Most states in the region have enacted laws that prohibit, to one degree or another, the giving and receiving of domestic bribes. While not as common, foreign bribery is also prohibited in certain jurisdictions (eg, South Africa). In general, however, implementation and enforcement are still at a nascent stage, and there is often a perception that enforcement activity is hindered by a number of factors. These include:

- lack of resources for enforcement;
- conflict of interest among political decision-makers; and
- the exercise of political influence to hinder enforcement activity.

Certain jurisdictions have adopted national corruption commissions and are undertaking initiatives to address corruption, including in the oil and gas sector. In

---

23 Complaint, paragraphs 31-36, note 18 above. See also the following: Information at paragraphs 9-15, *US v Weatherford Int'l Ltd*, 4:13-cr-00733 (SD Tex 2013); Information at paragraph 31, *Securities & Exchange Commission v ENI, SpA and Snamprogetti Netherlands, BV*, 4:10-cv-02414 (SD Tex 2010).

24 See US DoJ press release, *Three Vetco International Ltd Subsidiaries Plead Guilty to Foreign Bribery and Agree to Pay $26 Million in Criminal Fines* (February 6 2007), available at www.justice.gov/opa/pr/2007/February/07_crm_075.html. See also the following: US DoJ press release, *Oil Services Companies and a Freight Forwarding Company Agree to Resolve Foreign Bribery Investigations and to Pay More Than $156 Million in Criminal Penalties* (November 4 2010), available at www.justice.gov/opa/pr/oil-services-companies-and-freight-forwarding-company-agree-resolve-foreign-bribery; US DoJ press release, *Parker Drilling Company Resolves FCPA Investigation and Agrees to Pay $11.76 Million Penalty* (April 16 2013), available at www.justice.gov/opa/pr/2013/April/13-crm-431.html.

southern Africa in particular, there has been growing attention to the widespread public outcry over potential corruption in the country's nascent energy sector. For example, on November 30 2014, the Tanzanian Parliament voted to dismiss senior officials of the Tanzanian government, including the Minister of Energy, in connection with allegations of corruption.[25]

Even in countries with a relatively developed anti-corruption law framework, the enforcement track record is either unclear or weak. South Africa, the only African country to have ratified the OECD Convention on Bribery, was recently chided by the OECD for a lax enforcement record. In its most recent report on South Africa's anti-corruption legal regime, the OECD noted that, since joining the convention in 2007 and establishing a "well-drafted" corruption law, the country had yet to prosecute a single case of foreign bribery.[26]

3.2 FCPA/UKBA: Lessons from enforcement in sub-Saharan Africa

Although several national governments and international organisations have established and implemented legal frameworks to combat corruption, rigorous enforcement of the FCPA has had the most significant effect on multinational oil and gas companies' approach to compliance in the region. Five of the 10 largest historical FCPA settlements are a result of enforcement actions against multinational oil and gas companies.[27] These enforcement actions have resulted in companies paying hundreds of millions of dollars in fines, and high-level executives, managers and other employees being held personally liable, including serving prison sentences. These are discussed in the case studies below.

By contrast, despite widespread anticipation, there has as yet been no UKBA enforcement in sub-Saharan Africa, and indeed no company has yet been successfully prosecuted by the UK Serious Fraud Office (SFO) under the UKBA. The SFO has, however, previously reached a settlement with an oil and gas company, MW Kellogg, on charges brought under a related pre-UKBA anti-corruption law, the Proceeds of Crime Act 2002. In addition, the SFO has announced a number of ongoing, large scale investigations of large corporations, including Rolls Royce, Barclays and biofuel company AgroEnergy plc. The long-term impact of the UKBA on anti-corruption compliance in sub-Saharan Africa remains to be seen. In the light of the SFO's apparent trajectory, its stated intentions with regard to foreign bribery prosecutions and the significant corruption issues in sub-Saharan Africa however, it is only a matter of time before the SFO brings a significant anti-corruption prosecution under the UKBA involving the region.

In the meantime, consideration of the enforcement history in several key FCPA actions is instructive with regard to the practical nature of anti-corruption compliance issues that arise in conducting business in sub-Saharan Africa.

---

25 See Kimberly Bennet, 'Tanzanian Parliament Votes on PM Resignation Amid Corruption Scandal' *The Jurist* (November 30, 2014), available at http://jurist.org/paperchase/2014/11/tanzania-parliament-votes-on-pm-resignation-amid-corruption-scandal.php

26 See OECD Working Group on Bribery, *Phase 3 Report on Implementing the OECD Anti-Bribery Convention in South Africa* (March 2014).

27 See Richard L Cassin, 'Alcoa Lands 5th on Our Top Ten List', *The FCPA Blog* (January 10 2014), available at www.fcpablog.com/blog/2014/1/10/alcoa-lands-5th-on-our-top-ten-list.html.

3.3 Facts of Key FCPA Enforcement Cases

(a) *The Vetco cases*

In early 2004, a group of private equity entities (the Acquirers) formed Vetco International Ltd (Vetco International) and through this new entity sought to acquire from ABB Ltd (ABB) several oil and gas companies and their subsidiaries, including ABB Vetco Gray Inc (Vetco US), ABB Vetco Gray UK Ltd (Vetco UK), Vetco Gray Controls Inc (Vetco Inc), and Vetco Controls Ltd (Vetco Ltd) (collectively, the Acquired Entities).[28] During the pre-acquisition due diligence, the Acquirers identified illegal bribery activity in Nigeria by some of the Acquired Entities related to the obtaining of contracts.[29] After a joint investigation into this matter, the Acquirers required ABB to disclose the conduct voluntarily to the US Department of Justice (DoJ) and requested that the DoJ should not take enforcement action against the Acquirers for FCPA violations prior to the acquisition.[30]

On July 6 2004 – prior to both the closing of the acquisition and the DoJ's response to the Acquirer's request for non-prosecution – the DoJ and SEC settled with ABB, Vetco US and Vetco UK for violations of the FCPA in Nigeria.[31] According to court documents, between 1998 and 2001, Vetco US and Vetco UK paid $1 million in bribes to officials of the National Petroleum Investment Management Services (NAPIMS), a Nigerian government agency that evaluates and approves bidders for contract work on oil exploration projects in Nigeria, in exchange for confidential bid information and favourable consideration for its bids by NAPIMS.[32] Vetco US and Vetco UK paid bribes directly to NAPIMS officials. Vetco UK also paid bribes through a Nigerian agent with whom it had a fraudulent consultancy agreement established to provide marketing and goodwill services.[33] The bribes comprised cash and gifts, such as country club memberships, cellphone bill payments and paid shopping excursions in the United States.[34]

On July 12 2004 – six days after the DoJ and SEC settlements – the DoJ responded to the Acquirers' request for non-prosecution in *FCPA Opinion Procedure Release* 2004-02 (the *Opinion Release*). In the *Opinion Release*, the DoJ stated its intent not to prosecute the Acquirers or Acquired Entities presently for violations that occurred prior to July 12 2004, provided that the Acquirers met certain terms and conditions. These included effectively instituting and implementing a compliance system, training, and other sufficient controls to deter and detect violations of the FCPA.[35] Despite the DoJ's requirements, four of the Acquired Entities settled with the DoJ

---

28 See Information, paragraphs 2-4, *US v Vetco Gray Controls Inc*, 4:07-cr-00004 (SD Tex 2007).

29 See US DoJ, *Opinion Procedure Release*, 04-02 (July 12 2004), available at www.justice.gov/criminal/fraud/fcpa/opinion/2004/0402.pdf.

30 *Ibid.*

31 See US DoJ press release, *ABB Vetco Gray Inc and ABB Vetco Gray UK Ltd Plead Guilty to Foreign Bribery Charges* (July 6 2004), available at www.justice.gov/archive/opa/pr/2004/July/04_crm_465.htm.

32 Information, paragraphs 3-37, *US v ABB Vetco Gray, Inc*, H-04-CR-279 (SD Tex 2004).

33 *Ibid.*

34 *Ibid.* Vetco US agreed to pay a criminal fine of $5.25 million to the DoJ. In addition, Vetco US and Vetco UK's parent company ABB agreed to pay the SEC $5.9 million in disgorgement of profits and a civil penalty of $10.5 million. See note 31 above.

35 *Ibid.*

and/or SEC between 2007 and 2008 for FCPA violations in Nigeria.

On February 6 2007, Vetco Inc, Vetco Ltd and Vetco UK (again) pleaded guilty to conspiracy to violate the bribery provisions of the FCPA.[36] According to court documents, from September 2002 to April 2005, the companies hired and authorised Panalpina Inc, a major international freight forwarding and customs clearing company, to make approximately $2.1 million in corrupt payments to NCS officials for preferential treatment in customs clearance and collection of tariffs and duties.[37] In calculating Vetco UK's penalty, the DoJ noted Vetco UK's prior guilty plea, prior DoJ directives in 2004 and the Acquirers' failure to comply with the *Opinion Release*.[38]

On February 6 2007, Aibel Group Ltd (Aibel), a subsidiary of Vetco UK, also entered into a Deferred Prosecution Agreement (DPA)[39] with the DoJ for the same underlying conduct, but was not required to pay a criminal or civil fine or to disgorge profits. On November 21 2008, however, Aibel admitted to non-compliance with its DPA and settled with the DoJ on the basis of the facts which the company had admitted in the 2007 DPA.[40] The DoJ noted that the case marked the third time an entity affiliated with Vetco International had pleaded guilty to violations of the FCPA and that the Acquirers had failed to follow the terms and conditions of the *Opinion Release*.[41]

(b) The Panalpina oil and gas industry sweep

On July 2 2007, in the wake of the 2007 Vetco settlements, the DoJ sent letters to 11 oil and gas companies, requesting information about their dealings with Panalpina Inc.[42] On November 4 2010, the DoJ and the SEC settled FCPA enforcement actions with Panalpina Inc and Panalpina World Transport (Holding) Ltd, a subsidiary of Panalpina Inc, (collectively, Panalpina) and six of Panalpina's customers: Pride International, Inc (Pride), Royal Dutch Shell plc and its subsidiary Shell Nigeria Exploration and Production Company Ltd (collectively, Shell), Transocean, Inc (Transocean), Tidewater Inc and its subsidiary Tidewater Marine International, Inc (collectively, Tidewater), Noble Corporation (Noble), and GlobalSantaFe Corp.[43] On April 16 2013, the DoJ and SEC settled with a seventh Panalpina customer, Parker Drilling Company (Parker).[44]

According to court documents, between 2002 and 2007, Panalpina offered an

---

36 See press release of February 6 2007 at note 24 above.

37 Information, paragraphs 31-32, *US v Vetco Gray Controls Inc*, 4:07-cr-00004-1 (SD Tex 2007). Vetco Inc, Vetco Limited and Vetco UK agreed to pay criminal fines of $6 million, $8 million and $12 million respectively. See press release of February 6 2007 at note 24 above.

38 See note 24 above.

39 A DPA postpones prosecution of an FCPA violation in exchange for any or all of the following: payment of a monetary penalty, co-operation with the government, compliance with remediation requirements and admission of relevant facts. See DoJ *Resource Guide*, note 4 above.

40 See US DoJ press release, *Aibel Group Ltd Pleads Guilty to Foreign Bribery and Agrees to Pay $4.2 Million in Criminal Fines* (November 21 2008), available at www.justice.gov/opa/pr/2008/November/08-crm-1041.html.

41 *Ibid.*

42 See Gibson and Dunn, *2010 Year-End FCPA Update* (January 3 2011), available at www.gibsondunn.com/publications/pages/2010Year-EndFCPAUpdate.aspx.

43 See press release of November 4 2010 at note 24 above; see also US Securities and Exchange Commission (SEC) press release, *SEC Charges Seven Oil Services and Freight Forwarding Companies for WIbidespread Bribery of Customs Officials*, available at www.sec.gov/news/press/2010/2010-214.htm.

44 See press release of April 16 2013 at note 24 above.

express courier service to its customers in Nigeria called Pancourier, through which Panalpina bribed NCS officials to circumvent certain time-intensive Nigerian customs laws, including required paperwork, inspection of products and customs fees.[45] In addition, Panalpina offered an express service for extensions of initial Nigerian temporary import permits, which were time-sensitive permits required to import high-value, specialised equipment into Nigerian waters.[46] Specifically, Panalpina bribed NCS officials to obtain permit extensions that were not permitted under Nigerian law in order to help its customers avoid the time and cost of removing the equipment from Nigerian waters.[47]

In addition to its actions in Nigeria, between 2006 and 2008, Panalpina paid approximately $4.5 million in bribes to Angolan customs officials through a similar scheme, to induce them to overlook incomplete or inaccurate documentation or to avoid customs duties or fines.[48] Panalpina also paid millions of dollars in bribes to Angolan government officials to secure contracts.[49]

Panalpina, Pride, Shell, Transocean, Tidewater and Parker entered into DPAs and agreed to criminal penalties with the DoJ.[50] These entities also settled with the SEC, together with Global SantaFe Corp.[51] Noble, Panalpina's other customer charged in the case, also settled with the DoJ and SEC.[52] Due, however, to Noble's "early voluntary disclosure, thorough self-investigation of the underlying conduct, full cooperation" and "extensive remedial measures," the DoJ imposed a non-prosecution agreement (NPA)[53] and Noble was subject to a fine substantially lower than those imposed on Panalpina's other customers.[54]

(c) *The Bonny Island Project*

In 1990, the Nigerian government collaborated with three international oil and gas companies to create a joint venture to develop a liquefied natural gas project on an island off the coast of Nigeria called Bonny Island (the Bonny Island Project).[55] In 1991, four companies, MW Kellogg Limited (Kellogg), Snamprogetti Netherlands BV (Snamprogetti), JGC Corporation (JGC), and Technip SA (Technip), formed a joint venture for the purposes of bidding on and performing engineering, procurement and construction (EPC) contracts for the Bonny Island Project.[56] Between 2009 and

---

45 Information, paragraphs 25-27, *US v Panalpina World Transport (Holding) Ltd*, note 18 above. Panalpina charged its customers a premium for the service and invoiced customers by recording bribes as "local processing fees", "interventions", "special handling" and "administration charges".

46 *Ibid* at paragraphs 32-36.

47 *Ibid*. Panalpina invoiced its customers for the bribe payments and characterised the payments as "TI interventions" or "TI recycling" costs.

48 *Ibid* at paragraphs 40-42.

49 *Ibid* at paragraphs 43-45. To generate cash for the bribes, Panalpina invoiced an Angolan government-controlled entity for a non-existent employee who was allegedly dedicated to working on the logistics for a particular project (ie, the 'ghost employee').

50 See press release of November 4 2010 at note 24 above.

51 *Ibld*.

52 *Ibid*.

53 An NPA is similar to a DPA, except that the DoJ does not file criminal charges but rather maintains this right in order to allow the company to demonstrate good conduct during the term of the DPA. See DoJ *Resource Guide* (note 4 above) at 75.

54 See press release of November 4 2010 at note 24 above.

55 Information, paragraph 14, *US v Kellogg Brown & Root LLC*, 09-00071 (SD Tex 2009).

2013, the DoJ and SEC settled with all joint venture partners, one consulting company and three individuals in respect of a bribery scheme to win a series of EPC contracts related to the Bonny Island Project.[57]

According to court documents, between 1995 and 2004, the joint venture paid or promised to pay Nigerian government officials, including those in the executive branch, in exchange for the award of four EPC contracts totalling $6 billion.[58] To carry out the bribery, the joint venture created a Portuguese-based 'special-purpose corporation' that entered into fraudulent consulting agreements with Marubeni Corporation (Marubeni), a Japanese trading company, for the payment of bribes to lower-level Nigerian government officials, and with Tri-Star Investments Ltd. (Tri-Star), a shell corporation run by Jeffery Tesler, for the payment of bribes to higher-level Nigerian government officials.[59]

Kellogg, Brown & Root LLC (KBR) (the successor company to Kellogg), Snamprogetti, JGC, Technip, and Marubeni entered into DPAs with the DoJ and agreed to pay criminal penalties. In addition, KBR and its former parent company Halliburton Company (Halliburton), Snamprogetti and its parent company ENI, SpA (ENI) and Technip settled with the SEC.[60] Three individuals also settled with FCPA enforcement officials: Albert 'Jack' Stanley, a former officer and director of KBR; Wojciech J Chodan, a former sales vice president of Kellogg; and Jeffery Tesler, a joint venture consultant with Tri-Star.[61] Stanley and Tesler were sentenced to 30 and 21 months in prison respectively, plus supervised release, and each was ordered to pay hundreds of millions of dollars in combined fines and restitution.[62] Chodan was sentenced to one year of unsupervised probation and ordered to pay hundreds of thousands of dollars in combined fines and restitution.[63]

---

56 *Ibid* at paragraph 4.

57 See US DoJ press release, *Former Officer and Director of Global Engineering and Construction Company Pleads Guilty to Foreign Bribery and Kickback Charges* (September 3 2008), available at www.justice.gov/opa/pr/2008/September/08-crm-772.html. See also the following: US DoJ press release, *Kellogg Brown & Root LLC Pleads Guilty to Foreign Bribery Charges and Agrees to Pay $402 Million Criminal Fine* (February 11 2009), available at www.justice.gov/opa/pr/2009/February/09-crm-112.html; US DoJ press release, *Technip S.A. Resolves Foreign Corrupt Practices Act Investigation and Agrees to Pay $240 Million Criminal Penalty* (June 28 2010), available at www.justice.gov/opa/pr/2010/June/10-crm-751.html; US DoJ press release, *Snamprogetti Netherlands BV Resolves Foreign Corrupt Practices Act Investigation and Agrees to Pay $240 Million Criminal Penalty* (July 7 2010), available at www.justice.gov/opa/pr/2010/July/10-crm-780.html; US DoJ press release, *UK Citizen Pleads Guilty to Conspiring to Bribe Nigerian Government Officials to Obtain Lucrative Contracts as Part of KBR Joint Venture Scheme* (December 6 2010), available at www.justice.gov/opa/pr/2010/December/10-crm-1391.html; US DoJ press release, *UK Solicitor Pleads Guilty for Role in Bribing Nigerian Government Officials as Part of KBR Joint Venture Scheme* (March 11 2011), available at www.justice.gov/opa/pr/2011/March/11-crm-313.html; US DoJ press release, *JGC Corporation Resolves Foreign Corrupt Practices Act Investigation and Agrees to Pay a $218.8 Million Criminal Penalty* (April 6 2011), available at www.justice.gov/opa/pr/2011/April/11-crm-431.html; US DoJ press release, *Marubeni Corporation Resolves Foreign Corrupt Practices Act Investigation and Agrees to Pay a $54.6 Million Criminal Penalty* (January 17 2012), available at www.justice.gov/opa/pr/2012/January/12-crm-060.html.

58 Information, paragraph15, note 55 above.

59 *Ibid,* at paragraphs 12-14.

60 See US SEC press release, *SEC Charges KBR and Halliburton for FCPA Violations* (February 11 2009), www.sec.gov/news/press/2009/2009-23.htm. See also the following: US SEC press release, *SEC Charges Italian Company and Dutch Subsidiary in Scheme Bribing Nigerian Officials With Carloads of Cash* (July 7 2010), available at www.sec.gov/news/press/2010/2010-119.htm; US SEC press release, *SEC Charges Technip with FCPA Violations* (June 28 2010), available at www.sec.gov/news/press/2010/2010-110.htm.

61 See press releases of September 3 2008, (December 6 2010 and (March 11 2011) at note 57 above.

62 See press releases of September 3 2008 and March 11 2011 at note 57 above.

63 See press release of December 6 2010 at note 57 above.

In addition, the UK SFO ordered Kellogg to pay a fine of $12 million.[64] "The SFO recognized that [Kellogg] took no part in the criminal activity that generated the funds", but pursued the case because the funds due to Kellogg were share dividends payable from profits and revenues generated by contracts obtained through bribery and corruption.[65] In commenting on the Kellogg case, the SFO noted that it demonstrated the range of tools that UK enforcement officials was prepared to use to prevent bribery.[66]

(d) *The EGGS Project*

In 2008 and 2013, the DoJ settled with the Willbros Group, Inc and Willbros International, Inc (collectively, Willbros) and Bilfinger SE (Bilfinger) respectively, for conspiring to make corrupt payments and falsifying books and records related to a project for the Eastern Gas Gathering System (EGGS) in Nigeria, a natural gas pipeline system operated through a joint venture between the Nigerian National Petroleum Corporation and two foreign oil companies.[67] According to court documents, Willbros and Bilfinger created a joint venture through which the companies' Nigerian-based subsidiaries made payments and promises to pay $6 million in bribes to Nigerian government officials between 2003 and 2007 in order to obtain a contract for the EGGS project.[68] To carry out the bribery scheme, Bilfinger and Willbros inflated their joint venture's bid for the EGGS contract by 3% and promised to pay Nigerian government officials the extra money if their joint venture won the contract.[69] The joint venture then submitted inflated invoices to the operator of the EGGS project and distributed 3% of the invoice payments to Nigerian government officials.[70]

Using fraudulent consultancy agreements, Willbros originally funnelled money to Nigerian government officials through two purported consultants operating consultancy companies in Nigeria.[71] A 2005 internal investigation at Willbros, however, revealed the illegal activity, and the company terminated the consultancy agreements.[72] Subsequently, certain individuals at Willbros were concerned that the failure to pay bribes to government officials would interrupt the company's Nigerian business.[73] These individuals orchestrated a series of internal and external company loans (including one from Bilfinger), extracted cash from a Willbros petty cash account in Nigeria and funnelled bribes indirectly to Nigerian officials through a

---

64 See note 26 above.
65 *Ibid.*
66 *Ibid.*
67 See US DoJ press release, *Willbros Group Inc. Enters Deferred Prosecution Agreement and Agrees to Pay $22 Million Penalty for FCPA Violations* (May 14 2008), available at www.justice.gov/opa/pr/2008/May/08-crm-417.html; see also US DoJ press release, *German Engineering Firm Bilfinger Resolves Foreign Corrupt Practices Act Charges and Agrees to Pay $32 Million Criminal Penalty* (December 11 2013) available at www.justice.gov/opa/pr/2013/December/13-crm-1297.html.
68 Information at paragraph 28, *US v Willbros Group, Inc,* 4:08-cr-00287 (SD Tex 2008).
69 *Ibid.*
70 *Ibid.*
71 *Ibid.*
72 *Ibid* at paragraph 32.
73 *Ibid* at paragraphs 32-36.

second consultant.[74] Bilfinger paid bribes using cash from the office safe at one of its Nigerian-based subsidiaries.[75]

Willbros and Bilfinger each paid criminal fines and entered into DPAs with the DoJ, and Willbros also settled with the SEC.[76] The DoJ also filed charges against three former Willbros executives – Jim Bob Brown, Jason Steph and James Tillery – and a former Willbros consultant, Paul Novak.[77] Brown and Steph were sentenced to serve 12 and 15 months in prison respectively, and ordered to pay thousands of dollars in criminal fines.[78] Novak was sentenced to over one year in prison and ordered to pay a criminal fine of $1 million.[79] In connection with the DoJ investigation, the SEC also settled with Brown, Steph, and two former, less senior Willbros managers.[80] Tillery remains a fugitive and has never been tried.[81]

(e) *Weatherford*

On November 26 2013, the DoJ and SEC settled with Weatherford International Ltd and its wholly-owned subsidiary, Weatherford Services Ltd (collectively, Weatherford) for FCPA violations in Angola and the Middle East.[82] According to court documents, Weatherford engaged in two bribery schemes in Angola between 2004 and 2008 to bribe Sociedade Nacional de Combustiveis de Angola, EP (Sonangol), a government-owned and controlled corporation with the sole right to explore, produce, manufacture, transport and market oil and gas in Angola.[83]

Under the first scheme, Weatherford established and operated a joint venture with two local entities controlled by Sonangol officials and their relatives and funnelled hundreds of thousands of dollars in payments to the officials and their relatives in exchange for lucrative contracts and inside information about competitors' pricing.[84] Despite indications of red flags and advice received from

---

74 *Ibid.*

75 Information, paragraph 21, *US v Bilfinger SE*, 13-cr-00745 (SD Tex 2013).

76 See press releases of May 14 2008 and (December 11 2013 at note 67 above.

77 See US DoJ press release, *Former Executive of Willbros Subsidiary Pleads Guilty to Conspiring to Bribe Foreign Officials in Nigeria and Ecuador* (September 14 2006), available at www.justice.gov/opa/pr/2006/September/06_crm_621.html. See also the following: US DoJ press release, *Former Executive of Willbros SubsIbidiary Pleads Guilty to Conspiring to Bribe Nigerian Government Officials* (November 5 2007), available at www.justice.gov/opa/pr/2007/November/07_crm_885.html; US DoJ press release, *Former Willbros International Executive and Consultant Charged in $6 Million Foreign Bribery Conspiracy* (December 19 2008), available at www.justice.gov/opa/pr/2008/December/08-crm-1137.html; US DoJ press release, *Former Willbros International Consultant Pleads Guilty to $6 Million Foreign Bribery Scheme* (November 12 2009), available at www.justice.gov/opa/pr/2009/November/09-crm-1220.html.

78 See *US v Jim Bob Brown*, 4:06-cr-00316-1 (SD Tex 2006), available at http://shearman.symplicity.com/?mode=form&Ibid=187 (last visited August 27 2014); see also *US v Jason Edward Steph*, 4:07-cr-00307-1 (SD Tex 2007), available at http://shearman.symplicity.com/?mode=form&Ibid=189 (last visited August 27 2014).

79 See *US v James K Tillery and Paul G Novak*, 4:08-cr-00022-1 (SD Tex 2008), available at http://shearman.symplicity.com/?mode=form&Ibid=185 (last visited August 27 2014).

80 See note 77 above.

81 See US DoJ press release, *Former Consultant for Willbros International Sentenced in Connection with Foreign Bribery Scheme* (May 3 2013), available at www.justice.gov/opa/pr/former-consultant-willbros-international-sentenced-connection-foreign-bribery-scheme.

82 See US DoJ press release, *Three Subsidiaries of Weatherford International Limited Agree to Plead Guilty to FCPA and Export Control Violations* (November 26 2013), available at www.justice.gov/opa/pr/2013/November/13-crm-1260.html.

83 Information, paragraphs 13-40, *US v Weatherford Services*, 4:13-cr-00734 (SD Tex 2013).

84 *Ibid.*

outside counsel to identify the beneficial owners of the joint venture, Weatherford did not conduct any meaningful due diligence before signing the final agreement with Sonangol.[85] In the second scheme, Weatherford bribed an Angolan official to renew Weatherford's oil and gas contracts.[86] Specifically, Weatherford entered into a fake consultancy agreement with a freight forwarding agent and then generated fraudulent purchase orders for services the freight forwarding agent never performed.[87] In turn, the freight forwarding agent generated fraudulent invoices and, when paid, passed at least some of the money on to the foreign official authorised to renew Weatherford's contracts.[88]

3.4 Impact of FCPA and UKBA enforcement actions

The cases outlined above support the following observations about conducting business in the oil and gas industry in sub-Saharan Africa.

- *The oil and gas industry in sub-Saharan Africa is at high risk for corruption.* In the Bonny Island cases, Stanley, Chodan, and Tesler admitted in their plea agreements that although they knew that it was unlawful to bribe foreign officials, they believed that support of Nigerian government officials, including top-level executive branch officials and high-level petroleum ministry officials, was necessary to win the Bonny Island Project EPC contracts.[89] In addition, Weatherford's original consultancy agreement with its Angolan freight forwarding agent included an FCPA clause prohibiting the freight forwarding agent from giving anything of value, directly or indirectly, to an official or employee of any government.[90] The freight forwarding agent rejected the FCPA clause, however, stating that "in view of the nature of the business I cannot accept the original wording."[91]
- *Enforcement officials expect companies to establish, implement, and maintain an effective compliance programme that is commensurate with that risk.* In the Weatherford case, the DoJ specifically noted that the company operated in an industry with a "substantial risk profile", yet failed to establish internal controls in areas such as third-party due diligence, anti-corruption risk management, and gifts, travel and entertainment.[92] The DoJ noted that prior to 2008, Weatherford did not have a dedicated compliance officer or compliance personnel. Furthermore, the company failed to translate its anti-corruption policy into any language other than English.[93] This scrutiny of compliance efforts, and the adequacy of compliance resources, can also be

---

85 *Ibid.*
86 *Ibid* at paragraphs 41-46.
87 *Ibid.*
88 *Ibid.*
89 See Plea Agreement at paragraph 18.c, *US v Albert Jackson Stanley*, 4:08-cr-00597 (SD Tex 2008). See also the following: Plea Agreement at paragraph 18.c, *US v Wojciech J Chodan*, 4:09-cr-00098 (SD Tex 2010); Plea Agreement at paragraph 18.c, *US v Jeffrey Tesler*, 4:09-cr-00098 (SD Tex 2011).
90 Information, paragraph 45, *US v Weatherford Services*, note 83 above.
91 *Ibid.* Weatherford acquiesced by removing the FCPA clause and inserting one requiring the freight forwarding agent to "comply with all applicable laws, rules, and regulations issued by any governmental entity in the countries of business involved".
92 Information, paragraph 9, *US v Weatherford Int'l Ltd*, 4:13-cr-00733 (SD Tex 2013).
93 *Ibid* at paragraphs 10-15.

expected under the UKBA – under which 'failure to prevent' bribery is an offence.

- *The FCPA poses serious monetary risks for companies.* In 2007, the fines imposed on the Vetco entities were unprecedentedly high. The joint venture partners in the Bonny Island cases agreed to fines that rank among the top ten highest FCPA fines ever (KBR at number 2; Snamprogetti at number 6; Technip at number 7; and JGC at number 8), with KBR's fine being the largest ever imposed on a US company.[94]

The cases outlined above also support the following general observations about the impact of the FCPA enforcement actions worldwide.

- *Companies must be aware of competitors' activities that may signal industry-wide risks.* In commenting on the Panalpina cases, the SEC stated that the investigations were triggered "after detecting widespread corruption in the oil services industry" (ie, the Vetco cases) and added that the agencies would "continue to focus on industrywide sweeps, and no industry is immune from investigation."[95]
- *The FCPA has a broad jurisdictional reach.* In the 2004 Vetco UK case, jurisdiction was based on the theory that a Vetco US employee acted as an agent for Vetco UK.[96] The SEC reached Panalpina by charging that it aided and abetted and acted as an agent of its US-issuer customers, even though Panalpina itself was not an issuer.[97] Historically, non-US companies have been the subject of more FCPA enforcement actions than US companies.
- *Non-US citizen employees will be held liable for violations of the FCPA.* The US extradited Chodan and Tesler from the United Kingdom to prosecute them in the Bonny Island cases.[98]
- *Parent companies must ensure that their subsidiaries are implementing policies and procedures.* In the Panalpina cases, the SEC alleged that Halliburton and ENI did not ensure that KBR and Snamprogetti implemented agent policies and procedures.[99] With regard to Halliburton, the SEC alleged that it conducted insufficient due diligence on Tesler because, firstly, it never identified the beneficial owners of Tri-Star; secondly, it did not seek to determine how Tesler would carry out his duties; and thirdly, it did not check all Tesler's references, some of which were false.[100]
- *Due diligence procedures for agents must go beyond a basic questionnaire.* In the SEC complaint against Technip, the SEC alleged that Technip failed to conduct sufficient due diligence on agents because it only required that its agents should complete a written questionnaire seeking minimal background

94 See note 24 above.
95 See press release of November 4 2010 at note 24 above.
96 Information, paragraph 39, note 32 above.
97 Complaint, paragraph 9, *Securities & Exchange Commission v Panalpina, Inc*, 4:10-cv-4334 (SD Tex 2010).
98 See press releases of December 6 2010 and March 11 2011 at note 7 above.
99 Complaint, paragraphs 30-36, note 18 above; Complaint, paragraph 31, *SEC v ENI, SpA and Snamprogetti Netherlands BV*, 10-cv-2414 (SD Tex 2010).
100 Complaint, paragraphs 30-36, note 18 above.

information and did not require additional procedures, such as conducting an interview or background check and following up on responses to the written questionnaire.[101] A Technip senior executive admitted that Technip's due diligence procedures were a perfunctory exercise, conducted so that Technip would have some documentation showing purported due diligence.[102]

- *FCPA enforcement officials will prosecute companies that do not comply with DPAs.* The Vetco-Aibel case marked the first time the DoJ declared a breach of an FCPA DPA and prosecuted a company on the basis of the facts admitted in the earlier agreement. Prosecution of companies for non-compliance with a DPA is particularly relevant in the merger and acquisition context when companies are assessing the risk of a proposed transaction and negotiating transaction documents.
- *FCPA enforcement officials give meaningful credit to companies for voluntary disclosure and transparency.* For example, after learning of the Panalpina investigation, Noble discovered the improper payments through an internal investigation of its operations in Nigeria and voluntarily informed the DoJ of its investigation and findings.[103] Noble received a NPA as opposed to a DPA and received a penalty well below the low end of the US Sentencing Guidelines.

4. Anti-corruption conventions and protocols

In addition to the FCPA and the UKBA, the international community has also instituted measures to combat corruption in sub-Saharan Africa. When the FCPA first passed into law in 1977, US companies felt disadvantaged by its stringent provisions and feared losing business.[104] Shortly thereafter, the US government started lobbying for an international anti-corruption agreement to level the playing field.[105] It started by engaging in negotiations within the United Nations and then turned its attention to the Organisation of Economic Co-operation and Development (OECD).[106] Given the FCPA's advantageous terms to non-US companies, however, the United States struggled to negotiate an international agreement comparable to the FCPA until 1999, when the OECD finally agreed to the Convention on Combating Bribery of Foreign Public Officials in International Business Transactions.[107] In 2003, the United Nations and the African Union each agreed to an anti-corruption convention and, in addition, regional communities started to adopt anti-corruption protocols.

---

101 Complaint, paragraphs 30-31, *SEC v Technip SA*, 10-cv-02289 (SD Tex 2010).

102 *Ibid.*

103 See press release of November 4 2010 at note 24 above.

104 Jan Outers, Cedric Ryngaert & Ann Sofie Cloots, 'The International Legal Framework against Corruption', (2013) 14 *Melbourne J of Int'l L* 205 at 209. Reports varied in their estimates of how much business was lost annually to non-US companies because of the FCPA, with estimates of up to $45 billion in 1995. See Margo Cleveland *et al*, 'Trends in the International Fight against Bribery and Corruption', 90 *J of Int'l Ethics* 199 at 205 (2009).

105 Outers, Ryngaert & Cloots, *op cit* (note 104 above).

106 *Ibid.*

107 The OECD Convention on Combating Bribery of Foreign Public Officials in International Business Transactions came into effect in early 1999.

4.1 OECD anti-corruption convention

The OECD Convention on Combating Bribery of Foreign Public Officials in International Business Transactions, often called the OECD Anti-Bribery Convention (ABC), entered into force in 1999. The ABC was the first legally binding global instrument to prohibit the bribery of foreign public officials and became the driving force behind most international anti-corruption initiatives. All 34 OECD member states and seven non-member states have ratified the ABC, including one sub-Saharan African country, South Africa.

The ABC strongly resembles the FCPA and generally requires member countries to criminalise the bribery of foreign public officials, including authorisation and aiding and abetting of such bribery. The ABC obliges member countries to investigate and, where appropriate, prosecute those who offer, promise or pay bribes to foreign public officials, as well as to impose heavy penalties. The OECD Working Group on Bribery in International Business Transactions is responsible for monitoring implementation of the ABC. Each member state periodically undergoes a rigorous peer review that includes an in-depth assessment of the state's domestic anti-bribery laws and their implementation and enforcement.

4.2 United Nations Convention Against Corruption

The United Nations Convention Against Corruption (UNCAC), which entered into force in December 2005, is the first global anti-corruption framework aimed at creating universal standards. In all, 171 countries have signed the UNCAC, including most sub-Saharan African states, with the exception of Chad, Equatorial Guinea, Eritrea, Somalia, Sudan and South Sudan.

Like the ABC, the UNCAC requires its signatories to criminalise bribery but goes much farther in both scope and specificity. Unlike the ABC's focus on supply-side bribery of public officials, the UNCAC definition of bribery includes both the giving and receiving of bribes in the public and private sectors. The UNCAC's private sector provisions are similar to those of the FCPA in establishing recordkeeping and internal controls standards, while also promoting corporate codes of conduct, compliance programmes and best practices for companies.[108] The UNCAC also deals with several preventative measures, including adopting policies to prevent corruption, designating a body to co-ordinate and oversee the implementation of policies, establishing appropriate procurement systems, using both the civil and the criminal law to facilitate the recovery of state assets, and developing enhanced accounting and auditing standards for the private sector. In 2009, the UNCAC also adopted a review mechanism that consists of peer review and country visits if necessary. Finally, UNCAC's international co-operation chapter, which is largely self-executing, establishes mandatory extradition obligations where there is dual criminality,[109] as

108 Lucinda Low, *The United Nations Convention Against Corruption: The Globalization of Anticorruption Standards*, Remarks at the Annual International Bar Association Conference: The Awakening Giant of Anti-Corruption Enforcement (May 4-5 2006), available at www.steptoe.com/assets/attachments/2599.pdf.

109 Dual criminality applies to an offence that is a crime in both the country requesting extradition as well as the country receiving the extradition request.

well as guidelines for providing mutual legal assistance or transferring criminal proceedings "in the interests of the proper administration of justice".

4.3 African Union Convention on Preventing and Combating Corruption

In 2003, African heads of state adopted the African Union Convention on Preventing and Combating Corruption (AUCPCC). The AUCPCC, which came into force in August 2006, provides wide-ranging mandatory measures, including provisions on corruption prevention and criminalisation, regional co-operation, asset recovery, transparency of political fundraising, and commercial corruption. The AUCPCC does not, however, require sanctions or liability for legal persons. The AUCPCC established the African Union Advisory Board on Corruption to monitor implementation of the convention's requirements, but thus far the Board has focused on establishing its own organisational structure, while its strategic plan indicates that it will take an additional year to build its organisational efficiency. The Board's monitoring mechanism is not expected to be as rigorous as that of the ABC.

As the most comprehensive African-based regional anti-corruption convention, the AUCPCC signifies the consensus of African states in the areas of prevention and criminalisation of corruption and harmonises these states' anti-corruption measures with the objective of strengthening African development. Of the 54 member states in the African Union, 35 have ratified the AUCPCC.

4.4 African regional community anti-corruption protocols

The Southern African Development Community[110] Protocol against Corruption (the SADC Protocol), which entered into force in 2003, establishes five categories of obligation in order to promote and harmonise anti-corruption efforts at the national level:

- preventative measures (eg, codes of conduct for public officials and procurement transparency);
- criminalisation of bribery;
- anti-money laundering measures;
- co-operation; and
- implementation of anti-corruption efforts.

The SADC Protocol, however, lacks an efficient implementation mechanism.[111] Of the 15 SADC member states, 13 have ratified the SADC Protocol.

The Economic Community of West African States Protocol Against Corruption (the ECOWAS Protocol), which is similar to the SADC Protocol, provides for a wide range of preventative measures. Only Ghana has ratified the ECOWAS Protocol, however, and it has not yet entered into force.

Finally, the East African Community (EAC), which comprises Uganda, Tanzania, Rwanda and Burundi, has drafted the Protocol on Preventing and Combating

110 The SADC comprises Angola, Botswana, Democratic Republic of Congo, Lesotho, Madagascar, Malawi, Mauritius, Mozambique, Namibia, Seychelles, South Africa, Swaziland, Tanzania, Zambia and Zimbabwe.

111 Outers, Ryngaert & Cloots, *op cit* (note 104 above) at 231.

Corruption. Differences among the EAC member states on whether to give prosecutorial powers to their respective anti-corruption agencies have, however, hampered the signing of the convention.[112]

4.5 Impact of anti-corruption conventions and protocols

Given the relatively recent implementation of anti-corruption conventions and protocols in sub-Saharan Africa, the impact of these anti-corruption initiatives remains to be seen. However, the authors offer a few observations on the current and potential impact of the anti-corruption conventions and protocols previously discussed.

- Despite almost no participation by African states, the ABC is relevant for multinational oil and gas companies operating in sub-Saharan Africa, because state parties to the ABC, including several OECD member states and Russia, are home to several large multinational oil and gas companies.
- According to Transparency International, the implementation of the UNCAC is a "promising but uneven start with room for improvement in a number of areas".[113] It notes several specific areas of concern for UNCAC implementation: firstly, establishing a follow-up process to address member states' implementation of the recommendations made in country reports; secondly, speeding up the review process; thirdly, increasing transparency by publishing more of the country reports from the review process; and fourthly, providing technical assistance to governments of member states.[114]
- Along with the UNCAC, the AUCPCC has the potential to have the greatest impact on the African content. The implementation of comprehensive and strong national anti-corruption laws across Africa is, however, still nascent.
- The collective resources of the United Nations and the African Union in implementing, enforcing, and harmonising anti-corruption measures may prove more beneficial for the African continent than the SADC, ECOWAS and EAC regional protocols. Regional alliances have, however, historically proved to be more effective in Africa, such as in the economic context.

4.6 Other international developments: the World Bank and the IMF

In the midst of the United States' efforts to negotiate an international anti-corruption agreement, the World Bank in the early 1990s became aware of the fact that a "substantial part of its loans were diverted through corrupt practices".[115] Historically, despite its influence in the world of politics and economic relations, the World Bank had not engaged in anti-corruption initiatives because it believed that anti-corruption constituted a policy issue beyond the scope of its charter.[116] In 1996,

---

112 Fred Oluoch, 'Regional agencies seek more powers to fight corruption', *The East African*, June 28 2014, available at www.theeastafrican.co.ke/news/Regional-agencies-seek-more-powers-to-fight-corruption/-/2558/2364780/-/dbp3te/-/index.html.

113 See Transparency International, *United Nations Convention Against Corruption: Progress Report 2013* at 4, available at www.transparency.org/whatwedo/pub/un_convention_against_corruption_progress_report_2013.

114 *Ibid.*

115 Outers, Ryngaert & Cloots, *op cit* (note 104 above) at 213

however, the World Bank declared corruption a "cancer" and deployed a number of administrative instruments to combat fraud and corruption.[117]

In 2007, the World Bank adopted a new strategy to combat corruption on the basis of three pillars.[118] Firstly, the World Bank supports initiatives to help countries strengthen their governance, including initiatives in effectiveness, transparency and accountability.[119] Secondly, the World Bank aims to improve the impact of its own development funds by improving the integrity of its own projects.[120] Thirdly, the World Bank works with other international actors to co-ordinate and harmonise approaches in countries where governance poses a significant challenge for development.[121]

One key feature of the World Bank's administrative instruments has been its suspension and debarment system. Under this system, the World Bank has imposed 239 suspensions and sanctioned 224 firms or individuals as of June 30 2013.[122] Two-thirds of the bank's reported sanctions decisions affect just five sectors – health care, transportation, agriculture, water and energy.[123] Geographically, the suspended entities have had projects spanning the globe, though the World Bank has homed in on Africa, which has been the subject of one-third of the total number of investigations conducted by the bank.[124] Finally, although the World Bank's public statements focus on bribery and other forms of corruption, the vast majority of its sanctions cases to date have involved various types of low-level fraud that are easier to prove, such as forgery or misrepresentations in bidding documents.[125]

Like the World Bank, the IMF originally perceived governance issues as being outside of its economic goals and hesitated in pursuing anti-corruption initiatives.[126] Between 1996 and 1997, however, "the IMF acknowledged the economic impact of corruption…and followed the World Bank" in incorporating good governance into its standards and practices.[127] The IMF issued a formal Transparency Policy and launched other efforts, such as its Standards and Codes Initiative, to promote anti-corruption efforts. The IMF also utilises conditionality provisions in its aid agreements.

The historically high volume of international development funds flowing into high-risk sectors in sub-Saharan Africa have made the World Bank and IMF powerful advocates in the fight against corruption in the region. The direct impact of World

---

116 *Ibid.*

117 *Ibid,* at 214.

118 See *The World Bank's Sanctions System: Tackling Corruption Through a Two-Tier Administrative Sanctions Process,* http://go.worldbank.org/EB6JXKU4Z0 (last updated November 24 2014).

119 *Ibid.*

120 *Ibid.*

121 *Ibid.*

122 See World Bank Office of Suspension and Debarment, *Report on Functions, Data and Lessons Learned 2007-2013* (2014) at 15, available at http://siteresources.worldbank.org/EXTOFFEVASUS/Resources/OSDReport.pdf.

123 See *Freshfields Bruckhaus Deringer, World Bank sanctions investigations: blacklist revisited* (August 2013) available at www.freshfields.com/uploadedFiles/SiteWide/Knowledge/World%20Bank%20sanctions%20-%20blacklist%20revisted.pdf.

124 *Ibid.*

125 See World Bank Office of Suspension and Debarment report (note 122 above) at 29.

126 Outers, Ryngaert & Cloots, *op cit* (note 104 above) at 214.

127 *Ibid.*

Bank and IMF initiatives is difficult to measure. These two organisations have, however, undoubtedly helped to reshape the global anti-corruption discourse through their unique and influential position in world politics and economics.

5. Conclusion

Although the level of corruption in sub-Saharan Africa has dropped somewhat in the past decade, corruption remains a major business challenge and poses legal, commercial and reputational risks for multinational oil and gas companies operating in the region.[128] Although FCPA and UKBA enforcement actions have incentivised many multinational companies to change their behaviour in operating in sub-Saharan Africa, it is clear that these enforcement actions are not enough. Eliminating corruption will require a continued effort by the international community through the regional and international anti-corruption initiatives described above. In particular, efforts by the member states of organisations in sub-Saharan Africa and major economic players in the region other than the United States, such as China, will be necessary. As the international community continues to develop and implement anti-corruption initiatives, companies must continue to evolve their understanding of compliance requirements and adapt their controls to the particular risks, business practices and challenges arising in the region.

128 On October 27 2014, the SEC "charged a global water management, construction, and drilling company headquartered in Texas with violating the Foreign Corrupt Practices Act (FCPA) by making improper payments to foreign officials in several African countries in order to obtain beneficial treatment and reduce its tax liability.... According to the SEC's order instituting settled administrative proceedings, Layne's misconduct occurred from 2005 to 2010. In addition to favourable tax treatment, the improper payments helped the company obtain customs clearance, work permits and relief from inspections by immigration and labour officials in various African countries." See US SEC press release, *SEC Charges Texas-Based Layne Christensen Company With FCPA Violations* (October 27 2014), available at www.sec.gov/News/PressRelease/Detail/PressRelease/1370543291857. See also note 16 above.

Financing of oil and gas operations in Africa

Bruce Johnston
Morgan, Lewis & Bockius UK LLP

1. Introduction

Had it been written a few years ago, this chapter would have been very different. The emphasis would have been on west Africa, on sales of oil and liquefied natural gas (LNG) to the United States and Europe, and on international oil companies and smaller companies. The emphasis then was on financing using the equity raised by international oil companies (IOCs), carry finance for the national oil companies (NOCs), and reserve base lending for the smaller operators.

Now, with the increased use of shale oil and gas in the United States, and the likelihood of increased exports of oil and gas from that country, the financing of oil and gas operations in Africa has changed significantly. Significant discoveries of oil and gas in east Africa have also lead to many changes.

This chapter does not deal with the financing of downstream operations in oil and gas, or the financing of oil trading (for example, letters of credit or forfaiting). The basic theme of this chapter is that commercial (ie, non-financing) decisions made early in an oil or gas project in Africa often preclude certain types of financing at later stages. Decisions about contracts, insurance, procurement strategy, risk transfer etc will usually mean that a full range of financing options is not available. This is often because decisions about financing are not made at the start of the oil or gas project.

The purpose of this chapter is therefore to examine the financing options for upstream oil and gas, LNG projects and oil and gas pipelines in Africa, and to set out the criteria for the availability of such finance. Only then can developers of oil and gas projects in Africa ask, at the start of a project, "from where will the project get its funding?" and use the answers to structure the project properly in order to enable the funding to be raised.

2. Upstream

Traditionally, the financing of upstream oil and gas can be summarised as follows:

- exploration for oil and gas is financed from equity;
- once oil or gas is discovered, the development of the oil or gas field is financed using reserve base lending from banks; and
- the production of oil or gas is financed using project finance from banks (or otherwise from projected cash flow).

Since 2008, increased regulation of banks (including under Basel III[1]) has meant that fewer banks are willing to lend to oil or gas projects in Africa, and long-term lending is less freely available. This has resulted in more finance coming from private equity and from non-bank lenders, and more trade-based lending.

Recent growth in African economies has also meant increased interest from investors in both debt and equity for African projects (not only oil and gas). As a result, there are many new investors, including many Africa focused debt and equity funds.

2.1 Gas versus oil

There are fundamental differences between financing oil projects and financing gas projects. These may be summarised as follows.

- There is a deep and liquid market in oil, both on a spot and a forward basis. By contrast, there is no international market for African gas, except in the form of LNG.
- Gas requires large expenditure to monetise it. There need to be pipelines or liquefaction facilities. Without such facilities, the gas may be worthless. For example, much of the associated gas in Nigeria is flared rather than exported or used in the domestic market.
- Domestic use of oil or gas reduces the need for large expenditure and infrastructure (though oil does need a refinery), but there are two associated difficulties. Firstly, domestic use often means that the purchase price of the oil or gas is significantly less than the international market price. Secondly, local currency is often used to pay for the domestic oil or gas, resulting in a currency mismatch between the revenue and the debt service (which is usually in US dollars).

2.2 Equity

The exploration phase in an oil and gas project is the most risky. The risk/reward ratio therefore needs to be the highest. Equity is the most appropriate tool for financing the exploration phase.

Equity is also more expensive than debt (but see 2.3 below) and operates to dilute the ownership of the sponsors.

The traditional model is distorted because the big IOCs can raise equity from the stock markets more cheaply than an oil project can raise debt. The IOCs therefore have a strong preference to finance oil and gas projects in Africa using equity rather than debt.

Despite this, taxation systems in many countries operate so that interest is tax deductible but dividends are not. This often means that there is debt financing of oil or gas projects in Africa which, in economic terms, is really an equity financing.

(a) Private placement

Many startup exploration companies will raise finance by issuing shares on a private placement basis. This involves the issue of shares to the management of the startup

---

1 See www.bis.org/bcbs/basel3.htm.

exploration company, to friends and family, to investors in previous businesses connected with the management, and to specialist private equity funds and family offices. Although there is no prospectus, there needs to be documentation, such as a shareholders' agreement, subscription agreement and other usual documents associated with a private placement. It should be noted that this is different from the private placement market in the United States, in which insurance companies and pension funds are the traditional investors.

(b) ***Private equity***

Private equity funds and sovereign wealth funds are increasingly looking at investments in Africa. Oil and gas projects with proven reserves are ideal targets for private equity.

There will need to be all the usual documentation associated with a private equity investment, including shareholders' agreements containing such features as 'tagalong', 'dragalong', 'ratchets', provisions dealing with management, and a plan for the 'exit'.

(c) ***Stock exchange***

Most of the large IOCs are listed on one or more of the major stock exchanges. They can raise debt and equity on those stock exchanges relatively inexpensively.

Stock exchanges are also a source of finance for smaller oil and gas companies in the exploration, development and production phases. It is relatively rare for a company that is still exploring for oil to be listed on the stock exchange. The rules of some exchanges (such as Perth, Vancouver and Toronto), however, attempt to attract and accommodate exploration companies, and these exchanges have a few examples of companies with only exploration assets.

More commonly, oil and gas companies will list on a stock exchange either in London (AIM), Toronto (TSX) or the Australian Stock Exchange (ASX) when they can demonstrate proven reserves and/or production. The initial public offer (IPO) serves two purposes. Firstly, it is a means for the initial investors to exit (ie, sell) their investment. Secondly, the process is often used as a method of raising additional financing.

An IPO is, however, a time-consuming and expensive mechanism. There is a need for the company to meet certain standards of corporate governance and to prepare a prospectus. Ongoing compliance with the listing rules, together with investor relations, are also onerous for a small company.

(d) ***Joint ventures***

The most common means of financing an oil and gas project in Africa is a joint venture (JV) with a larger company, such as an IOC. Such JVs are undertaken by smaller exploration and production (E&P) companies or by NOCs.

In those JVs, the IOC would provide both financing and expertise, in return for an equity investment requiring the IOC to fund and perform drilling obligations. This is known as a farmout.

2.3 Debt

Debt is an important feature of all oil and gas projects. Because of its risk/return nature, however, it may be inappropriate to the exploration phase of African oil or gas projects. In addition, debt raised with recourse to the oil or gas project only will be expensive when compared to the financing that can be raised by an IOC. As a result, many oil and gas projects do not have project-specific debt financing.

There are, however, many significant benefits of external debt finance, which include the following:

- the leverage associated with debt finance can enhance the return on equity. Debt finance is usually cheaper than equity finance;
- the discipline that comes with debt finance often means that the project assumes a lower risk profile; and
- the involvement of major banks, development finance institutions or export credit agencies may encourage governments not to interfere in the oil or gas project.

(a) Project finance

Project finance usually has the following features.

- The lenders' primary recourse is to the cash flow of the oil or gas project, rather than project assets or the assets of the project's equity investors. There is usually some form of recourse to the equity investor (ie, 'limited recourse').
- Once the oil or gas project is operational, its revenues are used to:
  - pay the cost of operating and maintaining the project;
  - pay principal and interest to the lenders; and
  - pay distributions to the equity investors.

- There is a high debt/equity ratio.
- The borrower is a special purpose vehicle (SPV) with no assets other than the oil or gas project. At the time that the money is lent (ie, before the oil or gas project is built), those assets will predominantly be project contracts.
- The equity investors may include the operator and/or offtaker for the project. Despite some inherent conflicts of interest, there is a unified interest that reduces contractual disputes.

(b) Reserve based lending

Reserve based lending (RBL) involves loans made against the net present value of future cash flows projected to be generated from certain identified oil or gas reserves. RBL in Africa tends to be limited to oil reserves which can be exported to the international markets (ie, the oil can be valued in US dollars using international market prices).

RBL uses a borrowing base that is calculated to determine the maximum amount that can be lent under the loan facility. It is calculated with a formula that uses the proved and probable reserves of oil and then applies the net present value to the cash flow likely to be generated from such oil reserves. The reserves figures are taken from an independent reserves report, with six-monthly updates.

As the borrowing base will fluctuate with changes in crude oil prices, it is common for the borrower to hedge oil prices, so that the borrowing base remains more stable and subject only to changes in interest rates, oil reserves, and operating and capital expenditure.

(c) ***Carry loans***

As mentioned at 2.2(d) above, many oil and gas projects in Africa are financed by the IOCs. Such financing often takes the form of a carry loan. In law, this is a debt, but commercially it is equivalent to equity. The usual terms require that the loan is only repaid from the cash flow of the project and, if there is insufficient or no cash flow, there is only repayment of principal or interest in part (or not at all). The borrower may be one of the JV participants or the JV company itself.

(d) ***Corporate loans and bonds***

Because of the creditworthiness of the large oil and gas companies, they are able to borrow money using their corporate balance sheet in a cheaper manner than an oil and gas project in Africa could borrow money. As a result, the typical joint operating agreement (JOA) structure often involves a large oil company financing its share of the E&P costs through a general issue of corporate bonds.

Some African projects will be able to use a structure similar to the 2004 bond issue for TengizChevroil (a company with an existing oil production), which raised money to fund the second phase of development. There were four major shareholders: ExxonMobil, Chevron, Lukoil and KazMunaiGaz. Both ExxonMobil and Chevron wanted to finance their share of the second phase by making loans to the company. Lukoil and KazMunaiGaz did not want to finance their share. TengizChevroil issued bonds in the international finance markets to raise money equal to the Lukoil and KazMunaiGaz shares of the development. Chevron purchased bonds from TengizChevroil to finance its share of the development (on the same terms as the bonds issued to the international finance markets). ExxonMobil lent money to TengizChevroil to finance its share (*pari passu* to the bonds).

(e) ***Islamic finance***

Islamic finance is increasingly common in the development of projects in the Middle East. It has featured in the financing of some African oil or gas projects. It is most commonly used where the finance comes from banks or investors in the Middle East. The basic structures are:

- *Murabaha.* The financier buys an asset from the supplier and sells it to the project on deferred payment terms with a fixed maturity date. The financier receives a deferred sales price consisting of the cost price plus a premium. The premium is generally based on a benchmark (such as LIBOR plus a margin).
- *Bai Salam.* This is a structure similar to a murabaha, and is used to provide working capital. The key difference from a murabaha is that the financier pays in full for the asset in advance, for supply on a pre-agreed future date. The financier receives a discount for advance payment which is calculated by reference to a benchmark (such as LIBOR plus a margin).

- *Istisna'a.* The financier pays an amount to fund the development of the project and acquires the asset on completion, when the financier will sell the asset to the project or lease it back under an ijara (see below).
- *Ijara.* The financier leases the asset to the project.
- *Sukuk.* This is a form of Islamic bond.

There are other forms of Islamic finance. Generally these are not used, or are not suitable, for the financing of oil and gas projects in Africa.

The key difficulties with using Islamic finance in Africa are:

- there is no international consensus on *Shari'a* interpretations;
- there is a lack of standardised documents in Islamic financing (although this is changing);
- there can be quite complicated intercreditor arrangements if Islamic financing is being used at the same time as conventional financing (see 3.5(c) below); and
- there are often tax disadvantages with the use of Islamic financing, especially in African countries which have little experience of the system.

(f) Prepayment facility

Prepayment facilities are increasingly being used to finance oil and gas projects in Russia. They are suitable for use in financing of oil projects in Africa. A prepayment facility is commonly provided by a trader in oil products (for example, Vitol or Glencore).

A prepayment facility is structured so that the trader prepays for the oil to be supplied by the project under an export contract between the project (as seller) and the trader (as buyer). The oil may be delivered to the trader for onward delivery to the end buyer, or delivered directly to the end buyer. The sale proceeds received by the trader from the end buyer repay the loan. Sometimes, the trader will syndicate the prepayment facility to a group of banks.

(g) PXF finance

A pre-export financing (PXF) arrangement involves a loan to the project company taking security over cash flows due to the borrower under confirmed orders from pre-agreed offtakers under export contracts. The cash flows under the export contracts are sufficient to repay the loan, and there is a mechanism which allows the lenders to use the cash flows to repay the loan in a default situation. Typically, the lenders take security over the sales contracts, the related letters of credit, a collection account into which payments under the sales contracts are to be made, and a debt service reserve account. If the currency of payment under the sales contract is not the same as the currency of the loan, a hedging mechanism is often also put in place.

The Loan Market Association has a standard loan agreement for pre-export facilities.

(h) Oil for loan swap

This funding mechanism is not that different from a pre-payment facility, except that it covers many years of supply of oil or gas. It has been used in the supply of oil and gas from Russia to China. Typically, the purchaser of the oil or gas would agree to lend a sum of money in return for delivery of oil and gas over a multi-year period. The author is not aware of this having been used in the financing of oil and gas projects in Africa, but it is something which should be considered, especially where Chinese oil companies are purchasers.

2.4 Derivatives

One of the biggest risks for lenders and investors in oil or gas projects in Africa is the fluctuation of prices in the oil or gas. This can be hedged by over-the-counter (OTC) derivatives or exchange-traded derivatives.

Hedging derivatives for oil are widely available. Those for hedging gas are less freely available, because there are fewer benchmarks for African gas and less trading of African gas in a spot market.

Hedging instruments include futures, swaps, options, swaptions and index linked loans.

2.5 Insurance

The financiers of an upstream project will often require insurance against damage to physical assets and political insurance.

Insurance against damage to physical assets will often cover both compensation for the cost of replacing the asset, and for the interruption of the business associated with the physical damage.

Political risk insurance tends to cover war, political violence and expropriation. It sometimes covers breach of contract with a government entity. The latter could cover breach of a licence to exploit an oil or gas field.

3. LNG projects

LNG projects involve large upfront capital expenditure. Self-funding is often beyond the capacity of all the participants in an LNG project. Even if some participants in the project are capable of funding their share, other participants may require that the project itself raises the finance rather than its shareholders.

3.1 External funding

The types of financing available for LNG projects in Africa vary, depending on the range of credit criteria, including the identity of the sponsors, the country risk involved, the offtake contracts and creditworthiness of the offtake parties, and the contractual structure of the LNG project.

3.2 Shareholders and offtakers

The shareholders in an LNG project typically look at their investment in the LNG project not so much as a method of getting a return, but rather as a means of getting their 'equity share' of the LNG produced by the project. Alternatively, it is a way of turning their 'stranded gas reserves' into cash. This often means that the LNG project involves tolling (see 3.3(b) below).

Despite this, an LNG project which is financed by debt will still need a substantial equity investment from its shareholders.

3.3 Bankability

As explained in the introduction to this chapter, earlier decisions about an oil or gas project in Africa often mean that a LNG project is not bankable.

The biggest problem is that procurement decisions are made to reduce project costs, which transfer risks to the LNG project company. Bankability of an LNG project depends on project risks being transferred to project counterparties. This usually means increased project costs, however. As a result, there is an internal tension within the developer of the project, between the development team and the financing team.

(a) Gas supply

An LNG project needs a sufficient and stable supply of natural gas to support the forecast sales of LNG for the project. This needs to be done through either a strong gas supply contract or the demonstration of sufficient proven reserves of natural gas (as certified by an independent reserves consultant).

This 'reserve risk' can be taken by the gas supplier, the project company or the LNG offtaker (although, if it is taken by the LNG project company, it is unlikely to be a bankable project).

(b) Offtake or tolling

Many LNG projects in Africa have, to date, been supported by long-term offtake contracts with major energy companies. Most have been structured on the assumption that the gas would be shipped to the US markets. Recently, however, there has been a fundamental shift in gas markets, with the significant use of shale gas in the US markets (leading to substantial decreases in US gas prices) and the increase in gas prices in the Asian markets. This has been combined with increased volatility in the gas markets generally, and the uncertainty caused by new LNG projects in the Middle East and Australia.

This is generally likely to mean that contracts for new LNG projects in Africa will not take the traditional form of an LNG offtake contract. Instead, new projects are likely to be undertaken on a 'tolling' basis. This means that the upstream owners of the natural gas will retain ownership of the gas while the LNG project company converts the gas into LNG. The upstream owners of the LNG will then be able to trade the LNG as they think fit. A tolling structure means that the LNG project company is taking neither gas reserve risk nor LNG price risk. The project company merely receives a tolling fee for converting the gas into LNG. That fee can be structured so that it is similar to the fee used in a power purchase agreement for an electricity generating project. This would involve a 'capacity charge' (which would cover the debt service and fixed costs of the LNG project) and a tolling charge (which would cover the operating costs of the project). The capacity charge would be payable even if the LNG plant were not running (ie, to cover the gas reserve risk), and the tolling charge would be payable when the gas was being tolled through the plant. The tolling arrangement would substantially reduce the risk profile of an LNG project, and reduce the costs of debt finance, by transferring most of the risk to the shareholders of the LNG project.

(c) *Financial ratios*

African LNG projects typically use a financial model to produce cash flow ratios that will form the basis for testing the project's ability to service its debt. The financial model determines the cash flow available for debt service (CAFDS) for a period (usually six months). The two key financial ratios that are used to determine the financial strength of the project are:

- *Loan life cover ratio.* This measures the ability of the project to produce enough cash flow to repay the debt over the life of the loan. This is done by comparing the discounted net present value of the projected cash available for debt service against the aggregate amount of the principal outstanding under the loan facility, for the period to the maturity of the loan.
- *Debt service cover ratio.* This measures the ability of the project to service principal and interest on the next one or more scheduled payment dates. The debt service cover ratio is often measured both on a forward-looking and backward-looking basis.

These two cover ratios play an important role in:

- determining the debt-to-equity ratio of the LNG project;
- being a trigger for the release of sponsor completion support (see 3.3(d) below);
- payments of distributions of equity and subordinated debt by the project company;
- the ability of the project company to use insurance proceeds to reinstate the project facilities following a major loss; and
- the occurrence of an event of default for breach of financial covenants.

(d) *Completion support*

Most LNG projects (both in Africa and elsewhere) have had some form of sponsor completion support. This involves the shareholders in the LNG project either guaranteeing the timely completion of the project facilities or, more usually, underwriting debt payments until completion has occurred. The key issue here is the definition of when completion has occurred. This is usually a date after completion of the construction of the LNG project facilities, and involves a period of successful operation (usually determined by the cover ratios mentioned at 3.3(c) above), but may also include all necessary government approvals, no continuing default, and funding of some reserve accounts.

During the period of completion support, there will typically be restrictions on the sponsors selling any of their equity or the imposition of tests about the creditworthiness of new sponsors.

Sponsors also typically negotiate a 'political risk carveout' to their sponsor support. This means that the sponsors are not liable in the event that completion is delayed or impeded by the occurrence of a political risk (see 3.3(f) below).

(e) ***Environmental and social aspects***

The environmental and social aspects of an LNG project are very important to the lenders. They are often under-estimated at the start of the project, leading to projects that are not bankable. Most multilateral lenders, export credit agencies and commercial banks will only lend to LNG projects that comply with the Equator Principles[2] (which are largely based on the environmental and social guidelines issued by the International Finance Corporation, part of the World Bank group). The Equator Principles tend to be a lot stricter than environmental and social requirements set out in local laws. There are specific IFC environmental, health and safety guidelines for LNG facilities (which are part of the Equator Principles).[3]

Some ECAs have additional environmental and social requirements.

(f) ***Political risks***

The assessment and mitigation of political risk is important for any financing of an African LNG project. Political risk is not unique to emerging markets, however. Political risk in oil and gas is also high in Europe and the United States, given regular changes to taxation, regulation and environmental standards, but it can usually be financed without political risk mitigation. Despite this, African political risk is perceived to be higher and risk mitigation is therefore a necessary requisite for debt financing of an LNG project.

Typical risk mitigation includes:

- the involvement of multilateral lenders creating a 'halo' effect, even if they do not directly insure or guarantee the political risk;
- host government agreements (governed by English law) which provide for compensation for political events;
- bilateral investment treaties (BITs);
- guarantees from export credit agencies; and
- political risk insurance (see 2.5 above).

(g) ***Local gas use***

A major challenge to an LNG project in Africa is the demand for gas by local industry and for domestic consumer use. The development of the gas field for the LNG project often means that gas is also available for domestic use (ie, instead of for export as LNG).

This is a problem because local political desire to divert gas for domestic use, rather than for export, may mean that there is insufficient gas for the LNG project (as happened with some LNG plants in Egypt) and/or that the LNG project is paid for the domestic gas in local currency (at a price lower than that paid for the LNG).

(h) ***Links with upstream financing***

The links between the LNG project (and its financing) and the upstream gas project (and its financing) can create a variety of problems. The core problem is that both

---

2 See www.equator-principles.com.
3 See www.ifc.org/wps/wcm/connect/87e7a48048855295ac04fe6a6515bb18/Final+-+LNG.pdf?MOD=AJPERES.

projects rely on each other. If the LNG project is not working, then neither is the upstream gas project (and vice versa). Neither project has alternative sources of supply or offtake.

This can give rise to a potential 'hostage situation'. The lenders to one project that is in financial difficulty can threaten to stop operations unless the lenders to the other project contribute to the rescue of the first project.

In addition, the gas supply agreement between the upstream project and the LNG project needs to continue operating if lenders to either project enforce their security and sell that project. A purchaser of the LNG project will want to know that the gas supply agreement cannot be terminated and is transferred. A purchaser of the upstream project will also want to know that the gas supply agreement cannot be terminated and is transferred.

3.4 Sources of debt finance

LNG projects in Africa have many sources of debt finance.

(a) Banks (local and international)

Traditionally, commercial banks have been one of the major contributors to the funding of African LNG projects. This has been done using a mixture of covered and uncovered facilities involving export credit agencies (see 3.4(b) below). The capital adequacy requirements for commercial banks has, however, tended to mean that project finance is less attractive than it previously was for those banks. As a result, the other sources of finance discussed below will play a more important role in the financing of future African LNG projects.

It is expected that African banks (and not only the large South African banks) will also play an important role in the financing of new African LNG projects. With many African countries imposing laws that require local content to be sourced in the construction of LNG projects, local currency financing will be important to fund such local content costs.

(b) Export credit agencies

Export credit agencies (ECAs) play a major role in the debt financing of most African LNG projects. Their primary role is to support the exports of a relevant country, although the terms on which they provide financing tends to be harmonised by OECD guidelines to which most ECAs have agreed.[4]

Most ECA finance for African LNG projects is provided by the ECA in the country of export of the equipment used in the LNG project. There may be several ECAs if the equipment is sourced in several countries (typically within Europe or United States). The ECA's support typically takes the form of guarantees or insurance policies, with the commercial banks providing the actual funding. The risks covered can be 'comprehensive', which covers all risks of nonpayment by the LNG project company (with the exception of between 10 and 15% of the loan), but can be limited to political risks only.

4 See www.oecd.org/tad/xcred/theexportcreditsarrangementtext.htm.

Some ECAs will also cover the equity investments made by sponsors based in their country.

(c) ***Development finance institutions (multilateral, regional and bilateral)***

Development finance institutions (DFIs) can take many forms, including multilateral lending agencies (such as the World Bank, European Bank of Reconstruction and Development and the International Finance Corporation), regional DFIs (such as the African Development Bank and the Islamic Development Bank) and bilateral DFIs (such as CDC, DEG, FMO, Norfund, OeEB, Proparco, SIFEM, SOFID and Swedbank).

Many multilateral lending agencies (MLAs) use an A/B loan structure, under which the MLA is the lender of record but the financing is sourced by commercial banks for the B loan part of the financing.

(d) ***Debt capital markets***

Financing of LNG projects using the debt capital markets has been common in the Middle East (including the Ras Gas II and III expansion projects in Qatar and the Oman LNG project). Properly structured African LNG projects should also be capable of accessing debt from the debt capital markets (including *Sukuk* bonds (see 2.3(e) above)).

(e) ***Islamic finance***

The types of Islamic finance described at 2.3(e) above should be capable of use in financing an African LNG project, especially one with Middle East lenders or investors.

(f) ***Non-bank lenders***

Non-bank lenders ('shadow banking') play an increasingly important role in financing worldwide. Possible non-bank lenders could include debt funds, insurance companies and pension funds. Those lenders tend, however, to focus on developed markets and are unlikely in the near future to finance African LNG projects for significant amounts.

3.5 Documentation

Most debt financing for African LNG projects uses loan documentation governed by English law and which is based on the standard forms published by the Loan Market Association (LMA). The development finance institutions prefer, however, to use their own forms of loan documentation (which tend to be based on that of the IFC). There has been discussion for some years of a proposal that the DFIs should start to use the LMA documentation.

(a) ***Common terms agreement***

On a large LNG project in Africa, there are likely to be multiple sources of financing (including all or most of those described above). This will necessitate the use of a common terms agreement to which all of the financing parties are signatories and which contains the financing terms that are common to all forms of financing. The common terms agreement will operate together with the individual facility agreements between the borrowers and the individual lending groups pursuant to which the actual loan disbursements will be made. The individual financing documents tend to be limited to those things which are specific to a particular loan (eg, margin, interest calculation fees and any additional requirements particular to that financing).

The common terms agreement typically sets out the following:

- conditions precedent;
- drawdown procedures;
- interest calculation and payment;
- prepayments;
- security requirements;
- taxes, increased costs and market disruptions;
- banking case and budget procedures;
- fees;
- intercreditor agent and security trustee;
- transfers;
- covenants;
- representations; and
- events of default.

(b) Intercreditor agreement

In addition to the common terms agreement, all lenders typically enter into an intercreditor agreement. The basis of this agreement is that all lenders agree to act collectively through a common agent in making decisions and taking actions in relation to the financing. Generally, no individual lender or lender group may operate independently in modifying or enforcing its rights under the financing documents. The intercreditor agreement usually includes provisions dealing with:

- voting entitlements for amendments, waivers and enforcement;
- decision-making procedures and majorities (including unanimous consent for a defined list of matters that are fundamental to the financing), super-majority decisions and majority lender decisions;
- procedures for taking enforcement action;
- timetable for decision-making;
- the sharing of payments both before and after a default; and
- the accession of new financing parties.

(c) Security

Lenders to an African LNG project will require security over the assets of the project. This typically includes first ranking security over:

- the share capital and subordinated debt of the LNG project company;
- the land, building and physical assets of the LNG project;
- the gas and LNG belonging to the LNG project (which will be none, if the gas is being tolled into LNG);
- the LNG project's rights to all material project contracts, including

offtake/tolling contracts and any concession agreement with the host government; and
- all bank accounts, including offshore and onshore accounts.

In some African countries, there will be constraints on the type of security and assets that can be secured, including:
- restrictions on foreign ownership;
- restrictions on mortgaging the land;
- legal restrictions over taking security on an uncompleted building (such as the project facilities); and
- large registration fees or taxes on the security.

All security is held by a common security trustee, enforcement being regulated by the intercreditor agreement. When Islamic financing is part of the project, the intercreditor arrangements need to reflect the enhanced position that Islamic lenders have in owning the assets, rather than having a security interest in them.

(d) Direct agreements

Part of the security package will usually include direct agreements with the counterparties of the material project contracts (including the government, the builder, offtakers and tolling parties). The direct agreements include provisions dealing with:
- constraints upon termination of the project contracts by the counterparties;
- collateral warranties from the counterparties direct to the security trustee;
- the ability of the security trustee (and the lenders) to 'step-in' to the project contracts in the place of the LNG project company; and
- the ability of the security trustee to novate the project contract from the project company to a new entity (often owned by different shareholders or by the banks).

3.6 Multiple trains

All LNG projects should be financially structured so that there can be multiple trains (either at the start of the project, or later). If properly structured, this allows the second (and third, fourth, etc) trains to have different shareholders and lenders, without the veto from a minority shareholder in, or the lenders to, another train.

This is best achieved through each train having its own project company, and the common assets (eg, the LNG jetty, gas supply pipelines) being vested in a separate special purpose company. The common facilities would be financed by the lenders to the first train, but such lenders' consent would not be needed for the common facilities to be used by later trains. The later trains would pay a fee to the common facilities company. A default by the first train would not prevent the common facilities being used by later trains.

4. Pipelines

Oil and gas pipelines have been an important feature in the development of oil and gas fields in Africa. Projects such as the Chad-Cameroon Pipeline and the West African Gas Pipeline have been major projects involving large capital expenditure. They have enormous financing needs.

4.1 Bankability

The bankability of African pipeline projects is not fundamentally different from that of African LNG projects (see 3.3 above). Early decisions about a pipeline project often mean that a pipeline project is not bankable.

(a) *Intergovernmental agreement and host government agreements*

Many oil and gas pipelines in Africa are cross-border. These require unique intergovernmental and host government agreements. In addition to the usual features that will be found in a host government agreement, the cross-border nature of the pipeline necessitates some harmonisation between the legal and tax requirements in the different countries, so that the project can comply with standard basic sets of legal and fiscal requirements rather than with the highest common denominator (or having to deal with conflicting or overlapping requirements). The intergovernmental agreement and host government agreements used in the Baku-Tblisi-Ceyhan Pipeline from Azerbaijan through Georgia to Turkey have been published and provide a good template for oil and gas pipelines in Africa.

(b) *Oil/gas supply*

As with an LNG project, a pipeline project will require a reliable supply of oil or natural gas. Lenders to, and investors in, a pipeline project will remember the West African Gas Pipeline in which, after construction, it was discovered that there was insufficient gas for the pipeline downstream from Nigeria.

(c) *Transportation agreement*

The transportation agreement for the pipeline is the contract which provides the revenue for the pipeline project. It can take two basic forms: firstly, an arrangement in which the pipeline-owning company purchases the oil or gas from the sponsors (or suppliers); and secondly, where the users of the pipeline pay a fee to the pipeline company to enable it to use the pipeline to transport the oil or gas. The second structure can raise complications in some jurisdictions, especially where there are multiple users of the pipeline and each user's oil or gas is blended or mixed with that of the others. In such circumstances, it is difficult to say legally which user owns which oil or gas that is in the pipeline. Matters are complicated further if the quality of the oil or gas put into the pipeline varies from user to user.

Transportation fees can be based on $X per quantity of oil or gas. This requires some certainty, however, as to the quantity of gas that will be shipped on a daily or weekly basis. The alternative is the capacity/usage fee structure (as described at 3.3(b) above for a tolling agreement), in which the shareholders pay a capacity fee which covers the debt service and fixed operating costs and a usage fee that covers the operating costs.

(d) ***Common carrier versus producer pipeline***

A significant legal issue (and political risk) for a pipeline project is if the pipeline needs to be a 'common carrier' rather than a 'producer pipeline'. This could be an initial requirement or something that arises later as a result of a change in the law (ie, a political risk). A producer pipeline is a monopoly that can only be used by its owners (or with the agreement of its owners). A common carrier is a pipeline that is available for use by anybody who can meet the quality criteria for the oil and gas and pay the necessary fee.

(e) ***Financial ratios***

The financing of a pipeline project will depend on its financial ratios (mainly the loan life cover ratio and debt service cover ratio), which are described at 3.3(c) above.

(f) ***Completion support***

The completion support from sponsors should be similar to the requirements for LNG projects (see 3.3(d) above). A strong EPC contract with creditworthy builders should, however, reduce their requirements for sponsor support. Where there are different builders in different countries for a cross-border pipeline, this will increase the need for sponsor support.

(g) ***Environmental and social aspects***

The environmental and social issues for pipelines tend to be greater than for LNG projects (see 3.3(e) above). This is partly because of a history of oil and gas pipeline leaks and the displacement of local populations. This situation is exacerbated with longer pipelines.

As a result, the environmental and social issues (and the Equator Principles – see 3.3(e) above) form an important part of the financing an African oil and gas pipeline.

(h) ***Political risks***

There are more political risks in a cross-border pipeline project than in an LNG project, because the former will cover both more than one country and a greater area than the several hectares involved in an LNG project. This includes the risk that the pipeline will be designated as a 'common carrier' (see 4.1(d) above).

(i) ***Links with upstream financing***

The links between an upstream oil or gas field and the pipeline (and the financing of both) can cause similar problems to those in an African LNG project (see 3.3(h) above). The interdependence of the upstream project and the pipeline (and the related intercreditor issues) often leads to difficult negotiations.

4.2 Sources of debt finance

The sources of finance for an African pipeline project are similar to those for an African LNG project (see 3.4 above). It all depends on the risk profile of the project and its bankability.

5. Conclusion

The financing of African oil and gas projects is not too different from the financing of such projects worldwide. There is, however, a perception of greater political risk, which requires more political risk mitigation and different lenders. Local financial markets are less developed, which means more cross-border lending in US dollars. National oil companies lack the expertise and financial resources to develop some projects. Projects can take longer to develop, which may lead to early decisions that impede a later financing.

In time, however, the methods and sources of financing oil and gas projects worldwide will be used in Africa.

The growing and evolving role of African national oil companies

Bjorn-Erik Leerberg
Simonsen Vogt Wiig

1. Why the interest in petroleum and state control?

Roughly $2 billion worth of petroleum is traded every day. That makes it one of the most important commodities traded in terms of value. The immense value, the resource rent it represents and its importance in energy supply and economic development, make it impossible for any government not to be deeply involved in petroleum production, consumption or use. Taxes imposed on petroleum represent substantial contributions to the income of most state budgets. Ninety countries obtain a substantial portion of their tax revenue from petroleum. Petroleum production and sale affect the balance of payments and the appreciation of currencies. They affect companies' operating costs and profitability, ordinary people's purchasing power and employment.

It is not only the value of petroleum that interests us; it is also its importance as a raw material and its use and impact on every aspect of modern society. Any analysis of government, and of the relationship between government as a resource owner and regulator, state enterprises and international oil companies (IOCs), must been seen in its historic context.

When the oil sector is discussed, there is a tendency to label perceptions and characterise industry players. National oil company (NOC) is a frequently used label. Are 'national' oil companies really the same as the sense in which they are commonly understood? Are they all one of a kind and the same? The short answer is no. A more comprehensive answer depends on the historical viewpoint and the observer's perception of the industry, as much as the functionality of petroleum companies. The purposes of NOCs will vary, depending on policy and governance systems.

State participation is often perceived as 'resource nationalism' and is viewed with much scepticism. "The rise to prominence of national oil companies has shifted the balance of control over most of the world's oil and gas reserves."[1] Many industry commentators seem alarmed by this fact. The sentiment is understandable if government involvement is seen as politically undesirable, even where government holds property ownership in an asset.

Discussion of government intervention and the place of NOCs is highly

1 Jorge Leis, John McCreery & Juan Carlos Gay, *National oil companies reshape the playing field* (Bain & Company report, 2012).

politicised. The political symbolism is there, but the reality of economic and industrial needs has quickly overshadowed the political aspects.[2] It is safe to say that the assertion of government control over national oil companies is perceived very differently, depending on the historical legacy. Therein lies an interesting general debate which also affects the perception of the changing or evolving role of African national oil companies.

2. Ownership of natural resources – does it matter?

Approximately 90% of remaining known conventional oil and natural gas resources and roughly 75% of production capacity are controlled by governments or entities owned or controlled by governments.[3] Unconventional resources have recently had a profound global impact on markets. This does not, however, alter the importance of conventional resources or who controls them.

A prominent example of private resource ownership is US onshore.[4] In many respects, US onshore represents the cradle of the modern oil industry. When US oil brought its practices, experience and attitudes to new petroleum provinces, African jurisdictions were not exempted. Private ownership of petroleum resources is, however, by far the least commonly practised system around the world. In almost every petroleum province, it is the state that has title to petroleum resources in the ground.

In the early days of the industry, sovereigns treated petroleum resources in the same manner as any other assets under their rule. Outside the United States, oil exploration and production were, to a large extent, controlled by state monopolies. Even so, they were fairly quickly auctioned to private entrepreneurs and private oil companies (POCs).[5] The first concessions awarded for exclusive oil exploration and production in the Middle East and in north African states reflect this characteristic. Rights were obtained through a licence with the sovereign (under an agreement or contract governed by contract law principles), under which the foreign investor paid the sovereign owner royalties for the right to exploit the resource.

3. Oil, hydrocarbons or petroleum – understanding the non-renewable resource

Historically, the industry focused on oil extraction. This understanding was practised by industry, included in contractual arrangements and used in regulatory instruments. Understanding of the resource and its characteristics has, however, evolved. The term 'petroleum' is used in this chapter, rather than the traditional terms 'oil' or 'hydrocarbons'. This is not coincidental. The broader use and legal implications of the term 'petroleum' may originally have been triggered by the

---

2 Valerie Marcel, *Oil Titans: National Oil Companies in the Middle East*, Royal Institute of International Affairs (RIIA), London (2006), p 4.

3 International Bank for Reconstruction and Development, *National Oil Companies and Value Creation*, World Bank Working Paper No 218 (2011), Executive Summary; Marcel, *op cit* (note 2 above), p 1.

4 US offshore resources are not subject to private property ownership. Theoretically, this could have been the case if instituted by state or federal law, both within the territorial sea and on the continental shelf.

5 POCs are companies owned and controlled by private capital and involved in exploration, production and the onward sale of petroleum as commodities – regularly referred to as 'upstream' activities.

resource management and policy principles instituted by Norway in the 1970s.[6] Several of these principles were later codified, including a prohibition against wasting petroleum which was later translated into a general prohibition against gas flaring on the grounds of reservoir pressure management and environmental protection.

Deposits routinely contain hydrocarbons other than crude oil, which under ordinary atmospheric conditions is a liquid. Other components are important commercially as well as from a resource management and optimal depletion point of view. Various hydrocarbons are gaseous under normal atmospheric conditions. They change character as a result of processing or storage conditions. Many deposits contain additional components, such as inert gases, which may not only be valuable for their pressure properties, but also have direct commercial value.

For resource owners, the total depletion of all deposits and the ultimate recovery rate of each deposit are of fundamental importance. The situation is not the same for private investors. Investors' activities are not limited by the finite resources of a single sovereign state. This fundamental difference impacts upon the organisation and activities of resource owners, regulatory authorities and NOCs alike. Government resource management initiatives cannot, therefore, generally be viewed as unwarranted resource nationalism.

The implementation of resource management principles has varied in speed and consistency. It has depended greatly on conditions in the petroleum province in question, resource characteristics, industry structure and the legal relationship between IOCs, NOCs and the state as resource owner, regulator and resource rent collector. The degree of control exercised by the state over NOCs and the format for extending exclusive rights fundamentally affect how this plays out.

Several resource-rich countries (most African producing countries among them) have flared associated natural gas not used for oil production purposes.[7] A growing awareness of the consequences of this wasteful practice has risen among industry players, bureaucrats and politicians. The realisation has mounted that flaring reduces oil recovery rates, impacts upon security of supply, and inflicts a huge loss of natural gas volumes on the economy, including for electricity generation.

Resource owners have, due to resource conservation and climate concerns, increased their focus on resource management and improved oil recovery initiatives. Policies, regulatory frameworks and project-oriented decisions have been adjusted. Governments' interaction with NOCs has also been affected. Irrespective of the

---

6 The core component of the petroleum policy was debated and accepted by the Norwegian Parliament (Stortinget) in 1972. The debate resulted in the adoption of a common approach to sector policy development. The approach has been adopted in general by all political parties, regardless of the government in power. Norway is a parliamentary democracy, based on a constitutional monarchy, which has had both majority and minority governments since the advent of the petroleum sector there in 1963.

7 It has been estimated that Nigeria in 2008 lost 2.5 bcf/d (billion cubic feet per day) to flaring, which amounts to the approximate equivalent of European daily natural gas consumption. Even after implementing its first LNG projects, Nigeria continued to flare substantial volumes of associated natural gas. See African Development Bank, *Oil and Gas in Africa* (2009, Oxford University Press), p 61. In order to curb further the problem of flaring, the Nigerian authorities introduced a new initiative in 2014 which was aimed at monitoring flaring: see www.petroleumafrica.com/nigeria-launches-gas-flare-tracking-system.

resource base, governments have realised that the extraction of petroleum is no longer only a question of oil. The volatility of oil and gas prices has added to the urgency. Energy needs all over the African continent have also substantially increased since independence from colonial rule. Population growth is not the sole cause of increased demand. Even in the least developed economies, new technologies are available which impact upon education, health care and consumer electronics, such as mobile telecommunications. All require a steady supply of electricity. Concern for climate change consequences and discussions on the security of energy supply have only accelerated this trend.

4. The consequences of a globalised world

There has been movement over the past few years towards stricter health and safety standards. Furthermore, deviations from environmental protection standards are tolerated less and less. Such shifts in attitude have much to do with the ability of interest groups and the media to report on major accidents and incidents in real time.

Focus group activity has impacted upon attitudes and influenced policies in OECD countries. Other countries are following suit. Corporate governance requirements increasingly imposed on IOCs provide one example. Pressure to improve transparency in order to combat tax evasion provides another. The latest push in anti-corruption initiatives involves country-by-country reporting and a requirement to disclose beneficial ownership. These initiatives were not conceived or evolved specifically to address the petroleum sector or African NOCs. Even before being implemented in African jurisdictions, however, these initiatives have indirectly affected the way governments and African NOCs can and will operate in the future.

Further changes will also be forced to the forefront as a result of legitimate grievances. They may be expressed by local stakeholders, international focus groups, a new breed of investment funds, international financial and development institutions or bilateral aid donors. All of them will require certain standards to be met as a condition of financing or aid to be made available.

Investors from open and transparent societies and economies will be challenged by interest groups at home. Investors will increasingly be influenced or challenged, first and foremost in those states with a vibrant civil society, but also later in less open societies. Governments and their NOCs in Africa and elsewhere are or will be impacted upon as well. How deep the impact will be and how fast the transition will occur depends in each case on the conduct of government administrations and the performance of state monopolies. They will, moreover, depend on whether political elites produce results in societal development and poverty eradication; the wider the gap, the faster or harder the fall.

Regulatory measures protecting third party interests and rights from potentially negative effects of industry activities are likely to continue, regardless of the presence of any NOC. It may prove easier for governments to implement measures where there is no state or private monopoly.

Sovereign states, NOCs and IOCs will all be affected by these shifts, which will have commercial, operational and economic impacts. Governments and NOCs will in the future be no less immune to this than IOCs. The implementation of new measures may have come at a slower pace in many African jurisdictions by comparison with industrialised economies. The difference will be in timing, but governments and industry players will be compelled to comply.

5. What is a national oil company?

5.1 What does 'national' mean?

Are NOCs really as homogenous as most commentators seem to assume? Is the term 'national' useful? Is a company national only if it is entirely owned and controlled by the political leadership of a sovereign state? If that is the case, what do we then call private companies that are granted privileged access to resources on the basis of the nationality of their owner, place of incorporation or principal place of business?

Company laws establish the rules and requirements of corporate ownership and governance requirements. Legal requirements regularly determine and identify companies as local or national. In many cases, the qualification is a prerequisite to permitting certain activities or the key to obtaining specific privileges. It is not uncommon in the extractive industries that only the state or companies owned and controlled by nationals or citizens of that state may conduct petroleum activities upstream and downstream or have access to privileges conferred by law.

Several NOCs were, at their inception, truly national, in the sense that they were entirely government-owned and controlled. Some NOCs have, however, moved beyond this, becoming partly state-owned or controlled companies. Some companies no longer even have the exclusive right to resources but have retained privileged access. This development trajectory has not yet materialised with most NOCs in Africa. It may be more accurate to describe most NOCs as state oil companies.[8] They are entirely owned and controlled by the state[9] and members of the executive branch also tend to be involved in the running of their daily operations, as well as in strategic decisions.

Historically, IOCs have predominantly been headquartered and managed from Europe or the US. Early European NOCs were often not state-owned oil companies[10] in the manner in which they are known today. They did not enter the scene as a result of resource-related nationalisation. European companies were established for different needs and strategic interests when compared to the motivations leading to nationalisations in non-OECD countries. Early and mid-20th century European state-owned commercial companies[11] were established to achieve security of supply, in order

---

8 A restatement of this approach is included in the Mozambican Petroleum Law 2014 (note 8 above), article 4(6) which states: "The Government shall provide funding for Empresa Nacional de Hidrocarbonetos EP its sole representative, to invest.....in the oil and gas business."

9 Several authors seem to follow the approach expressed by Marcel, *op cit* (note 2 above) at p 5, where she states: "I use a minimalist definition of an NOC: it is a company with at least 51 percent state ownership that is active in the exploration and production of hydrocarbons – in other words the 'upstream'."

10 Examples of state-owned companies that have become IOCs are PETRONAS (Malaysia), PERTAMINA (Indonesia), Statoil (Norway), OMV (Austria), MOL (Hungary) and YFP (Argentina). Examples of IOCs that were previously state-owned are Total (France), ENI, previously Agip (Italy), and BP and BG Group (both UK). Examples of IOCs that were never state-owned are Exxon, Chevron and Anadarko.

11 Bernhard Taverne, *Petroleum, Industry and Governments: A Study of the Involvement of Industry and Governments in Exploration for and Production of Petroleum* (3rd Edn, 2013, Kluwer Law International BV, The Netherlands), p 30.

to cater for industrial needs, economic development and control of access to markets for products. African states with petroleum potential, on the other hand, generally became independent during the Cold War. This may have contributed to their early tendency to lean more towards more socialist or even communist solutions.[12]

5.2 The first 'national' oil companies

It is not an easy task to describe briefly the general structure of NOCs, their *raison d'être*, and their complement of activities, functionality and responsibilities. It takes an even larger canvas to compare trends and the challenges surrounding these companies today with the situation at the time of their formation. To generalise with respect to the diversity of the African continent is even harder. It is therefore useful to start with some general history.

The strategic importance of oil began to make its mark around the time of World War I.[13] It prompted several European governments to take political and legislative steps to secure or control and supervise the supply of oil.[14] The first state-owned oil company is said to have been created in 1908 by the Emperor of Austria-Hungary. Many European countries followed suit. Albeit through different techniques, Britain and France (among others) established such controls. The British government notably took control of the Anglo-Persian Oil Company[15] by acquiring 51.7% of its shares in 1914.[16] The First Lord of the Admiralty, Winston Churchill, considered securing oil a strategic necessity to modernise the British Royal Navy.[17] After World War I, it also became impossible for France to be dependent on the goodwill of

12 Even non-socialist regimes were, however, concerned with petroleum product availability for the general economy and its citizenry. A case in point is the National Nigerian Petroleum Company (NNPC). See James Baker Institute Policy Report No 35, *The Role of National Oil Companies in International Energy Matters*, James Baker Institute Policy Report No 35 (2007) (James A Baker III Institute for Public Policy, Rice University), p 7.

13 Otherwise referred to as the Great War of 1914-1918.

14 France instituted import controls which developed into state monopolies in the mid-1920s. These legislative regulatory barriers against foreign control of supply and distribution of oil were not entirely abolished until Law 92-1443 of December 31 1992, which abrogated the customs regime introduced by the Law of March 16 1928 and the import regime introduced by the Law of March 30 1928. See André Philippon, 'The French Example. The 1928 Laws: Longevity and Effectiveness of the Approach to Creating and maintaining a National Oil Industry in a Consumer Country – Appearances and Realities', in Alain Beltran (Ed) *A Comparative History of National Oil Companies* (2010, PIE Peter Lang SA, Brussels), p 45.

15 The Anglo-Persian Oil Company had, during World War I, acquired British Petroleum, a German-controlled oil distribution company in Britain, and used the latter to market its Romanian production there.

16 Daniel Yergin, *The Prize: The Epic Quest for Oil, Money and Power* (1991-2012, Simon & Schuster, London), pp 143-148. The share purchase securing British government control had not been completed by the time World War I broke out: see p 157.

17 See First Lord of the Admiralty memorandum entitled 'Oil Fuel Supply for His Majesty's Navy', June 1913. This policy was subsequently implemented through a parliamentary bill debated and approved in June 1914, which authorised the British government to acquire the majority stake in a private company. It was not clearly stated in the bill that the target for acquisition was the Anglo-Persian Oil Company. See also Yergin, *op cit* (note 19 above), p 146.

18 France did not relinquish its control until 1992 over what stemmed from the 1920s legislative initiatives (see note 17 above) that led to what today is known as Total. In 1953 France established Entreprise de recherche et d'activités pétroliers (EARP) and its subsidiary Société nationale Elf Aquitaine (ELF). These companies were subsequently all privatised. The privatisation of British state interests in BP (the successor to Anglo-Persian) and the indigenous British National Oil Corporation (BNOC), a 100% UK government-owned company, was completed several years earlier. The chapter of UK government ownership of oil companies was firmly closed during the Thatcher era.

undertakings such as Standard Oil and companies outside French national control, such as Royal Dutch Shell and Anglo-Persian.[18] The victors of the conflict also had to carve up the spoils of war. Compagnie Française des Pétroles (CPF) was created in 1924 to take over German holdings in Turkish Petroleum.[19]

The background and context leading to the formation of European state-owned companies differ materially from the circumstances surrounding those NOCs established outside Europe. Irrespective of whether they were formed during the first wave, as in Argentina or Mexico,[20] or subsequent to World War II and the collapse of colonial empires,[21] or in connection with the oil price shocks of the 1970s and 1980s,[22] these NOCs were formed to control both production and domestic markets.[23]

During the 1970s, it was not really petroleum that was nationalised or 'reformed', but rather the oil sector. Thus the name given to the state-owned companies was 'national oil companies'. These were, however, national in the sense that the state either owned or controlled a substantial part of the companies that existed prior to the dismantling of the colonial empires. Several of today's multinational enterprises (MNEs) or IOCs, such Total and ENI,[24] began life as state-owned oil companies (SOCs) in the consumer countries. Their activities had often started out at the supply end and developed step-by-step upstream towards the source, culminating with control from deposit to the petrol pump.

State corporate governance exercised over NOCs often includes the involvement of the president of the republic or the energy minister. The same practice is seen under absolute monarchies, such as several of the SOCs in the Arabian peninsula. A substantial number of state entities are not true companies, nor are they established and governed pursuant to generally applicable corporate law. If established as entities with legal personality, NOCs tend to be subject to special laws or particular rules or regulations.

5.3 General discussion of the concept

There is a substantial difference, both materially and legally, between a commercial company and a sovereign state. Commercial companies or corporations such as MNEs consist of several companies established and operating in several jurisdictions at the choice of the owner.[25] Commercial companies, particularly those listed on

19 Philippon, *op cit* (note 17 above), p 21.

20 BP (1914), Argentina Yacimientos Petrolíferos Fiscales (YPF) (1922), France (CFP) (1924), Chile and Italy (Agip) (1926), Uruguay (1931), Peru (1934), Bolivia (1936) and Mexico (Petróleos Mexicanos (Pemex)) (1938).

21 Examples are Iran (NIOC) (1951), Brazil (Petrobras) (1953), India (ONGC) (1956), Kuwait (KPNC) (1960), Saudi Arabia (Petromin) (1962) and Algeria (Sonatrach) (1965).

22 Among these are Libya (1970), Nigeria (NNPC) (1971) and Egypt (EGPC) (1976), later followed by EGAS (2001) and Ganope (2002).

23 Several national oil companies have had the task of subsidising petroleum products for domestic consumption. An example in the African context is Nigeria's NNPC. See James Baker Institute, *op cit* (note 15 above), p 7. See also International Bank for Reconstruction and Development, *op cit* (note 3 above), pp 26-27 (on 'Subsidies and Noncommercial Objectives').

24 Agip (Azienda Generale Italiana Petroli) was a state oil company set up by the Mussolini government in 1926. From the beginning, Agip was tasked not only with supply and distribution, but also with undertaking exploration and production. See Pier Angelo Toninelli, 'Energy Supply and Economic Development in Italy: The Role of the State-owned Companies', in Beltran, *op cit* (note 17 above), p 132.

25 Peter T Muchlinski, *Multinational Enterprises and the Law* (2nd Edn, 1999, Blackwell). See, in particular, chapters 3 and 4. See also Nick Mathiason, *Piping Profits*, a report for Publish What You Pay, Oslo, Norway (2011).

stock exchanges, are owned by a large number of legal or physical persons. In many cases, owners are not even domiciled in the jurisdiction where the ultimate parent company is headquartered. A company may, at the whim of its owners, easily change its character, its domicile or even be wound up. A commercial company conducts its business to achieve optimal returns on its capital for the owners. State-owned oil companies regularly lack the ability to operate under a corporate structure along the lines of commercial companies such as IOCs.

The establishment of NOCs may be attributed to certain base conditions. The governments of newly formed sovereign states were disadvantaged by at least three basic asymmetries when compared with IOCs: in relation to information, agency and bargaining power.[26] The agency issue arises from the basic notion that natural resource ownership stems from state sovereignty. Sovereignty is attributable to the people. In many resource-rich countries, the state and its administrative organs are, for numerous reasons, still not fully answerable to its people.[27] The formation of NOCs and the creation of OPEC have been relatively successful strategies in overcoming asymmetries in information and bargaining power at government level, though not in relation to their populations.

African producers are generally not members of OPEC,[28] nor do all African producers have traditional state-owned or controlled companies. Agency problems are not automatically terminated by the creation of a state-owned company alone. Several African countries still struggle with agency and are likely to continue to do so at least in the near future.

The formation of OPEC represented a general shift in terms both of functionality and mandates of state-owned oil companies. It also further increased the predominance of such companies. OPEC appeared alongside a more consistent trend of nationalisations, principally in the Middle East and Latin America. In this context, it is natural to draw a distinction between developments in Africa north and south of the Sahara. Major discoveries and mature petroleum provinces existed in north Africa at the time of OPEC's formation. OPEC was formed prior to the west African oil boom that would include the growth of large producers such as Nigeria and Angola.

Government intervention and nationalisation occurring around the time of OPEC's formation also happened before east Africa had really attracted any genuine interest. The importance of east Africa would only coincide with the oil industry realising that natural gas was a desirable hydrocarbon resource, not merely an inconvenient consequence of the discovery of oil. This came about as a result of technological developments, increases in energy demand, the need for diversification of supply, oil price hikes, growing resistance to nuclear power and rising concerns associated with climate change. Natural gas, no longer dependent on pipeline transport, became the preferred 'go-to' fossil fuel in the OECD and ASEAN

---

26 George Soros, Foreword to Macartan Humphreys, Jeffrey D Sachs & Joseph E Stiglitz (Eds) *Escaping the Resource Curse* (2007, Columbia University Press).

27 Humphreys, Sachs & Stiglitz, *op cit* (note 29 above), pp 26-34.

28 OPEC had 12 member states in December 2014. No African states were among the founding members of that organisation. OPEC's African member States were, as at December 2014: Algeria (1965), Angola (2007), Libya (1962) and Nigeria (1971). Gabon (1975) left the organisation in 1995.

regions. Coupled with increased interest in new petroleum provinces came the introduction of Chinese state-owned companies. Chinese companies rushed to Africa in order to secure long-term supplies for that country's energy-hungry and expanding economy. The Chinese acted in much the same way as European state-owned companies had done a century before: they used political connections to establish trade links for the purpose of obtaining energy supplies.

5.4 Traditional functions of state oil companies

The purpose of state-owned oil companies has, more often than not, been linked to functionalities other than optimal return on investments to owners. Invariably, NOCs of this kind are owned and controlled by a single entity – the state. In post-colonial Africa, this has inevitably meant a republic with a particular set of constitutional or other governance attributes.[29]

NOCs are commonly owned or controlled by state organs. Only in exceptional cases are they listed on a stock exchange. In many cases, a NOC is a company in name only.[30] Several state-owned companies function merely as an extension of government institutions and state organs. The variety of legal and organisational structures is vastly different and does not only relate to the administrative and legal tradition structures adopted by the previous colonial powers.

The territorial 'lock-in' effect of sovereign states is another element which, given trends in economic development, natural resource management and energy supply, affects government thinking in a manner different from that of commercial entities. States do not have the ability to forum shop with regard to available resources. To protect against the vulnerability arising out of the geographical lock-in effect, newly independent states have felt compelled to introduce measures in order better to protect their perceived national interests.

The traditional motivation and function of early state-owned oil companies, whether they were large consumers or producers, was for the state to control a fundamental aspect of a large part of its economy. Apart from the vital economic interest of the state, there were political imperatives associated with oil's impact on development. Strategic, including military, concerns were also important, not least for large consumers. For resource owners, state-owned companies offered a rapid solution to bring government closer to technical and commercial decision-making. It enabled input to be made to resource development and depletion policies, control to be exercised over prices for locally consumed petroleum product, and acted as an employment creator.

---

29 In order to exercise authority and obtain recognition, a sovereign state must fulfil certain base criteria beyond independence, the control of territory and the presence of a government. Governmental authority exercised over a population must comply with minimum public international law standards. The government must also have in place a governance structure meeting certain minimum qualitative and quantitative criteria. See Sir Ian Brownlie & James Crawford, *Brownlie's Principles of Public International Law* (8th Edn, 2012, Oxford University Press), pp 128-136.

30 A case in point is the description of Nigeria's NNPC: see Mark C Thurber, Ifeyinwa M Emelife & Patrick RP Heller, 'NNPC and Nigeria's Oil Patronage Ecosystem', in David G Victor, David R Hults & Mark C Thurber (Eds), *Oil and Governance* (2012, Cambridge University Press), p 701. With regard to Algeria, see Marcel, *op cit* (note 2 above) at pp 83-84 and 86. Also see John P Entelis, 'Sonatrach: the political economy of an Algerian state institution', in Victor, Hults & Thurber, *op cit*, p 568.

Other elements associated with the benefits of national or state-owned oil companies are the ability to reduce information asymmetry in relation to IOCs. This is particularly important in relation to development plan approvals, including insight into the optimisation of production profiles, production schedules and the application of technology to allow higher depletion rates. The state-owned company may be used as a tool to implement health, safety and environmental (HSE) standards and to facilitate government regulatory oversight and resource owner interest (including rent collection).[31]

Without state-owned or state-controlled NOCs, it might be difficult for government to implement policies of a more societal nature. These aspects come on top of the need to build technical and commercial capacities related to the sector or to the economy in general, and to enable fast track development of other needed infrastructure, such as communications, energy supply (electricity), water supply, sanitation and health care, to name but a few.

Compared to POCs or IOCs, the purpose, mandate and responsibilities of state-owned NOCs are normally outlined in legislation.[32] Company mandates are, in addition, regularly detailed in their documents of incorporation or statutes. Most NOCs have more than a commercial mandate. Governance and development aspects of state ownership have had a predominant position in NOC mandates. The popularity of such initiatives has not disappeared, but appears to have been weakened as many African economies have started to grow and the ideological aspects of the Cold War have melted away. Governments, including those on the African continent, increasingly seem to be taking a more pragmatic view. Compelling NOCs or IOCs to perform outside their core competencies may not be the most effective and cost-efficient way to implement fundamental infrastructure needs.

An increasing number of governments are embracing the notion that it is in their own interest, as well as that of development, to be able to benchmark the performance of sector players. State-owned monopolies (or indeed any monopolies) are not optimally suited to serve this purpose. The associated corporate governance and transparency issues frequently associated with state-owned monopolies, and the apparent delay in rent collection because of the need to build a robust corporate structure, are also increasingly factored in.

Some state-owned companies had additional regulatory obligations at the outset of their existence. Several companies worldwide, including in Africa, have had their regulatory mandates removed or curtailed at a later stage.

The trend in the separation of commercial and regulatory functions is likely to continue. The governance environment surrounding state-owned oil companies in Africa is thus shifting, in common with other oil producing regions.

---

31 International Bank for Reconstruction and Development, *op cit* (note 3 above), pp 23-25.

32 See, in the case of Uganda, the Petroleum (Exploration, Development and Production) Act 2013. Sections 42-46 of this act replace the Petroleum (Exploration and Production) Act 1985, which contained no such provisions. Another example is the Ghana National Petroleum Corporation Act 1984 which, through the Petroleum Commission Act 2011 (Act 821), redefines the mandate of the country's NOC, the GNPC.

5.5 Resource nationalism

Henri Madelin explained the concept of 'resource nationalism' as being embodied in policies implemented in north Africa in the late 1960s and 1970s. Resource nationalism activity was pursued with:

> *revolutionary fervour directed towards removing all vestiges of former subservience. It assumes a socialist color in order to be better designed to signify collective rights to interests accused of the three vices of being foreign, capitalist and private.*[33]

The most prominent practices at that time were nationalisation or expropriation. In many cases, it was not the resource that was expropriated, but rather the exclusive right to exploit it,[34] along with associated infrastructure and other assets. Commentators have, however, extended the use of the term resource nationalism to embrace situations where governments have initiated varied forms of stricter regulatory requirement.

Not many nationalisations have occurred in more recent years. Of those, only one occurred in Africa, in Chad.[35] This may have contributed to a resurgence of fear of resource nationalism in the form of expropriation. These nationalisations, however, occurred predominantly following privatisations that had been challenged as flawed.[36] They also followed a fast and massive surge in crude oil prices.

Resentment against government involvement has not been limited only to resource ownership. It has frequently been expressed in relation to other types of government involvement, whether regulatory or commercial.

Every industrial and commercial activity must deal with changing regulatory requirements. Regulation of markets has proved to be necessary, time and time again. Government intervention in this regard is not necessarily detrimental to an industry, particularly if it is predictable in approach and transparent in its implementation. Regulation may assist in making the industry more transparent, accountable and competitive. It would, however, have substantial negative effects if governments could not apply the experience gained to the improvement of conditions, or intervene in ongoing practices and forms of conduct that lead to demonstrably unacceptable results.

Government intervention is problematic, however, where its aim or result is the removal of transparency, accountability and predictability. Equally problematic are deliberate attempts to remove or to reduce drastically the gains of foreign or domestic investors from their efforts and investments.

Protection against pollution, the improvement of working conditions, the protection of health and the provision of utilities for the development of the

---

33 Quote from Henri Madelin *Oil and Politics* (1975, English translation) Saxon House, at p 66 by Marcel, *op cit* (note 2 above), p 2. See also Ekim Arbatli, *Political Regimes, Investment Risk and Resource Nationalism: an Empirical Analysis*, available at http://regconf.hse.ru/uploads/7da62134fab330f54f067e5cd2e603c40298cd7e.pdf.

34 If analysed from the perspective of expected resources in place, most African countries rank behind their peers in the Middle East (outside of north Africa), Latin America (Venezuela) and Russia (in terms both of oil and natural gas). The reserves controlled by state-owned NOCs in Africa, however, dwarf even the largest IOCs, such as ExxonMobil, Royal Dutch Shell and BP. Libya is the African country recognised as having the largest oil reserves, followed by Nigeria and Algeria.

35 The last five nationalisations worldwide were those in Bolivia, Chad, Ecuador, Russia and Venezuela, all in 2006. See Arbatli, *op cit* (note 36 above), p 1.

36 Stiglitz, *op cit* (note 29 above), pp 34-38 ('Experience with private control and economic efficiency – The Lessons of Russia').

economy and society are universal requirements. Regulatory initiatives in these areas may limit or curtail activities and negatively affect the profitability of ongoing ventures. The mere fact that they may limit absolute freedom of enterprise does not, *per se*, earn such initiatives the character of resource nationalism, however. Only when they are discriminatory in nature or purpose may they be considered as such.[37]

Among other things, radically changing ownership or disposal rights and introducing tax hikes that are unrelated to the capture of windfall profits not associated with investors' efforts may amount to nationalisation. Measures taken prior to the award of exclusive rights need to be seen differently.

While government participation in commercial activities may be labelled as state capitalism, it does not automatically result in the end of free markets. Scandinavian economies may vouch for this. Yet, state participation in commercial ventures is ideologically opposed by many and considered undesirable from an economic efficiency point of view by others.

There are two main reasons why owners of resources may want to partake in commercial ventures. Firstly, non-renewable resources represent, for most sovereign states, part of their capital base. The extraction of resources, and the efficiency with which this is performed, substantially affect the realised value of assets. The extraction process represents the conversion[38] of assets from real to capital assets. The resource owner naturally feels entitled to a substantial portion of the resource rent – even a qualified majority share of it. In the same way as an asset owner is unlikely to hand over to a broker the entire profit realised as the result of an asset sale handled by that broker, the state should not be expected to hand over the resource rent to IOCs or POCs. The broker gets a fee for his services; he does not keep the profit from the sale.

Secondly, the renewed fear of resource nationalism may really be linked to high oil prices. Many contracts operate under stabilised fiscal terms negotiated at much lower prices. Most contracts do not allow governments to collect windfall profits resulting from price hikes. If the gap between what the IOC takes and the government receives becomes too wide, stakeholders commonly become agitated. Fiscal and regulatory initiatives in most jurisdictions have been markedly tempered, given the size of price increases seen in the period up to the autumn of 2014. With a cycle of rapidly falling crude oil prices occurring yet again, the motivation for restrictive measures is likely to wane.

6. African state-owned oil companies

6.1 A brief history of state-owned oil companies in Africa

Newly independent states (and African states have been no exception) have secured control over natural resources either through the nationalisation of foreign investor

37 Reid W Click & Robert J Weiner, 'Resource nationalism meets the market: Political risk and the value of petroleum reserves', (2010) 41 *Journal of International Business Studies* 783, cited by Arbatli, *op cit* (note 36 above), who describes 'resource nationalism' as "a set of strategies that domestic elites employ for increasing their control over natural resources in a given country at the expense of foreign participation and investment." (at p 4).

38 Humphreys, Sachs & Stiglitz, *op cit* (note 29 above), p 9.

rights and assets or by licensing the entire national territory and maritime areas within their jurisdiction to a state-owned oil company. Angola[39] and Libya are two examples of this practice.

The first state-owned companies operating in Africa were not African but European. The first African state-owned oil company of the type with which the industry became familiar in subsequent years was Sonatrach in Algeria.[40] Under the Evian Accords of March 19 1962, the Algerian independence movement succeeded France in controlling Algerian petroleum resources.[41] Sonatrach[42] was originally established as a pipeline and marketing company. Subsequent renegotiations concluded in 1965 secured for Algeria the majority interest, culminating in the gradual nationalisation of all foreign petroleum assets between 1967 and 1971. Nationalisation meant the end of the previous concession regime in Algeria and introduced a new approach to national control over resources and activities.

Sonatrach was not the first state-owned oil company to arise out of nationalisation. Following both world wars, a number of former colonies initiated substantial nationalisations. The petroleum sector was no exception to this process. The nationalisations by President Cardenas in Mexico (1938) and Prime Minister Mossadegh in Iran (1951) represent such earlier examples. In the African context, Libya nationalised American-controlled assets in 1970.

6.2 The functions of African state-owned oil companies

African NOCs are predominantly state-owned. This does not imply that they are all state monopolies in the upstream sector (for example, the National Iranian Oil Company (NIOC) since the 1979 Islamic Revolution, Petróleos de Venezuela, SA (PDVSA) in Venezuela (occasionally) or Gazprom in the former Soviet Union). In several African countries, the state-owned oil company co-existed early on, if not always happily, with foreign investors.

The number of African state-owned oil companies has steadily increased over time. This happened quite quickly in some countries. In others, the process took longer.[43] The difference in speed is often related to the relative economic importance of the sector in each country. The structure and mandate of state companies still vary substantially.

State-owned oil companies are normally distinctly different from IOCs. The

---

39 See Angola's Petroleum Activities Law (Law 10/04 of November 12 2004), which replaces, in particular, the general Petroleum Activities Law (Law 13/78 of August 26 1978). Articles 4(1) and (2) appoint, subject to article 44 of the same law, the Sociedade Nacional de Combustível de Angola, Empresa Pública – (Sonangol, EP) as the national concessionaire and holder of mining rights.

40 Sonatrach's predecessor was the Société national de recherche et d'exploitation des pétroles en Algérie SN REPAL (National Company for Exploration and Utilization of Oil in Algeria), which was established in 1946 as a joint venture between the Bureau de recherche de pétrole (BRP) and the Algerian colonial government of that time. See Samir Saul, 'SN REPAL, CPF and Oil-Paid-in-Francs"', in Beltran, *op cit* (note 17 above), p 99.

41 Preferences for French companies remained in place during a transitional six-year period: see Saul, *op cit* (note 43 above), p 108.

42 Société Nationale pour Transport et de la Commercialisation de Hydrocarbures (National Company for the Transport and Marketing of Hydrocarbons), which was established on December 12 1963.

43 The South African NOC, Petro SA, is a 100% state-owned company established in 2002 as a result of the Mineral and Petroleum Resources Development Act 2002.

NOCs of some north African OPEC members may have reached the threshold and are close to becoming MNEs.[44] Outside Africa, several companies initially created as national champions, such as PETRONAS, Petrobras and Statoil, have moved on to become MNEs.

Few African national oil companies are labelled national companies without having complete upstream, downstream or combined mandates. The Kenya National Oil Corporation (KNOC) appears to be an exception, since its primary function is more akin to a data centre. KNOC does not participate in development and production activities or in marketing and sales.[45]

Many African regimes initially associated themselves with Marxist ideology in relation to their economic structures after achieving independence. These regimes tended to establish state-owned monopolies. When the Cold War ended, they opened up to foreign investors. Collaboration has normally taken two alternative forms: agreements either with local POCs, or with foreign direct investors or IOCs as collaborators with the state oil company.

Following the 1955 Law[46] Libyan oil activities soon expanded with the assistance of several IOCs. Law 13 of 1968 established the general National Oil Corporation (later to become the Libyan National Oil Corporation (LNOC)) and directed the state company to assume the responsibility for all oil sector operations. Following the revolution that deposed the King in 1969, this law was replaced by the 1970 Law, which was further complemented by decision 10/1979 of the General Secretariat of the General People's Congress. The decision resulted in a reorganisation of the state oil company and defined a broader scope of responsibility. These enlarged powers included ensuring the realisation of the petroleum sector development plan objectives and providing for the new LNOC to become an integral part of the development of the national economy.

An interesting observation with regard to African states is the way in which they have developed along different lines when compared to previous practice. Two examples illustrate this. Uganda codified the legal foundation for the establishment of a state-owned oil company through revised petroleum legislation enacted in 2013. The legislation did not change the basic premise of the production sharing contract-based system. Under the new system, however, the commercial interests of the state as resource owner are managed by a company, not by the relevant ministry and the Petroleum Export and Production Department (PEPD), thus moving commercial management out of the administration.

The opposite trend has taken place in Ghana with regard to its state-owned company, the Ghana National Petroleum Corporation (GNPC). GNPC previously had commercial as well as regulatory functions. Recent legislation has, however, removed regulatory tasks from the GNPC and transferred them to the Petroleum

---

44 In the case of OPEC, Saudi Aramco, the Kuwait Petroleum Company and PDVSA are state-owned companies that have invested downstream, including in shipping, and outside their home territories. Compared to 'thoroughbred' IOCs, these overseas activities are still relatively limited.

45 Mwinda Nyaga, 'Kenya', in Dr Eduardo G Pereira & Prof Kim Talus (Eds), *Upstream Law and Regulation: A Global Guide* (2013, Globe Business Publishing, London).

46 Law 25/1955.

Commission.[47] An identical development could be seen in Mozambique in 2001,[48] when Empresa Nacional de Hidrocarbonetos (ENH) the state-owned oil company, lost its monopoly on upstream petroleum activities. All of ENH's regulatory functions were taken over by the relevant ministry and then delegated, initially to the Direccao Nacional de Carvao e Hidrocarbonetos (DNCH) a subordinate directorate, and subsequently to the Instituto Nacional de Petroleo (INP).

Separating the roles and functions associated with commercial interests from regulatory responsibilities is a new trend in the context of African petroleum. Clarification of roles has obvious positive transparency implications. The potential for more accountable and predictable regulatory and industry environments will benefit investors and local stakeholders. In the case of Uganda, this may forebode more active government participation. Uganda is, however, a landlocked country and therefore faces difficulties in attracting foreign investors, so that a state-owned oil company may be required for financial and operational reasons to get production off the ground.

Administrations seem to have initiated a process whereby the various roles of government in relation to industry interests are separated from regulatory functions. To some extent, this has assisted framework conditions to become more transparent and predictable. In other cases, it has served to reveal that past monitoring, benchmarking and control practices have been insufficient. Past practices have not served resource owner and rent collector well. Equally, they have not served the interest of third party stakeholders (other than IOCs) as well as should or could be expected. Changes of approach have undoubtedly resulted in tighter regulatory control that will open the way to enlarged government control, though not necessarily intervention. For those believing in unabated free enterprise, this may be unwelcome and therefore be negatively labelled and even described as resource nationalism. For most other stakeholders, these initiatives are welcomed as opening up the economy and enabling civil society to monitor the conduct of elected representatives and government administrators.

Ghana and Mozambique have reorganised their governance and removed regulatory power from state-owned companies. In subsequent bidding rounds, Mozambique opened up to foreign investors and awarded new standardised exploration and production concession contracts (EPCCs) rather than the previously individually negotiated production sharing agreements. Under the EPCCs, the state (through ENH) was awarded a nominal carried interest during the exploration phase. In Ghana the government took over regulatory functions and licensing from the GNPC, but did not change the general approach of production sharing contracts.

If properly structured and enforced, clarification and separation of roles will assist IOCs in demonstrating that they are compliant. This will also assist them in demonstrating compliance with growing demand for documentation of conduct arising from anti-corruption legislation at home. Ultimately the separation of

47 See the Ghanaian National Petroleum Corporation Act 1984 and the Petroleum Commission Act 2011 (Act 821).

48 See Mozambique Petroleum Law (3/2001 of February 21 2001), revoking Law 3/81 of October 3 1981.

regulatory and commercial interests in the petroleum sector will assist competent IOCs in gaining the upper hand in competition for access to resources and production rights. Clarity in role allocation and making regulatory framework requirements a matter for the public domain will, if adequately managed, reduce the window of opportunity for corrupt and non-competitive acreage awards and project approvals. If, however, regulatory powers are not exercised in a transparent and accountable manner, government initiatives in this domain may end up having the same negative effect on industry as previous methods of nationalisation or the imposition of unchecked state-owned companies. There cannot be an African solution to this. The solution must be global.

Dispute resolution involving oil and gas assets in Africa

Mark Beeley
Vinson & Elkins

1. Introduction

The potential for disputes concerning the oil and gas industry is generally high. Across the production chain, from upstream hydrocarbon extraction through refining and downstream sales, the amounts of money at stake frequently confront very significant numbers of interlocking contracts with multiple parties, and inevitable disagreements arise. Typically, these disagreements are worth millions of US dollars. Africa is no different from anywhere else in the world in this regard. Africa, however (with its multiplicity of jurisdictions, evolving legal traditions and high levels of both foreign direct investment (FDI) and political risk), presents different practical challenges for resolving those disputes in an efficient, timely and satisfactory fashion.

2. Arbitration v the courts and court interference in arbitration

As with the majority of countries involved in energy disputes, the first choice of many participants in the African oil and gas sector (and in particular for non-African origin investors) is arbitration. On paper at least, this choice minimises the level of local court interference, allows for cross-border enforcement of any resulting award and gives the parties a measure of control over who hears their dispute. Due however to a mix of restrictive hydrocarbon laws reserving certain matters to the courts, frequent scepticism that arbitration gives an advantage to the 'foreign' party, a greater willingness on the part of courts to interfere with the arbitration process and a penchant for associated disputes (eg, claims brought by 'agents', local 'fixers' and introducers), a substantial body of African oil and gas disputes are also resolved through the domestic courts. This is done either directly or indirectly via the 'backdoor', where, despite a clear agreement to arbitrate, the process is either disrupted by local court interference or the real battleground becomes the domestic enforcement of any resulting arbitral award.

It is, of course, impossible to make anything more than the most general points about dispute resolution systems across 54 countries – particularly given the diverse mix of legal systems, reflecting the historic impact both of common law legal systems and multiple civil law legal systems (and, in places, the impact of multiple religious laws). There are, however, certain trends that can be anecdotally observed, and a certain degree of empirical evidence to support them.

Generally speaking, the African continent is no stranger to arbitration. This process was a well understood and used concept in Ptolemaic Egypt, and has since appeared across the continent in the form of customary arbitration, as well as from the legacy of the various colonial legal systems. Despite this early start, however, and with some exceptions, international arbitration (as the term is understood internationally) remains a misunderstood and poorly supported concept in much of Africa (particularly in sub-Saharan Africa). This is especially the case in the oil and gas sector, where the combination of high stakes, national interest and divergent nationalities all too often leads to domestic court interference.

This is the key issue. There is nothing particularly surprising about most arbitration practices or procedures in Africa *per se*, but there is an unfortunately high dependence on the local courts to support such matters (including by showing restraint). While some jurisdictions have enthusiastically embraced arbitration, others remain sceptical, with judiciaries seeing arbitration as a poor cousin to the courts and being all too willing to allow rogue parties to violate arbitration agreements and bring disputes before the courts instead. In some cases, courts have even gone so far as to enjoin parties from participating in an arbitration, particularly where a domestic party is being made a respondent in a foreign-seated arbitration. It is not an irregular experience for parties, arbitral tribunals and legal representatives involved in an offshore-seated arbitration against a sub-Saharan African respondent to be ordered not to participate in an arbitration by the home court of that respondent. While such orders are often ignored by the international tribunal, and the arbitration proceeds, doing so creates significant risk to enforcement of an award. It is not difficult to argue that it would be against the public policy of a country to enforce an arbitral award obtained in breach of a court injunction in that country.

Even where the court's involvement is entirely proper, and by contrast with counterpart western courts (which may well have originally served as the inspirations for most African court systems), users often find its process slow and inefficient, with frequent adjournments and cases being heard in piecemeal over the course of months rather than in one block until the proceedings are concluded. Unpredictability is also a common feature, with many of the relevant legal systems still only starting to develop a reliable corpus of legal precedents applicable to complicated commercial matters (and in particular as to the conflict of laws analyses that arbitrations so often require). Furthermore, judges often make decisions based either on policy concerns above and beyond the law or on a simple lack of experience and understanding of what is frequently a specialist and complex area.

Regrettably, parties also still face corruption, or at least significant bias, with many international parties being rightly concerned about home town advantage. While there is a tendency to generalise about the extent of corruption in African nations, the author's experiences at least suggest that it can often constitute a significant obstacle to the just and effective disposal of disputes by both courts and arbitral tribunals. This is particularly an issue for oil and gas companies, a sector which has global corruption issues and is under fierce regulatory scrutiny. In matters involving agency agreements (including royalty interests) and land, it is all too common for large multinational oil companies to find themselves locked in years of court proceedings with a private individual who has no objectively meritorious case, but who does have an improper influence over the court process.

Concerns as to speed and reliability of African litigation are being combatted in part by the incremental spread of specialised and better funded commercial courts, for which judges are given specialist training, tailored procedural rules and a much needed professional support staff. Such courts can now be found, for example, in Tanzania, Uganda and Ghana. Such specialist courts are welcomed, particularly in cases in which certain African states have reserved particular hydrocarbons-related matters (eg, environmental matters, taxation and rights of ownership) exclusively to the courts. This may sometimes create snags where foreign-seated arbitrators have jurisdiction to decide a matter, only for the award ultimately to prove unenforceable domestically, as being contrary to public policy.

All of these factors lead to a situation in which, irrespective of whether a party is dealing with a domestic or foreign-seated arbitration, court intervention can be expected both in the arbitral process itself and at the stage where enforcement of any resulting award is sought.

3. Growth in the use of arbitration in Africa: domestic and international trends

All that being said, there is evidence that the use of arbitration is growing and with it, a greater sense of reliability of the process. It is now the starting point in most African model form production sharing contracts to offer to resolve disputes with operating companies by arbitration, typically under either the United Nations Commission on International Trade Law (UNCITRAL) or the International Centre for Settlement of Investment Disputes (ICSID) regimes. Whereas the battle may originally have been concerned with going to arbitration at all, the negotiating 'hot spots' nowadays are more often concerned with seeking to agree a neutral (and typically offshore) 'seat' or juridical place of arbitration, and on obtaining a valid sovereign immunity waiver (a matter which remains all too often a point of disagreement, and which is not meaningfully assisted by bilateral investment treaty (BIT) provisions or by bringing claims under the ICSID Convention). Similarly, as foreign investors have brought the Association of International Petroleum Negotiators (AIPN) and other standard form operating agreements and like instruments into their African projects, and with the increased focus on local partnering (including many domestic companies now buying out external partners), the idea of commercial arbitration in the African oil and gas sector has increasingly become the norm, irrespective of whom the dispute will involve.

In a survey of 54 African countries[1] as at 1 September 2014, despite all of those countries having some form of arbitration laws (whether on a 'stand alone' basis or as part of a civil code), only 18.5%[2] of those countries had adopted the UNCITRAL Model Law on International Commercial Arbitration (the Model Law), which might be considered surprising given that this law was developed in particular for emerging

1 For the purposes of this survey, all member states of the African Union (including all currently suspended states) were included, except for the Sahrawi Democratic Arab Republic. In addition, Morocco, a former member of the African Union (currently excluded over its role in the disputed territory of Western Sahara), was also included. A current list of African Union member states may be accessed at www.au.int/en/member_states/countryprofiles.

2 Based on the list of adopting jurisdictions maintained by UNCITRAL and available at www.uncitral.org.

markets. Those countries not adopting the Model Law appear to have two preferences. The first preference is to retain 'inherited' arbitration laws from former colonial powers. These laws are now often grossly behind the times in terms of modern practice, however; for example, in some countries the English Arbitration Act of 1889 (!) remains the model form. The second preference is to have effectively 'unique' combinations of arbitration laws, which create traps for the unwary with contradictory results and/or ambiguities, but which also contribute to the growth of individual arbitration centres. Bodies of case law and precedent are developing in each jurisdiction, but remain a long way short of forming a reliable corpus with sufficient depth to promote certainty of outcome.

Perhaps reflecting strong levels of FDI, 83%[3] of countries are signatories to the Washington Convention on the Settlement of Investment Disputes between States and Nationals of Other States 1965 (the Washington Convention), which allows for investment disputes between a state on the one hand, and a foreign investor on the other, to be settled by ICSID or 'World Bank' arbitration. This trend is also reflected in the high number of BITs existing and in force with countries throughout the continent, with 96% of those surveyed being parties to BITs (474 in total) and 26% being state parties to the multilateral OIC Investment Protection chapter (discussed below). These treaties provide individuals and companies with both investment protection rights and access to international arbitration directly against the state if those rights are violated. Given the levels of political risk often perceived across the continent, such protection mechanisms are increasingly important to oil and gas investors, and may provide some degree of protection against targeted taxation, unexpected upheavals in the relevant legal regime and, in the most extreme cases, the direct taking of property and investments.

The prevalence of BITs and the high uptake of arbitration under the Washington Convention, coupled with well understood political risks, has (perhaps predictably) led to a number of publicly known investment treaty cases against African states, of which approximately 15% concern investments in oil and gas or in related industries (eg, power and energy infrastructure). Despite the seeming willingness of African states to enter into investment protection treaties, no African signatories have ratified the Energy Charter Treaty 1994, a multilateral investment protection treaty aimed expressly at investments in the energy sector. This is an increasingly important consideration in the minds of investors in oil and gas, and the absence of this treaty means that investors need to be more creative in ensuring that they have meaningful treaty coverage, including taking advantage of some less-tested paths (see, for example, the discussion of the OIC below).

Equally, despite the high level of ratification of the Washington Convention, ratification of the New York Convention on the Recognition and Enforcement of Foreign Arbitral Awards 1958 (the New York Convention), which permits cross-border enforcement of commercial arbitration awards, is lower, with only 59% of African countries surveyed having ratified it.[4] This has the consequence that, for

3 Based on the list of signatories maintained by ICSID and available at https://icsid.worldbank.org/ICSID/FrontServlet?requestType=ICSIDDocRH&actionVal=ContractingStates&ReqFrom=Main.

approximately one in three African countries, there is little in the way of standard enforcement mechanisms, leaving the parties at the mercy of local court processes and domestic arbitration laws, many of which are in the formative stages and are consequently unpredictable. In addition, many users have found the process of trying to enforce foreign arbitral awards in Africa very variable, irrespective of whether or not the New York Convention has applied, with varying degrees of political and other influences often creating significant risks to enforcement, despite a sound (on paper) legal mechanism. By way of further complication, unwary award creditors may find that, despite the application of the New York Convention, little or no effort has been made to make domestic laws conform so as to give it effect. There is a need to take early advice from local counsel when dealing with such cases, in order to ensure a good understanding of not only what the law says, but also how it is applied in practice, which may be a very different proposition.

With regard to commercial arbitrations themselves, there is also a slowly growing trend towards the use of international arbitration institutions by domestic African participants. For example, in 2012 the Paris-based International Chamber of Commerce (ICC) received 759 new filings for arbitration, which included 127 parties from Africa.[5] Despite this significant level of usage, only five of these arbitrations were seated in Africa, which demonstrates the degree of uncertainty, even among African parties, as to the domestic legal frameworks that support arbitration. A similar trend may be observed in arbitrations conducted through the London Court of International Arbitration (LCIA), an institution which African parties have traditionally been less willing to embrace than the ICC, with 8% of parties to the 290 new cases registered in 2013 coming from the African continent. It remains the case that the vast majority of African arbitrations are conducted either under domestic arbitration regimes (eg, the Arbitration Rules set out in the First Schedule to the Nigerian Arbitration and Conciliation Act 1990) or are entirely *ad hoc* in nature.

Consistent with the global trend towards regionalisation in arbitration, an increasing number of arbitration centres have opened across the continent. One of oldest and most well-established of these is the Cairo Regional Centre for International Commercial Arbitration (CRCICA), which celebrated its 35th anniversary in 2014. Further centres may now be found in Rwanda (the Kigali International Arbitration Centre), Nigeria (the Lagos Regional Centre for International Commercial Arbitration) and Kenya (the Nairobi Centre for International Arbitration), as well as in Algeria, Benin, Burkina Faso, Cameroon, the Democratic Republic of the Congo, Ethiopia, Ghana, Ivory Coast, Lesotho, Libya, Madagascar, Mali, Morocco, Senegal, South Africa, Swaziland, Tunisia and Zimbabwe. These centres do not merely provide hearing room facilities, but also seek to promote arbitration locally, including by way of educating local practitioners, the judiciary and lawmakers in international arbitration practice with a view to increasing the reliability and usability of arbitration in their countries. This is, of course, a good thing both for arbitration users and host governments.

---

4 Based on the list of signatories maintained by UNCITRAL and available at www.uncitral.org.

5 ICC Court Bulletin, Vol 24(1), p 7.

It is clear from the above discussion that, as can also be seen in developing regions elsewhere around the world, there have been growing trends towards the establishment of individual arbitration centres. These are often (legitimately) driven by hopes of tapping into the revenue that can be attracted to a country that becomes a regional arbitration hub. There are, however, also growing trends in favour of multilateral arbitration solutions. These include the *Organisation pour l'Harmonisation en Afrique du Droit des Affaires* (OHADA), the *Organisation of the Islamic Conference* (OIC) *Investment Protection Chapter* and the *LCIA-Mauritius International Arbitration Centre* (LCIA-MIAC). These relatively new entrants to African dispute resolution should be on the radar of those involved in African oil and gas. They are explored in more detail below, not least because their efforts span the continent and may lead incrementally to a more informed and perhaps more unified approach.

4. OHADA: A new dawn for dispute resolution in Africa?

The evolution and expansion of OHADA is being keenly watched by those with an interest in dispute resolution in Africa. Originally signed by the 14 African Franc zone states at Port Louis in Mauritius on October 17 1993, OHADA's constitutional treaty came into effect on September 18 1995 and was later substantially revised, with the revised treaty entering into force on March 21 2010. OHADA now includes 17 member states.

Operating under a framework of commercial laws deriving largely from modern French law, the original goal of the signatory states was to harmonise outdated business codes, which often dated back to the colonial era, and thus facilitate trade and investment in order to promote economic development.[6] This included addressing the resolution of business disputes.

While OHADA clearly has a far broader remit than dispute resolution, its impact in this area can be profound. Among nine uniform acts that OHADA members have ratified, the Uniform Act on Arbitration (UAA) is applicable to both individuals and corporate entities alike. Based on the UNCITRAL Model Law, the UAA was adopted by the OHADA member states on March 11 1999 and entered into force 90 days later. Upon entry into force in a new OHADA member state, the UAA immediately becomes applicable to all arbitrations. Although the UAA is stated as superseding any conflicting domestic arbitration legislation, any previously existing national legislation covering arbitration that does not conflict with it will remain in force; this was recognised in a decision of the Common Court of Justice and Arbitration (CCJA) on April 30 2001. This feature will likely increase the complexity and length of disputes held under the auspices of the OHADA.

Uniquely, OHADA law specifically favours arbitration as a method for resolving commercial disputes and has the advantage of applying to all types of arbitration where the registered office of an entity is in a member state. OHADA law also contemplates an institutional arbitration organised under the auspices of the CCJA,

---

6 Although there is no official English translation, a rough translation of the Preamble to the revised treaty includes the wording, "Determination to make the harmonisation of business law a tool continuously strengthening the rule of law and legal and economic integration." See http://www.ohada.com/traite-revise.html.

although that body does not itself act as an arbitral tribunal. Arbitration under the procedural rules of the CCJA strongly resembles ICC procedure and the rules themselves are broadly similar to those of the Dubai International Arbitration Centre and the Singapore International Arbitration Centre. Any arbitral award rendered in an OHADA member state may be enforced within any other member state by obtaining an *exequatur*. Under the UAA, the granting of an *exequatur* may only be refused in very limited circumstances.

The UAA covers both domestic and international arbitration and its rules apply to "any arbitration when the seat of the Arbitral Tribunal is in one of the member states" (article 1). Thus, if an arbitration clause merely specifies that the seat of the arbitration will be in an OHADA member state, the UAA will apply, though the clause may also state that the arbitration will take place under the specific framework of the CCJA. Under article 14 of the UAA, parties "may directly or by reference to arbitration rules, determine the arbitration procedure; they may also subject this procedure to a procedural law of their choice". The UAA thus provides an important contemporary framework for dispute resolution in Africa. The environment in which it operates, however, inherently breeds a number of significant practical challenges to its effectiveness.

As a 2011 World Bank paper on OHADA points out, any assessment of the organisation must take account of the milieu in which it operates:

> *OHADA member states are all low-tier countries crippled by structural problems and most of them have experienced numerous calamities since the creation of OHADA, including humanitarian crisis, military coups and the collapse of democratic governments.*[7]

Lack of resources is far from the only deficiency affecting OHADA. The Organisation spans a vast geographical area, encompassing west and central Africa and stretching out to the Comoros Islands, off the coast of Madagascar. Although the CCJA is intended to act as a court of final appeal across Africa, it has been noted that, by 2010, a majority of the appeals heard came from within hydrocarbons-rich Ivory Coast.[8] By contrast, a party in the Comoros Islands would perhaps be more reticent to resort to an appeal to the CCJA, for reasons of practicality and cost.

Moreover, although membership of OHADA is open to any member state of the African Union, the application of OHADA law has already raised numerous difficulties, due to the differing nature of the judicial systems and the fact that French remains the working language of the organisation, by virtue of article 42 of the OHADA treaty. OHADA has faced particular hostility in the common law regions of Cameroon, where the Southern Cameroons National Council and other legal associations have complained of marginalisation and an attempt to wipe out the English cultural, legal and linguistic heritage.[9] Asking an English-speaking common law judiciary to apply a constitutional treaty with no official translation from the

---

7 Renaud Beauchard & Mahutodji Jimmy Vital Kodo, *Can OHADA Increase Legal Certainty in Africa?*, World Bank Justice & Development Working Paper Series (2011), at 5.

8 *Ibid*, at 22.

9 Justin Melong, *Implementation of OHADA laws in a bilingual and bijural context: Cameroon as a case in point* (2013), available at http://revue.ersuma.org/no-2-mars-2013/etudes-21.

French text inherently presents major difficulties; in the Cameroonian case of *Akiangan Fombin Sebastien v Fotso Joseph & others*, Justice Ayah Paul refused to apply the OHADA treaty on the ground that, by being available only in French, its application to the Anglophone region was thereby excluded.[10] Essentially, OHADA faces a 'Catch 22' situation: any tweaks to the framework of the organisation to incorporate differing judicial systems may result in a further drain on resources; unlike a comparable European body, however, there is little money available to fund a large bureaucracy and an army of translators.

Aside from structural deficiencies, and as has already been noted, corruption remains a key issue in obtaining effective legal process. In Kalm's study in Cameroon, all of the lawyers interviewed complained about corruption in the judiciary and stated that the OHADA system has had very little impact on this.[11] Dickerson also noted that, while the CCJA is well respected for its integrity, legal professionals in Cameroon were quick to acknowledge that the CCJA's transparency has not eradicated corruption in the national judicial systems, a problem compounded by the perception that political corruption is endemic.[12] Nevertheless, the development of arbitration in member states, a key pillar of OHADA law, has begun to offer a viable alternative to the regular judiciaries.

5. Old dog, new tricks? Arbitration under the OIC Investment Agreement

In a recent (2013) arbitration seated in Singapore and conducted under the UNCITRAL Arbitration Rules, a tribunal held, for the first time, that the Agreement on Promotion, Protection and Guarantee of Investments Among Member States of the Organisation of the Islamic Conference 1981 (the OIC Investment Agreement) provided a mechanism for investors to sue ratifying member states.[13] The award on jurisdiction (the Al-Warraq Award) was subsequently heralded as "a fabulous discovery that will open a new perspective to arbitration and to investment in the Islamic world"[14] and may have substantial ramifications in the field of investor-state arbitration for the 27 African nations of the Organisation of Islamic Cooperation(OIC).[15]

The OIC is the second largest intergovernmental organisation after the United Nations, with a membership of 57 states spread across four continents. Member states of the OIC account for almost two-thirds of the world's proven crude oil and natural gas reserves, at 62% and 63% respectively, and include some of the largest producers in Africa, such as Nigeria, Algeria and Libya.[16] Despite this, the OIC Investment Agreement has received remarkably little attention since it was initially

10 Vernon Valentine Palmer, *Mixed Jurisdictions Worldwide: The Third Legal Family* (2nd Edn, 2012, Cambridge University Press), at 669.

11 Gustav Kalm, *Building Legal Certainty through International Law: OHADA Law in Cameroon* (2011) p 19, Working Paper No 11-005, Buffett Centre for International and Comparative Studies, available at www.cics.northwestern.edu/documents/workingpapers/Buffett_11-005_Kalm.pdf.

12 CM Dickerson, 'Harmonising Business Laws in Africa: OHADA Calls the Tune', Columbia Journal of Transnational Law, Vol 44 (2005), 17 at 70.

13 The Award on Jurisdiction was issued in June 2012 in a dispute between Hesham Al-Warraq, a Saudi businessman, and the Republic of Indonesia, concerning the nationalisation of a bank in the wake of the 2008 Global Financial Crisis. It is available at: http://www.italaw.com/cases/documents/1528

14 Walid Ben Hamida, 'A Fabulous Discovery: The Arbitration Offer under the Organization of Islamic Cooperation Agreement Related to Investment', (2013) 30(6) Journal of International Arbitration 636.

15 Formerly known as The Organisation of the Islamic Conference.

ratified in 1981 and the OIC itself has yet to provide clarification on various outstanding issues emanating out of the Al-Warraq Award.

The OIC Investment Agreement was approved and opened for signature by resolution 7/12-E of the Twelfth Islamic Conference of Foreign Ministers, held in Baghdad, Iraq, in June 1981. Thus far, however, only 14 of the 27 African OIC member states have ratified it. Although a multilateral treaty, and couched in different language, its provisions will be familiar to anybody who is accustomed to dealing with BITs.

Under article 1 of the OIC Investment Agreement, the definition of 'Investor' is interpreted broadly, so as to encompass:

- governments of other OIC member states;
- a natural person with qualifying nationality in an OIC member state; and
- a corporate person incorporated in an OIC member state.

The OIC Investment Agreement contains various provisions that are comparable with those commonly found in BITs, including a most favoured nation provision (article 8) and expansive expropriation protections (article 10). There is, however, no specific article according fair and equitable treatment to investors.

Where a dispute arises, the OIC Investment Agreement permits reference to international arbitration directly against the state, up until the time a standing judicial body is set up to hear such claims. In that regard, one of the organs contemplated by the OIC framework is the International Islamic Court of Justice (IICJ), which is referenced in article 14 of the OIC Charter as having been established in Kuwait in 1987 with a remit to act as the "principal judicial organ" of the OIC "upon the entry into force of its statute".[17] Although a draft statute was approved by Resolution 11/13 at the Third Islamic Summit Conference, there is no tangible evidence to demonstrate that the court even exists. As George Burn, counsel to the successful claimant in the Al-Warraq case, has pointed out:

> *The picture is a confusing one, but it is beyond debate that the International Islamic Court of Justice, if it has been established at all, has been established only in name. For this reason alone it cannot be considered as the 'organ for the settlement of disputes arising under the Agreement'.*[18]

Accordingly, the OIC Investment Agreement currently offers a mechanism for bringing disputes against states only by way of arbitration.

The degree to which the Al-Warraq Award heralds a new dawn in investment treaty disputes across Africa will depend largely on whether it remains a one-off or whether other arbitral tribunals will follow the same path. In that regard, and as at the time of writing, commentators are closely watching a second case, brought against

---

16 *Current Stance of Energy Resources and Potential in OIC Member Countries*, Organisation of Islamic Cooperation Statistical, Economic and Social Research and Training Centre for Islamic Countries (December 2012), at 1, available at www.sesrtcic.org/files/article/459.pdf.

17 A copy of the English language version of the OIC's Charter is available at www.oic-oci.org/is11/english/Charter-en.pdf.

18 George Burn, *The Invisible MIT: The Curious Case of the Agreement for the Promotion, Protection and Guarantee of Investments among Member States of the Organisation of the Islamic Conference* (2014) (unpublished article on file with the British Institute of International and Comparative Law).

Egypt, in which the claimant party has applied to the OIC Secretary General to appoint an arbitrator, the respondent state having failed to do so. Despite initial requests for the Secretary General of the OIC to make a default appointment of an arbitrator having initially been made in April 2014, there are no public indications that it has yet done so.[19] Investment treaty watchers will continue to hold their breath.

Notwithstanding the more positive indicators previously discussed, it is clear that the OIC could do much more, and addressing the current state of investor-state arbitration is paramount. A delegation from the Saudi-Egypt Business Council that was due to meet with the Secretary General lamented the "urgent need at this time to revitalize the role of arbitration within the organization",[20] and stated that the OIC needs to clarify its position on a number of unresolved matters stemming from the Al-Warraq Award if it is serious about creating a positive investment climate to boost intra-OIC trade. The OIC's April 2014 report on the implementation of the Ten Year Programme of Action highlights the importance of the OIC Investment Agreement, noting that it:

> *provides for the commitment of OIC member states to creating, in their respective countries the necessary and favourable conditions for promoting intra-OIC investment and to offer various incentives for free movement of capital.*[21]

If the OIC were to begin to address the various outstanding issues relating to the application of the OIC Investment Agreement, it would provide an invaluable arbitral tool for many investors in the African continent.

6. The LCIA-MIAC Arbitration Centre

While the use of the major international arbitration institutions has been slow to take off in Africa, as discussed above, there is incremental growth in that direction. Consistent with this, the Mauritian Government and the LCIA entered into a joint venture in July 2011 to launch the LCIA-MIAC Arbitration Centre, with the intention of providing an 'institutional' arbitration centre within Africa, with its own set of bespoke rules and a Secretariat which is making active efforts to identify the best African arbitrators and increase the use and sophistication of arbitration across the continent.

While LCIA-MIAC is, of course, not the first arbitration centre in Africa (and nor will it likely be the last), it does represent a stepping stone between the benefits of local centres possessing knowledge of the unique features of their domestic markets and the experience and expertise of the LCIA as a very long-standing arbitration centre. Accordingly, the user has the benefit of a locally 'savvy' English/French dual language Secretariat, the staff of which can tap into the LCIA's long experience and, in particular, have access to the LCIA's extensive diligence and knowledge of arbitrators. Equally, the addition of the LCIA brand may well serve to attract

---

19 Luke Eric Peterson, 'Viability of Investor-State Arbitration Under Inter-Islamic Investment Treaty Now Lies in Hands of Secretariat, Following Petitions to OIC', *IA Reporter* (July 31 2014).

20 Khamees Al-Saadi, *IDB Aims to revive troubled Saudi investments in Egypt* (August 17 2013), available at www.arabnews.com/news/461480.

21 *Report of the OIC General Secretariat on Implementation of the OIC Ten-Year Programme of Action Submitted to the Thirtieth Meeting of the Follow-Up Committee to Standing Committee for Economic and Commercial Cooperation of the OIC*, OIC/COMCEC-FC-30/2014 (May 7-8 2014) at 6. Available at www.comcec.org/UserFiles/File/30.isedak-izleme-kitap/EN/30FC-D(2)-eng-OIC.pdf.

arbitrators who may not otherwise be willing to sit in a case under the auspices of a centre with which they are unfamiliar.

To be truly successful, the LCIA-MIAC will have to overcome the reticence many domestic African parties have traditionally felt in relation to the LCIA. Despite being a truly international body, with an outstanding reputation, some African parties have focused heavily on the fact that the 'L' in the initialism stands for London, and have concluded that this represents an institutional bias towards parties from western Europe. This prejudice has not affected the ICC International Court of Arbitration in the same way, despite the fact that it is based in Paris. The centre will also need to overcome the general preference towards *ad hoc* or non-administered arbitration, with African states in particular generally preferring to employ the UNCITRAL Arbitration Rules for significant oil and gas contracts rather than agreeing to institutional arbitration. Where this is the case, it may be worthwhile for a negotiator to accept the demand for UNCITRAL arbitration, but seek to 'bolt on' an administrative body to assist in the arbitral process. Both the LCIA-MIAC and the International Bureau of the Permanent Court of Arbitration at The Hague are (among others) willing to provide this service. This approach may represent a compromise, in that the state will not feel as though it has submitted to an arbitral institution, but the arbitral process will still benefit from the support that a good secretariat can render to it.

7. Conclusion

Dispute resolution in Africa, particularly in the oil and gas sector, requires more than good technical lawyering in order to reach a successful result. Across most of the region, it is vital to have an inside track on not only the law, but also the unwritten procedures, the degree to which court interference can be anticipated and managed and, ultimately, real world pragmatism about whether an award or judgment realistically stands any prospect of enforcement.

Upfront attention should be paid to structuring deal documents to ensure the most stable dispute resolution process, and thought should be given before anything is signed as to how to enforce any award. When dealing with states, sovereign immunity waivers are key, and upfront consideration should also be given to enforcement treaties and whether, in reality, there is any successful track record of the law being applied as written. Having good, reliable, and 'street wise' advice from a local law firm as part of this planning process is highly recommended, as is considering whether deal structures will allow for offshore money flows that might be used for enforcement purposes.

All that being said, dispute resolution in Africa is making steady strides in the direction normally expected by western European-trained lawyers and their clients, and a particularly strong set of arbitration and litigation specialists, as well as arbitrators, are emerging from across the African continent. Effective dispute resolution can be achieved with a little bit of planning, the right resources, the right amount of diligence regarding the playing field, and a willingness to hold one's nerve and play a long game.

The author would like to express his thanks to Mr Ben Wilkins for his help in researching this chapter.

Decommissioning in Nigeria

Olubunmi Fayokun
Aluko & Oyebode

1. Introduction

A number of historical developments have taken place down the years in relation to the ownership of interests in the Nigerian oil and gas industry, following the first commercial discovery of oil in Oloibiri, Delta State in 1956. Examples of such developments include the grant to the Shell D'Arcy Company of an oil exploration licence in 1938 by the British colonial government, under a Sole Concessionaire Arrangement (the Arrangement) concluded pursuant to the Mineral Oils Ordinance of 1914, which applied to the entire territory. The Arrangement was subsequently replaced by traditional joint venture arrangements (JVAs) after Nigeria joined the Organisation of Petroleum Exporting Countries (OPEC). The the country was obliged, as a condition of OPEC membership, to take control of its oil and gas industry in line with OPEC resolutions. Another significant development was the introduction of production sharing contracts (PSCs) in 1973, which assisted in alleviating the challenges faced by the country in the early 1990s with regard to meeting cash call obligations under the JVAs.

As the oil acreages held under the JVAs approach the end of their productive lives, there have been a number of divestments by international oil companies (IOCs) operating in the Nigerian oil and gas sector. These include:

- the sale of the interests held by Shell Petroleum Development Company (SPDC), Total Exploration and Production Nigeria Limited and Nigerian Agip Oil Company Limited in an unincorporated SPDC joint venture with the Nigerian National Petroleum Corporation (NNPC); and
- the ongoing divestment programme of Chevron Nigeria Limited, involving five shallow water blocks that are estimated to hold as much as 250 million barrels (bbls) of oil reserves.[1]

The IOCs are reputed to have earned in excess of $7 billion from the divestments, which have created an effective platform for the active participation of indigenous oil and gas companies in the upstream sub-sector of the Nigerian oil and gas industry.[2]

The divestments, which involved the negotiation of sale and purchase agreements (SPAs) and other ancillary transaction documents, required the determination of how certain liabilities of the IOCs under the JVAs between the IOCs

1 www.vanguardngr.com/2014/08/divestment-pengassan-seeks-listing-iocs-stock-exchange.

and the Federal Government of Nigeria (the Federal Government) – for example, decommissioning obligations – were to be addressed. The negotiations were particularly important because the existing joint operating agreements (JOAs) between the Federal Government and the IOCs do not specifically address the decommissioning and abandonment of the oil blocks. Furthermore, the existing legal framework does not currently provide for the allocation of responsibilities with regard to the decommissioning obligations of the parties in such JVAs. The absence of a comprehensive legal framework for decommissioning has created uncertainty for all the parties involved in the divestment process with regard to the financing of decommissioning and the enforceability of decommissioning obligations.

This chapter provides an analysis of the existing legal framework for decommissioning in Nigeria and presents an overview of some of the challenges pertaining to decommissioning in the Nigerian oil and gas sector.

2. Decommissioning

Decommissioning refers to the treatment of derelict facilities used for oil and gas operations during the productive life of a project. The term decommissioning, which was historically referred to as abandonment,[3] is defined as:

the process by which options for the final status of structures at the end of their working life are assessed for their dismantling, physical removal, disposal or modification ...[4]

Decommissioning has also been referred to as:

the process in which the operator of an offshore oil and gas installation goes through to plan, gain government approval and implement the removal, disposal or re-use of a structure when it is no longer needed for its current purpose.[5]

Decommissioning may be carried out in relation to both onshore and offshore oil and gas operations and involves activities such as the plugging and capping of wells, the dismantling and removal of (among other things) huge platforms, pipelines, sub-sea installations and floating equipment, the recycling of steel materials, the closing of landfills and land rehabilitation.

The process of decommissioning extends beyond the treatment of physical assets or installations, as there are also environmental effects to consider. The environmental hazards which the disposal of redundant onshore and offshore installations poses have necessitated regulation of the condition of the environment

---

2 Some of the local oil and gas companies that have benefited from the ongoing divestments include: ND Western Ltd, which acquired Oil Mining Lease (OML) 34 from SPDC; Elcrest E&P, which acquired OML 40 from SPDC; Shoreline Natural Resources Ltd, which acquired OML 30 from SPDC; Lekoil Ltd, which acquired OML 113 from Panaro Energy; Seplat plc, which acquired OMLs 4, 38 and 41 from an SPDC consortium; and, most notably, Oando plc, which is currently in the process of acquiring ConocoPhillips' Nigerian business unit for a record sum of $1.65 billion: see http://businessdayonline.com/2014/08/divestments-acquisitions-in-oil-gas-sector-stringing-the-deals-together/#.VBrZM5RdV1Y.

3 Mark Saunders, 'XXX', in Martyn R David (Ed), *Upstream Oil and Gas Agreements* (insert year of publication and publisher), suggests that the use of the term decommissioning evolved in the industry, as the term 'abandonment' connotes the surrender of ownership rights or the leaving behind of one's obligations.

4 World Bank, Oil, Gas and Mining Policy Operations Unit, *Towards Sustainable Decommissioning and Closure of Oil Fields and Mines: A Toolkit to Assist Government Agencies*, Version 3.0 (March 2010).

5 http://www.kimointernational.org/WebData/Files/Decommissioning/oildecommissioningreport1.pdf at p 7.

following the completion of oil and gas operations.[6] Given these additional environmental considerations, decommissioning activities need to be efficiently carried out, in order to ensure that the impact of the process poses minimal or no risk to the environment and the public. Accordingly, it is imperative that the issue of decommissioning is adequately addressed and that decommissioning obligations are clearly set out at the onset of any oil and gas transaction, preferably before the grant of government consent to undertake operations.

In a bid to assist governments in creating comprehensive regulation systems that will ensure that decommissioning is treated as an integral component of oil and gas operations, the Oil, Gas and Mining Policy and Operations Unit (COCPO) of the World Bank published (originally in 2009) a tool kit (the Toolkit)[7] to serve as a resource in the development of flexible but systematic regulatory approaches to key components of a sustainable decommissioning and closure planning and implementation process.[8] The creation of such comprehensive regulations has become imperative, due to:

- the increased number of oilfields approaching the expiry of their productive lives; and
- the huge financial implications of the environmental restoration and rehabilitation measures that necessarily follow decommissioning.

Some of the countries that have developed comprehensive regulatory and fiscal frameworks for the closure or decommissioning of exploration and production (E&P) facilities (including the provision of financial mechanisms for undertaking decommissioning) include the United States of America, the United Kingdom and Norway. Other oil producing countries, including Nigeria, are expected to enact comprehensive decommissioning legislation in compliance with the recommendations of the World Bank and the International Maritime Organisation (IMO) in the near future.

3. Decommissioning in Nigeria

The Petroleum Act 2004[9] (the PA) is the primary piece of legislation currently governing onshore and offshore exploration for oil and gas in Nigeria. While it does not include specific provisions regulating the decommissioning of oil and gas installations and pipelines, section 9(i)(b)(iii) of the PA empowers the Minister of Petroleum Resources to make regulations for the prevention of pollution of water courses and the atmosphere. By virtue of the PA, other primary and subsidiary legislation which relates more specifically to decommissioning has been passed, including the Oil Pipelines Act 2010 (Cap O7, Laws of the Federation of Nigeria), the Petroleum (Drilling and Production) Regulations (the Regulations), the Oil and Gas

6 Natalia Meza Lomonaco – *How to Finance Decommissioning in the Offshore Petroleum Industry? The Role and Importance of Decommissioning Funds.*

7 Note 4 above.

8 The Toolkit was designed and prepared with the support of Environmental Resources Management, Inc (ERM).

9 Cap P10, Laws of the Federation of Nigeria.

Pipelines Regulations 1995 and the *Environmental Guidelines and Standards for the Petroleum Industry of Nigeria* (EGASPIN) issued in 2002 by the Department of Petroleum Resources (DPR) – the regulatory authority charged with oversight of activities in the oil and gas industry in Nigeria.

The existing legislative framework on decommissioning in Nigeria is consistent with the partial and non-removal approach to decommissioning permitted by article 60(3) of the United Nations Convention on the Law of the Sea (UNCLOS) 1982, which provides:

> *Any installations or structures which are abandoned or disused shall be removed to ensure the safety of navigation, taking into account any generally accepted international standards established in this regard by the competent international organisation. Such removal shall also have due regard to fishing, the protection of the marine environment and the rights and duties of other States. Appropriate publicity shall be given to the depth, position and dimensions of any installations or structures not entirely removed.*[10]

By virtue of regulation 46(3) of the Regulations, upon the termination of an oil prospecting licence or an oil mining lease, the licensee or lessee is required, subject to the rights of the owners of the surface land or other persons having a legal interest in the relevant area or any portion of it, to remove all buildings, installations, works, chattels and effects erected or brought by the licensee or lessee onto the relevant area for or in connection with its operations. The Minister of Petroleum Resources is, however, empowered to purchase any such buildings, installations, works, chattels or effects at a written down value.

Furthermore, the Regulations provide:

> *Every borehole or existing well which the licensee or lessee intends to abandon shall, unless the Director of Petroleum Resources ['DPR'] otherwise permits in writing, be securely plugged by the licensee or lessee so as to prevent ingress and egress of water into and from any portion or portions of the strata bored through and shall be dealt with in strict accordance with an abandonment programme approved or agreed to by the Director of Petroleum Resources.*[11]

In relation to pipelines used in oil and gas operations, the Oil and Gas Pipelines Regulations (OGPR) 1995[12] make provision for the decommissioning of pipeline systems. By virtue of regulations 23 and 24, a licensee intending to discontinue or abandon a pipeline, whether partially or completely, must make an application to the DPR, giving at least three months' notice of its intention to do so. The application must be accompanied by necessary documentation, including a statement setting out the reasons for the discontinuation of the pipeline system or

---

10 Although there appears to be a conflict between the provisions of the 1958 Geneva Convention on the Continental Shelf (the Geneva Convention) and the UNCLOS (as the Geneva Convention advocates the total removal of installations following decommissioning, while the UNCLOS and the IMO Guidelines of 1989 (see note 15 below) allow the partial removal of installations), article 311(1) of the UNCLOS provides that that convention shall prevail over the Geneva Convention as between state parties. As the IMO has been recognised as the "competent international organisation" by the UNCLOS, the IMO Guidelines would be regarded as the "generally accepted international standards". Accordingly, partial removal is regarded as the general rule in Nigeria, while total removal of installations has been adopted under certain specified conditions.

11 Regulation 36(2).

12 SI 14 of 1995.

its ancillary facilities and the proposed method to be used for discontinuing operations. Upon the grant of approval for discontinuation or abandonment of the pipeline by the DPR, the licensee is required to disconnect the pipeline from other facilities and purge it of petroleum liquid or gas, using water or inert material capped at both ends with moisture-resistant materials. In the event of a decommissioning of the pipeline, the licensee is required to obtain the approval of the DPR by submitting the proposed work programme for the decommissioning.

Under the EGASPIN,[13] decommissioning is sub-classified into onshore and offshore decommissioning and the process is required to incorporate remediation and restoration programmes. Decommissioning programmes are required to be planned in tandem with the objectives and implementation methodology drawn up at the inception of a project. The licensee or lessee is required to decontaminate, dismantle and remove structures in an appropriate manner from oil and gas installations and facilities after such installations/facilities have been abandoned and decommissioned.

In relation to onshore decommissioning, the licensee or operator is required, among other things, to:

- obtain appropriate permits from the DPR;
- isolate wells from the surface;
- plug and abandon downhole according to permit criteria;
- place surface cement plugs below cellars to allow removal of surface components while avoiding any significant adverse effect on the environment; and
- close the pit appropriately.

The EGASPIN regulations also make provision for the procedure for decommissioning equipment or facilities and pipelines or flowlines.

In relation to offshore decommissioning, operators are required to remove completely all abandoned installations:

- standing in a depth of less than 100 metres of water and weighing less than 4000 tonnes in air; or
- placed on the seabed, excluding the deck and the superstructure.

Furthermore, installations or structures placed on any continental shelf or in any exclusive economic zone must be designed to allow for the entire removal of such installations upon the discontinuance of their use.

As stated previously, there is currently no comprehensive legislative framework for decommissioning in Nigeria and, as a result, obligations in relation to decommissioning have, in recent oil and gas transactions, been incorporated into the transaction documents relating to them.

With reference to the recent divestments by certain IOCs of interests held via JVAs with the Federal Government, decommissioning liabilities were transferred to the purchasers of the interests. This was due to the fact that the JOAs with the Federal

13 Page 286.

Government did not expressly provide for the treatment of the decommissioning obligations in relation to the relevant acreages. The provisions of JOAs in relation to decommissioning are limited to the duties and powers of the operating committee, which include determination of the selection, scope, timing and locations, testing, completion, plugging and abandonment of all wells and facilities for joint operations and of any change in the use or status of any such wells and facilities (article 3.1(i)) and the abandonment and salvage of joint property or any portion thereof (article 3.1(vi)).[14]

While the JOA directs the operator to undertake its duties in accordance with good industry practice and applicable regulations, which include observing existing provisions of the law, there remains a void concerning the allocation of responsibilities relating to decommissioning and the attendant financial obligations for undertaking decommissioning activities. In view of the looming expiry of the productive lives of relevant acreages, it has become necessary for contracting parties to make provision in their transaction documents for the allocation of decommissioning obligations/liabilities in relation to the future decommissioning of those acreages.

4. Decommissioning under the proposed Petroleum Industry Bill

The Petroleum Industry Bill [7](PIB or the Bill) seeks to provide a more robust regulatory framework for decommissioning in Nigeria, in compliance with both recent policy developments and international standards and the non-binding IMO *Guidelines and Standards for the Removal of Offshore Installations and Structures on the Continental Shelf and in the Exclusive Economic Zone* 1989 (the IMO Guidelines).[15]

Under clause 362 of the PIB, the terms decommissioning or abandonment are defined as:

> *the approved process of cessation of operations of oil and gas wells, installations and structures, including shutting down an installation's operation and production, total or partial removal of installations and structures where applicable, chemicals, radioactive and all such other materials handling, removal and disposal of debris and removed items, environmental monitoring of the area after removal of installations and structures.*

The PIB anticipates the integration of decommissioning as an integral component of oil and gas operations, which must be determined at the onset of an oil and gas transaction. In this regard, the PIB proposes that a licensee or lessee who has discovered oil or gas in commercial quantities would, in accordance with the provisions of the Bill, be expected to submit a field development plan for the commercial discovery to the proposed Upstream Petroleum Inspectorate (the Inspectorate) as well as a commitment to undertake the work described in the development plan in a manner acceptable to the Inspectorate.[16] More importantly,

---

14 G Etikerentse, *Nigerian Petroleum Law* (2nd Edition, date, name of publisher).

15 Article 1.1 of the IMO Guidelines states that the removal of abandoned or disused offshore installations or structures on any continental shelf or in any exclusive economic zone is required, except where non-removal or partial removal is consistent with the IMO *Guidelines*.

16 Clause 179 of the PIB.

the approval by the Inspectorate of such a development plan would be predicated upon the inclusion by the licensee, in its development plan, of an acceptable decommissioning and abandonment plan.[17] Failure by the licensee to submit a development plan pursuant to the PIB could result in the revocation of its licence.[18]

Upon the enactment of the PIB into law, operators involved in both onshore and offshore oil and gas operations would be required to undertake such decommissioning and abandonment activities in accordance with both good oilfield practice and regulations implemented by the Inspectorate, subject to the guidelines and standards set by the IMO with regard to offshore petroleum installations and structures.[19] The decommissioning activities of such operators would be subject to the prior approval of the Inspectorate and would include the submission of a decommissioning programme to the Inspectorate providing:

- an estimate of the cost of the proposed measures;
- details of measures proposed to be taken in connection with the decommissioning of disused installations, structures or pipelines, as the case may be;
- clear descriptions of the method to be employed in undertaking the work programme, which should be in line with best oilfield practices and environmental standards; and
- steps to be taken to ensure the maintenance and safeguarding of health, safety and the environment where any installations, structures or pipelines are to remain disused and in position, or are to be partially removed.[20]

The PIB seeks to take into account the likely effects of decommissioning in relation to the present and future effects on the environment and, to that extent, seeks to ensure that activities in connection with decommissioning are undertaken in a manner that guarantees sustainable environmental management.[21]

To ensure that decommissioning-related obligations are effectively undertaken, the PIB seeks to provide for the Inspectorate to "recall" (ie, require) a licensee or lessee responsible for the decommissioning or abandonment programme with respect to a licence or lease that has expired to carry out its decommissioning and abandonment obligations.[22] Given, however, that the operations would have been concluded, it may be necessary for further provisions to be included in the Bill for the creation of a security, such as a guarantee or a bond prior to approval of the decommissioning work programme. Such a requirement would compel the licensee or lessee to comply with a recall by the Inspectorate to perform its decommissioning obligations as a precondition for release of the security by the Inspectorate.

Under the PIB, in the event of a surrender or relinquishment of a licence by a licensee, that licensee would be required to comply with all requirements of the law

17 *Ibid*, clause 179(3)(e).
18 *Ibid*, clause 179 (4).
19 *Ibid*, clause 204.
20 *Ibid*, clause 204(5).
21 *Ibid*, clause 204(8)(d).
22 *Ibid*, clause 204(9).

with regard to the relinquishment and decommissioning of installations and the reclamation of land, upon giving to the Downstream Petroleum Regulatory Agency a minimum of 12 months' notice in writing of its intention to cease its activities, unless a shorter period is stipulated in its licence.

Under the Bill, the Minister of Petroleum Resources would be empowered to issue regulations on abandonment and decommissioning processes and procedures, where such regulations are absent at the commencement of production, while the Inspectorate is empowered to issue directives to affected licensees or lessees in relation to the decommissioning and abandonment of oil, gas, or bitumen installations within their licence or lease area, as the case may be.[23]

For the purpose of ensuring that financing of decommissioning operations is adequately provided for, the Bill makes provision for an abandonment fund to be set up by the lessee for the purpose of abandonment, decommissioning and/or disposal, with the approval of the Inspectorate. Such funds would be accessible to the Inspectorate in the event that the lessee should fail to carry out its decommissioning obligations in relation to the relevant acreage.[24]

The Bill appears to suggest that environmental obligations in relation to oil and gas operations would be applicable retroactively.[25] Therefore, while there are currently no specific provisions relating to decommissioning, the purchasers of oil and gas interests pursuant to the recent divestments by the IOCs would, upon the enactment of the Bill, be required to comply with the obligations relating to environmental protection, including decommissioning and abandonment. Although such provisions would increase the cost of acquiring interests in the oil and gas sector, they would also result in the better protection and management of the environment during and after completion of the productive lives of oil and gas projects.

Under the PSCs, pursuant to which the operators fund the operation of oil and gas projects and merely receive a share of the production as compensation for capital, exploration and operating costs,[26] ownership of the concessions is held by the NNPC. Upon cessation of such projects, the obligation to decommission would remain vested in the NNPC. It is therefore important that measures are put in place for the provision of funds during the productive life of projects, in order to ensure that the required financing is available at their expiry to fund their closure or decommissioning. In order to avoid any difficulties that may arise in connection with the retention of funds for decommissioning under such PSC operations, it is advisable that the definition of 'cost oil' in the PSC be amended to include decommissioning costs.[27]

By virtue of the Bill, it is clear that the Nigerian legislature proposes to adopt an all-encompassing approach to onshore and offshore decommissioning and

23 *Ibid*, clause 205.

24 *Ibid*, clause 204(11).

25 Clause 200(2) of the PIB states that operators engaged in oil and gas operations commenced prior to the enactment of the PIB would, upon commencement of the Bill as an act, be required to submit an environmental management plan within one year of the passage of the Bill into law.

26 Etikerentse, *op cit* (note 13 above)

27 Lomonaco, *op cit* (note 6 above).

abandonment by taking into account international recommendations and creating laws that reflect the peculiarities of the Nigerian oil and gas industry. The PIB seeks to provide for the allocation of decommissioning obligations, the financing of decommissioning costs, and the maintenance of the environment and of the socio-economic conditions of any persons who might be directly affected by upstream petroleum operations.[28]

5. Financing decommissioning

The nature and complexity of a project plays a pivotal role in the financing of the decommissioning activities required in connection with disused facilities upon the expiry of the project and the closure of oil and gas operations. A variety of factors, including the location and type of facility, the number of structures to be removed, water depth and weight associated with the structure, the number and depth of wells and conductors, the removal method(s), and transport and disposal options, would need to be considered in arriving at the most suitable financial structure to be included in the decommissioning plan to be submitted to the relevant authorities prior to the decommissioning of an oil and gas project.

In recognition of the huge financial outlay required for decommissioning, particularly in relation to offshore installations, the more recent approach is to retain, partially or totally, larger and deeper installations of more than 100 metres, while totally removing installations in shallow waters. Consideration is also being given by stakeholders to the re-use of assets decommissioned from offshore installations in onshore oil and gas operations.[29]

Financing the decommissioning of oil and gas projects has become a major concern in the Nigerian oil and gas industry, in view of the pending decommissioning of a number of acreages. Given that neither the JOAs between the Federal Government and the IOCs nor the PSCs provide for the retention of funds for decommissioning during the productive life of a project, it is envisaged that decommissioning activities may be delayed upon the closure of a project or be left to the responsibility of the Federal Government, which may be required to have recourse to the national budget for the purpose of ensuring that decommissioning activities are carried out.

In order to ensure that decommissioning is adequately and promptly carried out after the closure of an oil and gas project, the COCPO has suggested a number of financial assurance mechanisms in relation to financing for the restoration and rehabilitation of the environment following oil and gas operations, including setting up decommissioning funds, issuing letters of credit, or requesting a bond or a guarantee to be issued by a financial institution or a parent company for the benefit of the appropriate agency in relation to the decommissioning obligations arising upon the expiry of an oil and gas project.

While existing provisions of Nigerian law do not make specific provision for the

28 Clause 200(2) of the PIB.

29 Article 1.2 of the IMO *Guidelines* suggests that installations may be applied for purposes other than the primary purpose for which they were originally designed and installed.

allocation of financial obligations relating to decommissioning, the PIB seeks to introduce a fund to be maintained and operated during the continuance of productive operations, the purpose of which would be the financing of decommissioning and abandonment activities upon the expiry of such operations.[30] The Bill also, as stated previously, seeks to introduce a creative provision which would empower the Inspectorate to recall licensees or lessees for the purpose of undertaking decommissioning obligations arising upon the closure of oil and gas operations.

6. Conclusion

While the PIB has proposed extensive amendments to the current legislative framework relating to decommissioning and abandonment in Nigeria, it has yet to be enacted into law. It is anticipated that, once the PIB has taken effect as an act, it would serve as the compendium of laws regulating operations in the oil and gas sector and address present deficiencies in the existing legislative framework for decommissioning in the country.

In view of these lacunae in the existing legislative framework and the imminent challenges in connection with the efficient and prompt undertaking of decommissioning operations in the oil and gas sector, it may be necessary for additional regulations to be issued under the PIB, once enacted. The objective of the regulations would be to address such challenges and to ensure that the abandonment of onshore and offshore oil and gas operations do not have a negative impact on the environment.

30 Decommissioning funds is one of various financial assurance mechanisms suggested by COCPO in the Toolkit that are available to an operator, a co-venturer, a state and other duty holders to ensure that sufficient funds are reserved to return the areas affected by oil and gas operations to an environmental and socially acceptable condition when activities cease and the project is no longer generating revenues.

About the authors

Kevin Atkins
International partner, Chadbourne & Parke LLP
katkins@chadbourne.com

Kevin Atkins is an international partner in the corporate department of Chadbourne & Parke in London. He specialises in the energy sector and has over 10 years' experience advising on international cross-border upstream oil and gas transactions, joint venture arrangements and energy projects. He has worked on a number of the highest profile upstream transactions across Africa. He is familiar with the issues facing investors and host governments during the bidding and licence award stages of an upstream investment in Africa and has advised both buyers and sellers in acquisitions and disposals, as well as investors and lenders on the optimal and most bankable structures for upstream investments in Africa.

Sarah Banco
Associate, Akin Gump Strauss Hauer & Feld LLP
sbanco@akingump.com

Sarah Banco is an associate in the international trade group at Akin Gump Strauss Hauer & Feld, based in Washington DC. Ms Banco regularly assists US and international clients in understanding and navigating US export control, sanctions and anti-bribery laws. She also assists clients with a variety of transaction related matters, including the Committee on Foreign Investment in the United States. Ms Banco has counselled clients in a variety of industries, including aerospace, defence, electronics, investment funds, logistics and freight forwarding, oil and gas, education and transportation. Her experience includes leading internal investigations and audits, developing compliance programmes, developing export and sanctions licensing strategies and conducting due diligence exercises and contractual negotiations.

Mark Beeley
Partner, Vinson & Elkins
mbeeley@velaw.com

Mark Beeley is a partner in Vinson & Elkins' international dispute resolution practice group, based in London and Dubai. Mr Beeley's practice is primarily focused on international dispute resolution in the energy sector, with a particular focus on upstream disputes. He has more than 10 years' experience in disputes involving arbitration and litigation in West and East Africa, as well as in the Middle East and North Africa region. In addition to acting as counsel, Mr Beeley sits as an arbitrator.

Adam Blythe
Senior associate, Bracewell & Giuliani (UK) LLP
adam.blythe@bgllp.com

Adam Blythe is a senior associate at Bracewell & Giuliani (UK) LLP, specialising in upstream oil and gas transactional work, with a particular focus on sub-Saharan Africa. Mr Blythe has extensive experience in Nigeria, Tanzania, Ghana and Mozambique.

Larry Bottomley
Chief executive officer
Chariot Oil and Gas Limited

Larry Bottomley has worked in the oil and gas industry for more than 30 years and has a significant track record of building exploration and production businesses on the international stage, delivering transformational growth and shareholder value. Mr Bottomley has worked across a broad spectrum of exploratory and business development roles worldwide, as well as in senior management roles with Perenco SA, Hunt Oil, Triton Energy and BP. He has a strong background in integrated geosciences, team management and relationship building. A key aspect of his work has been in the creation, development and delivery of significant drilling programmes that have led to the discovery and development of giant oil fields.

Olivier Chambord
Partner, Morgan, Lewis & Bockius UK LLP
ochambord@morganlewis.com

Olivier Chambord is a partner in Morgan Lewis's business and finance practice. He focuses on international project development, cross-border and domestic mergers and acquisitions and private equity transactions, with an emphasis on energy petrochemical and commodities industries. He has worked on a diverse mix of upstream, midstream and downstream oil and gas assets, petrochemicals, soft commodities projects and mergers and acquisitions throughout Europe and Africa.

Mr Chambord represents oil and gas, mining and petrochemicals companies and investors on acquisitions of oil blocks, hydrocarbon assets, upstream, midstream and downstream assets, as well as their participation in refinery joint ventures.

Mr Chambord has been listed in a number of legal guides, including the International *Who's Who of Oil and Gas Lawyers* and *Legal 500.*

Ben Donovan
Partner, DLA Piper
ben.donovan@dlapiper.com

Ben Donovan is a US and UK-qualified energy and projects partner in the London office of DLA Piper. Mr Donovan has represented various energy clients, government and parastatal entities, as well as lenders in the development, acquisition, financing, restructuring and divestiture of oil and gas, power, pipeline, refinery and petrochemical projects, with a particular emphasis on projects in Africa. Mr Donovan lived for several years in South Africa and has been working on African energy projects for nearly 20 years.

He has been listed as a leading individual in projects by *Chambers and Partners* and a leading lawyer in energy and projects for Sub-Saharan Africa in the *IFLR/Petroleum Economist Energy and Infrastructure Guide.*

Olubunmi Fayokun
Partner, Aluko & Oyebode
olubunmi.fayokun@aluko-oyebode.com

Olubunmi Fayokun is a partner at Aluko & Oyebode. She has extensive experience in all aspects of corporate and commercial law, with particular emphasis on energy and natural resources law.

Ms Fayokun has advised on a significant number of energy transactions, including the development of a greenfield independent power producer (IPP) project, the development, financing and implementation of the first IPP project in Nigeria and the acquisitions, by various international oil companies, of participating interests in Nigerian oil blocks. She continues to advise major oil and gas companies operating in Nigeria.

Ms Fayokun graduated from the University of Ife, Ile-Ife, Nigeria in 1984 with a bachelor's degree in law and was admitted to the Nigerian Bar in 1985.

She is recognised as one of the world's leading

lawyers in oil and gas by *Who's Who Legal* and is a member of the Association of International Petroleum Negotiators.

Alex Green
Commercial manager, Chariot Oil and Gas Limited
Alexg@chariotoilandgas.com

Alex Green has 25 years of experience in the business development, commercial and financial aspects of the upstream oil and gas sector. He began his career as a petroleum economist for Clyde Petroleum, subsequently working as a corporate planner for BG Plc and later moving to become group economics manager for Paladin Resources. At Paladin, Mr Green led successful joint venture negotiations, managed the oil and gas sales arrangements for the group and ran the financial and commercial analysis in the company's business development team. At Chariot Oil & Gas, he has been responsible for the commercial aspects of farm-out processes, as well as negotiations with host governments, joint venture partners and service providers, which has led to the successful negotiation of farm-out agreements, joint operating agreements, production sharing contracts, seismic and drilling contracts.

Marc Hammerson
Partner, Akin Gump Strauss Hauer & Feld LLP
mhammerson@akingump.com

Marc Hammerson is a solicitor and partner at Akin Gump Strauss Hauer & Feld LLP in London. He is an experienced upstream energy lawyer specialising in both M&A and project development. He has worked in private practice and in-house, and was based in the Far East in the early 2000s. Mr Hammerson has degrees in law from Manchester University and the London School of Economics, and is a member of the Association of International Petroleum Negotiators.

Nnedinma C Ifudu Nweke
Senior counsel, Akin Gump Strauss Hauer & Feld LLP
nifudu@akingump.com

Nnedinma (Nnedi) C Ifudu Nweke is a senior counsel in the international trade group of Akin Gump based in the firm's Washington DC office. Ms Ifudu's practice focuses on various aspects of US and international trade controls and regulatory compliance that affect international trade and business, including US export controls, US and international economic sanctions and trade embargoes, US anti-boycott laws, the Foreign Corrupt Practices Act and the UK Bribery Act.

Ms Ifudu represents clients in international trade matters before many US government departments and agencies, including the departments of commerce, justice, state and the treasury. Ms Ifudu has helped clients in various industries to manage effectively due diligence investigations in connection with investment fund formation, mergers, acquisitions and other transactions. She advises clients on how to respond to US government enforcement investigations, develop and implement compliance policies and procedures, prepare voluntary self-disclosures and conduct internal reviews, audits and investigations.

Bruce Johnston
Partner, Morgan, Lewis & Bockius UK LLP
bruce.johnston@morganlewis.com

Bruce Johnston heads Morgan Lewis's international finance practice. He focuses his practice on a wide range of banking and finance transactions, including acquisition finance, leveraged finance, project finance, structured finance, trade finance and asset finance. He has experience in energy and infrastructure transactions throughout Europe, Russia, Africa, Asia, and the Middle East, as well as workouts and restructurings in many industries.

Jaelyn Edwards Judelson
Counsel, Akin Gump Strauss Hauer & Feld LLP
jjudelson@akingump.com

Jaelyn Edwards Judelson is a counsel in the international trade group of Akin Gump. Ms Judelson is currently based in Akin Gump's London offices and splits her time between the firm's offices in the United Kingdom and Washington DC. Ms Judelson's practice focuses on US law and policy affecting international trade and business, particularly in anti-bribery, the Foreign Corrupt Practices Act, export controls and economic sanctions.

Ms Judelson has counselled clients in a variety of industries, including aerospace, defence, investment funds, logistics, freight forwarding and oil and gas. Her experience includes advocacy for global multinational clients to avoid civil and criminal liability through the development of effective compliance programmes, managing global internal investigations and compliance matters and preparing voluntary self-disclosures and licensing strategies for multinational corporations.

John C LaMaster
Partner, Akin Gump Strauss Hauer & Feld LLP, London
jlamaster@akingump.com

John C LaMaster is an international energy transactional lawyer. His primary focus is on project development and mergers and acquisitions. He has over 30 years' experience in virtually all areas of the energy industry, including upstream, midstream and downstream oil and gas, electricity generation, biofuels, chemicals and petrochemicals. Mr LaMaster has worked on energy transactions throughout Africa, Europe, the Middle East, Russia and the former Soviet Union and the United States.

He holds a BA in economics and business administration from Vanderbilt University and a JD with honours from the Paul M Herbert Law Centre at Louisiana State University.

Mr LaMaster is highly rated by various legal directories, including a Band 1 ranking among leading individuals in oil and gas in the 2015 edition of *Chambers*.

Bjørn-Erik Leerberg
Partner, Simonsen Vogt Wiig
bjorn-erik.leerberg@svw.no

Bjørn-Erik Leerberg holds a law degree from the University of Oslo and is partner at Simonsen Vogt Wiig (SVW), Oslo. He has long and extensive experience as a senior civil servant and private practitioner on petroleum and energy activities, contracts, administrative and public international law.

MrLeerberg has developed the SVW upstream oil and gas practice in Norway and advises companies on Norwegian continental shelf establishment through production. He leads SVW's international petroleum practice, focusing on public international law, treaties and legislation and contracts and negotiations. His experience ranges from border disputes, joint development and unitisation and cross-border submarine pipelines to bid rounds, upstream and midstream legislation, concessions and contracts, pipelines, gas sales and mergers and acquisitions. His clients include international organisations, governments, energy and oil and gas companies and their suppliers with activities in Europe, Africa, the Middle East, the Far East and Latin America. Mr Leerberg lectures regularly on petrolem and public international law.

Christopher RK Moore
Managing director, Moyes & Co
cmoore@moyesco.com

Chris Moore is a managing director with upstream commercial advisers Moyes & Co, Inc. He provides a wide range of consulting services to a variety of clients on technical, financial and economic issues, particularly fair market valuations and expert witness testimony. His experience in economic analysis includes many of the world's fiscal regimes.

Mr Moore read natural sciences at the University of Cambridge. He joined BP as a geologist in 1975 and worked in Aberdeen, London and Tunis before joining Tricentrol in London, latterly specialising in economic analysis in corporate planning. He subsequently joined ARCO, working in London and its international headquarters in Plano, Texas, where he held various technical, commercial and management positions.

Mr Moore is a fellow of the Geological Society (London) and a member of the Society of Petroleum Engineers and the American Association of Petroleum Geologists. He is also a member of Association of International Petroleum Negotiators and co-chairs its economic evaluation and valuation workshops.

Caroline-Lucy Moran
Associate, Akin Gump Strauss Hauer & Feld LLP
cmoran@akingump.com

Caroline-Lucy Moran is an associate in the global energy transactions department of Akin Gump Strauss Hauer & Feld LLP in London.

Ms Moran has experience in international mergers and acquisitions, divestments, joint ventures, project development and equity capital markets transactions, with a particular focus on upstream and downstream oil and gas and power sectors.

Legal 500 UK recommends Ms Moran as a "valuable resource" for oil and gas work and *IFLR1000 Energy and Infrastructure Guide* recognises her as "up-and-coming" in her field.

Ms Moran has worked on transactions throughout Europe, Asia, the Middle East and West, East and Sub-Saharan Africa while based in London, Milan and Singapore. As a trainee she was seconded to one of the largest energy corporations in the world.

Ms Moran graduated from the University of Oxford in 2006 and was admitted as a solicitor of the Senior Courts of England and Wales in 2010.

Allison Soilihi
Associate, Morgan, Lewis & Bockius UK LLP
asoilihi@morganlewis.com

Allison Soilihi is an associate in Morgan Lewis's corporate and business transactions practice. Ms Soilihi represents oil and gas companies on acquisitions of oil blocks, hydrocarbon assets and upstream, midstream and downstream assets. She is experienced in drafting negotiations related to various petroleum agreements, including production sharing agreements, joint operating agreements, hydrocarbons transportation agreements, hydrocarbons supply agreements, establishment conventions, joint venture agreements and sale and purchase agreements related to the acquisition of petroleum assets. She also regularly provides assistance related to litigation matters regarding petroleum assets and the incorporation of local affiliates.

Tamer Soliman
Partner, Akin Gump Strauss Hauer & Feld LLP
tsoliman@akingump.com

Tamer Soliman is a partner in the international trade practice of Akin Gump Strauss Hauer & Feld LLP. After working for over a decade from the Washington, DC office, he now leads the firm's trade compliance and investigations practice in the United Arab Emirates. Mr Soliman provides strategic counsel on managing regulatory and legal risk in diverse global holdings and acquisitions. He also specialises in handling government enforcement actions and investigations in various regulatory matters. He advises corporate and government clients on a wide range of issues governing cross-border investments, joint ventures and sales, including in export control and International Traffic in Arms Regulations, anti-corruption, economic sanctions and import laws.

Mr Soliman has advised clients in various sectors, including engineering services, energy, defence and aerospace, private equity and logistics. He is a frequent speaker on trade compliance and investigations matters involving anti-corruption, export controls, sanctions and related issues.

Index